The PhDictionary

The PhDictionary

A Glossary of Things
You Don't Know
(but Should)
about Doctoral
and Faculty Life

HERB CHILDRESS

The University of Chicago Press · Chicago and London

2/14/17
LN
$20.00

HERB CHILDRESS is cofounder of the consulting firm Teleidoscope Group LLC. He has extensive professional experience as a teacher and administrator in higher education, most recently as dean of research and assessment at the Boston Architectural College. Childress is the author of *Landscapes of Betrayal, Landscapes of Joy: Curtisville in the Lives of its Teenagers.*

The University of Chicago Press, Chicago 60637
The University of Chicago Press, Ltd., London
© 2016 by The University of Chicago
All rights reserved. Published 2016.
Printed in the United States of America

25 24 23 22 21 20 19 18 17 16   1 2 3 4 5

ISBN-13: 978-0-226-35914-4 (cloth)
ISBN-13: 978-0-226-35928-1 (paper)
ISBN-13: 978-0-226-35931-1 (e-book)
DOI: 10.7208/chicago/9780226359311.001.0001

Library of Congress Cataloging-in-Publication Data
Names: Childress, Herb, author.
Title: The PhDictionary : a glossary of things you don't know (but should) about
    doctoral and faculty life / Herb Childress.
Other titles: Chicago guides to academic life.
Description: Chicago ; London : The University of Chicago Press, 2016 | Series:
    Chicago guides to academic life
Identifiers: LCCN 2015036893 | ISBN 9780226359144 (cloth : alk. paper) | ISBN
    9780226359281 (pbk. : alk. paper) | ISBN 9780226359311 (e-book)
Subjects: LCSH: Doctoral students—United States—Dictionaries. | Doctor of
    philosophy degree—United States—Dictionaries. | College teachers—United
    States—Dictionaries.
Classification: LCC LB2386 .C455 2016 | DDC 378.2—dc23 LC record available at http://
    lccn.loc.gov/2015036893

♾ This paper meets the requirements of ANSI/NISO Z39.48–1992 (Permanence of Paper).

Contents

Note: When describing the insider language of a community, defining one unfamiliar term sometimes requires the use of other, equally unfamiliar, terms. As you read through this glossary, you'll occasionally come across words in **boldface**. These words are the subjects of their own glossary entries.

Thanks

There are impossibly many people to thank for a project such as this. Some played a direct role in its creation; some supported its creator; some provided wisdom; and some played the role of the cautionary tale, the example of higher ed practices that I could best honor through being their 180-degree opposing force. I will limit my thanks here to those whose positive public recognition is necessary. Private recognition will be held for elsewhere.

First, thanks to my mother and brothers, who read to me, and read to me, and read to me, until finally at age three I started to read back. You cannot imagine how important it was to grow up with words.

I cannot overstate the importance of our Sylvania black-and-white console television, which later kept me company in the hours when no one else was available, and which taught me how to tell stories myself. Nor the spiritual power of WTRU-AM disc jockey Tom Andrews, whose focused loneliness helped me focus my own.

I appreciate a life of magazines and newspapers that taught me the power of topical attention and authorial voice. From *Boy's Life* through *The New Yorker*, from *Hot Rod* through the *San Francisco Chronicle*, I learned how to invite a reader into a conversation rather than essay at them.

And then, of course, there have been teachers. In the entry in this book on **teaching**, I recommend that you all make a list of the handful of teachers who changed your trajectory. Here's mine.

- Pastor John Beem, Bethlehem Lutheran Church, Muskegon Heights, Michigan
- Paul Klemp, sixth grade, Theodore Roosevelt Elementary School, Muskegon Heights, Michigan

- Andrew Grzeszkowiak, seventh grade, Our Redeemer Lutheran School, Muskegon, Michigan
- Robert Ribesky, English, Muskegon Community College
- Tom Turman, architectural design and drafting, Laney College
- Spiro Kostof, architectural history, University of California, Berkeley
- Heather Clendenin, landscape architecture, University of California, Berkeley
- David Littlejohn, journalism, University of California, Berkeley
- David Seamon, architecture and geography, Kansas State University
- Jerry Weisman, environment/behavior studies, University of Wisconsin–Milwaukee
- Judith Kenny, cultural/urban geography, University of Wisconsin–Milwaukee
- Tom Hubka, architectural history, University of Wisconsin–Milwaukee
- Linda Krause, art and architectural history, University of Wisconsin–Milwaukee
- John Goulet, fiction and creative writing, University of Wisconsin–Milwaukee

And then there is the first among equals who deserves his own entry: Paul Groth, cultural landscape geography, University of California, Berkeley. Paul was the first person with whom I shared the thought that I might become a college teacher. Not only did he not laugh at me; he gave me a serious look at what that life entailed, and strategies for how best to prepare for it. He taught me that my attention to everyday things could be a noble calling, because it felt noble when he did it. I still think of the difference between silos and grain elevators.

I appreciate the many friends from whom I've learned how higher ed works on the ground, whose brilliant work and laughing complaints have helped me understand things I'd have never otherwise known about the culture: Julio Rivera, Van Hillard, Andrea Chapdelaine, Andy Harris, Jenny Shanahan, Beth Paul, Nancy Hensel, Greta Boers, Simon Cook, Deb Carver-Thien, and dozens of colleagues in the Council on Undergraduate Research. And my friend Anthony Bernier, who understands as well as any what the journey costs.

Thanks to the students who stepped up and did more with my courses than I could ever have asked—far too many to name here. But specifically for Susannah Swearingen, whose decision to go to a doctoral program herself, and whose questions of content and of strategy, got me started thinking about this book in the first place.

Thanks to three specific friends in publishing: Susan Breen of the New York Pitch conference, who taught me how to write a credible book proposal; Jackie Cantor at Penguin, who has always encouraged my work even though it would never fit her own list; and Elizabeth Branch Dyson at the University of Chicago Press, whose steady championing of this project took it from Microsoft Word into your hands and improved it greatly along the way. Elizabeth, you're a *mensch*.

In absentia, thanks to my mother-in-law, Estelle, who invented herself and then pretended she'd always been there, but never, ever missed a chance to speak gratefully of her mentors. She was one of mine.

And final words of gratitude to my wife, Nora Rubinstein, who has helped me constantly to be true to the work and to believe in my own capacity for it. I met her after she'd written one of the most brilliant papers in our shared field, and I still seek out her guidance as we pursue our lunatic visions far too late into the nights. W, always.

Why Does This Book Exist?

Every tradition grows ever more venerable—the more remote its origin, the more confused that origin is. The reverence due to it increases from generation to generation. The tradition finally becomes holy and inspires awe.
FRIEDRICH NIETZSCHE, *Human, All Too Human*

In the early 2000s, I was teaching in the University Writing Program at Duke; it was one of my favorite jobs ever. But something caught my attention. I kept hearing my colleagues, all relatively recent PhDs, referring casually to things their mothers or fathers had once done as college faculty members or administrators. If it had been one or two people, I'd have left it alone; in any crowd, there are probably two plumbers or two golfers or two college faculty members. But this was a constant background sound, like a refrigerator motor or tinnitus. So I asked.

Fourteen of the twenty-six had one or both parents who were university faculty.

College teaching seemed to be a family trade, like mortuary work or circus acrobatics. And that finding gave sudden organization to a dense scatter of misunderstandings I'd had during my time in higher education. I was learning everything by myself, while many others had some firsthand experiences to draw upon. It seemed as though everything was a secret, but there was nothing quite so sinister at work, just the presumption that everybody involved in the enterprise simply *knew* these things.

The function of this book is to offer you some borrowed wisdom, to help you learn all the things that I learned. It's framed around common terms and built as a glossary; but each entry will have a little storytelling, some context, and will leave you able to put on the mask of the capable scholar even though you feel like an impostor. Every time you hear a term you feel you *ought* to know, look here.

Armed with *The PhDictionary*, I hope that you'll feel somewhat more confident as you enter a graduate program or start applying for academic jobs or your first research grant. Treat me as the Lewis and Clark for your westward expansion; I've found the quicksand and rapids and bandits on your behalf, so that you might have an easier and more knowable trip. I've also seen wonderful landscapes that I could never have predicted, and I hope that periodically you might take some strength on a bad day by reading a tale of delight. There are good places out there in higher education; I hope I'll be able to help you get there with fewer breakdowns.

As a pending or new doctoral student, then as an experienced doctoral student on the search for faculty work, and then again as an early-career faculty member moving toward tenure, you are not merely becoming an ever more capable professional. More centrally, you are becoming a member of a community, absorbing and embodying a specific culture. And cultures—their norms, values, language, taboos, and automatic responses—have to be understood from the details up.

We grossly misunderstand career training, and thus typically do a terrible job of it. Any career has three major components, of which we understand one: content knowledge. Colleges are excellent at providing content knowledge, the things our tribe knows that differentiate us from the other tribes and the things they know. But while content mastery is a crucial element of a career, it's not the only one.

A second component is purpose, a sense of why you're doing what you do. What is it that's joyful about this way of life? What keeps you going through hard nights? What do you want to be true because you've done this kind of work? What I knew at thirty-one—*all* I knew at thirty-one—was that I wanted to hang around college. I wanted to be a college teacher, to lead others to have the same kinds of pleasures I'd had. That's how I framed it: "a college teacher." I had no idea of the life of a college faculty member, no idea about research and tenure and publish-or-perish. I wanted to be the kind and intelligent man who helped other kids find joy in ideas.

We don't talk comfortably about purpose, and so we leave it to young people to find it for themselves. I learned the pleasures of research on my own, just as I had earlier learned how to write on my own, and why to write. I'd never had a more experienced confidante with whom I could moon over my dream life, someone who could adjust my romantic notions without destroying the romance. I'd never had someone with whom to test a plan, or someone to help me find fertile ground for my desires. I never knew I should have asked, and would never have known what to ask about. You don't know what you don't know.

A third component: careers also have logistical elements. You've got to learn to write a grant proposal, and learn where to send it. You've got to learn which journals might take your work, learn how to construct a new course, learn when to say yes to a committee assignment, and when to politely decline. You've got to learn how to attend a conference, learn how to choose which conference to attend, learn how to get reimbursed for your travel. You've got to learn how to choose a research committee, learn where the jobs are posted, and how to ask for and write letters of recommendation.

Thinking of your career as a form of cultural immersion is not often part of your formal training; it certainly wasn't part of mine. There were so many components of the ecosystem that remained invisible to me for far too long. Because I'm an ethnographer, a person who tries to understand a community's unspoken rules, I tended to correct my mistakes quickly. But I made a *lot* of mistakes that led to halted progress and terrible job choices and detours that let me see the holy land only from the next ridge over.

Higher education, even the subset devoted to doctoral study and early-faculty life, is vast, complex and contextual. A small, rich library—indeed, one or more dissertations—could be constructed about each of the 150 or so entries in this abbreviated dictionary. My goal here is not to be exhaustive, to account for every instance or circumstance, or to provide a full history of how things came to be the way they are. My work is much simpler: to make you aware of things you haven't considered as you make your way toward selecting a graduate program or entering the world of the faculty—to help you see things you have never imagined, things you can investigate locally and get help with.

In these definitions, I'm dealing with general norms of practice, and not all possible shades of implementation or peculiarities of custom. There will be exceptions to everything I put forth. But armed with these norms, you can always start a conversation by saying, "I know that [insert some practice here] often happens this way; is that true here as well?"

Although data on many aspects of higher educational practice is scarce, I've attempted to locate current data wherever available, and to label all conjecture as being such. However, as in all social endeavors, most of what matters here is interpretation rather than blunt inventory. I freely admit to having a point of view: that of what the journalist Alfred Lubrano calls "the Straddler," a person who has left a working-class upbringing for a professional adulthood, and who finds himself perfectly at home in neither community.[1] This is the ideal position from which to practice ethnography: finding things familiar enough to describe and categorize, strange enough to step back and analyze.

I also come from a particular academic background, a sort of middle ground between the social sciences and the humanities. So my own experience will be most immediately relevant to others in interpretive scholarship; I am not a laboratory or field scientist. I have, however, spent the past dozen years in leadership roles within the Council on Undergraduate Research, an organization originally founded by research chemists and still extensively populated by physical scientists. CUR has given me a great community of friends and colleagues in fields that I'd otherwise have no contact with, and their experiences as natural science faculty have guided many of my thoughts in this book.

I have some thoughts about structural problems in higher education and how the whole enterprise might be improved, and as you read, you'll almost certainly know what I think. But this is not particularly a book about what I believe should be different about higher ed. Rather, it's about what grad school and faculty life is like now, and what you should expect. I'm fifty-seven years old and have had the past twenty-five of those years in doctoral education and academic life, whereas I'm presuming that you are on the other end of that journey, looking forward, and have some specific needs and questions. As much as I might like many things to be different, my primary responsibility is to lead you through the landscape of higher education as it exists today, like an escort through a tough neighborhood.

One of my roles as that escort is to make sure you know that the neighborhood isn't safe. Planning to become a college faculty member is a better bet than planning to become a major league shortstop, but not by much. You need to take a cold-eyed look at the numbers, and determine whether the risk is acceptable and how much you're willing to invest in the gamble. If you're part of the one-in-six PhDs who will get a tenure-track faculty position, the rewards are enormous; maybe not financially, but at least you'll be economically comfortable and secure in employment, and will spend your life working with ideas and with students who occasionally are excited by

1. Alfred Lubrano, *Limbo: Blue-Collar Roots, White-Collar Dreams* (Hoboken, NJ: John Wiley and Sons, 2004).

them. It's a rare privilege, and it may be worth pursuing even if the outcome is far from certain. As the state lottery boards are fond of saying, "You can't win if you don't play."

But you need to know the odds, and you need to read the dour predictions just as carefully as you consider the rainbows and unicorns of success. The *Chronicle of Higher Education* essays by William Pannapacker (under the pseudonym Thomas H. Benton) are probably the best known in this genre, with titles including "So You Want to Go to Grad School," "Graduate School in the Humanities: Just Don't Go," and "The Big Lie About the 'Life of the Mind.'"

I can't pretend to advise you on whether or not you should try to get your PhD and work toward a faculty life. I spent five years of my young adult life training to become a professional bowler, which had far worse odds and far less payoff than academia. I worked in dead-end jobs to do it, enjoyed it, didn't spend a ton of money on it,[2] and moved on when I got to be twenty-five years old and realized I would never be quite good enough. I'm glad for that part of my life, now thirty years past, just as I'm glad for my PhD and subsequent experiences even though they never became the tenured dream. Knowing the odds didn't stop me from bowling for hours every day, and it may not stop you from grad school.

I also don't pretend to have encountered every possible circumstance. As you enter the fray, you may find yourself with questions for which this book does not prepare you. But I hope that I'll have helped you get in the habit of asking them, with at least the confidence that your lack of confidence is broadly shared.

I also want to make it clear, if it isn't clear already, that this book is not the work of a committee, winnowing the idiosyncrasies out of it to determine best practices. This book is drawn from my own experiences and those of folks I've met along the way, and it's aimed squarely at speaking in the vernacular of the communities from which I've come.

When I was teaching at Duke University, most of a tree fell on top of our program's offices during a ferocious ice storm. The deck outside was

---

2. This whole game changes if you're going to spend a lot of money and incur extensive debt in order to finance your doctoral program. It's one thing to do this and spend your time, but the state of student loan finance in America makes Pannapacker exactly right if you're thinking about borrowing for grad school. *Do not do it.* If you're committed to doing a doctoral program, make sure you have access to financial aid, teaching and research assistantships, and other opportunities to work your way through the program.

covered with frozen limbs, and part of the roof had been knocked off. At the same time, the campus was the only part of Durham that hadn't lost electricity, since the university could afford to underground all the utilities and hadn't had power lines knocked out. Since most of us postdocs lived somewhat near campus, many of us brought sleeping bags and camped in our offices for a few days, since it was too cold to live at home without power.

After a couple of days of constant work, the university's facilities crew finally made it around to our offices and began to clear the trees and debris. The temperature was near zero, and the crew members were working in bucket trucks and in the trees themselves, chainsawing the dead and damaged branches and lowering them by rope to be cleared away. Their work was brutally hard and considerably dangerous. While we were out watching them, the partner of one of our colleagues—an assistant professor of recent vintage in Duke's history department—walked over to join us. She watched with us for a moment, and then remarked, "Things like this just inevitably reenergize certain discourses of masculinity."

This, friends, is the culture you're about to enter: a culture that replaces labor with rhetorical maneuvers, a culture in which no one has ever lost a finger or ruined a knee on the job, a culture in which working outdoors at dawn at three degrees Fahrenheit is an event to be theorized. There are lots of wonderful things about this culture, but there's a vocabulary and a tone you're just not going to be accustomed to if you grew up in rural Vermont or industrial Michigan or California's Central Valley. Use this book and practice often; academia may always be a second language, but at least you'll be able to navigate its daily transactions.

Aa

ABD. Short for "All but **dissertation**," it marks the point at which a doctoral student has completed all of her coursework, passed her exams, and has her dissertation proposal approved. (It's also the point at which she can call herself a "doctoral **candidate**," rather than merely a "doctoral student.") People occasionally put ABD in the education category of their **CV**s, but probably shouldn't. It's a somewhat humorous attempt to have letters after your name before you get the three letters that count, though it can be a useful indicator of a colleague's progress toward degree. "How's Michelle doing at Emory?" "She's great, making good time ... ABD after only three years."

ABD also, though, marks a point of vulnerability in degree completion. Up to that moment, you're still a student, with courses, papers, exams, and **deadlines**. Someone else is managing your progress and setting your agenda—which, after more than twenty years of formal education, is familiar and comfortable. Once you're ABD, though, you're expected to act like a scholar rather than a student, and set your own pace, agenda, and standards for acceptable work. That's a huge transition, one that many students don't survive.[1] Couple that with the fact that ABD students may lose the opportunity for institutional support, and may move away to do fieldwork and thus lose the social encouragement of fellow students and daily contact with dissertation supervisors, and the end of the doctoral course has more obstacles than we'd like to admit.

1. The typical completion rate for students entering doctoral programs runs from less than half in the humanities to about two-thirds in engineering, and too much of that attrition happens after coursework is completed. Maureen Grasso, Melissa Barry, and Thomas Valentine, *A Data-Driven Approach to Improving Doctoral Completion* (Washington: Council of Graduate Schools, 2009), accessed April 27, 2015, http://www.cgsnet.org /cgs-occasional-paper-series/university-georgia/chapter-1.

The ABD represents a transitional moment from student to colleague. **Dissertation committee** members must recognize that this transition has both logistical and emotional components, and that both require management. Losing a student at this stage is tragic all around; the investment has been great, the commitment even greater. It's as if we have felled a tree, milled the lumber, kiln-dryed the boards, framed a house, and then never roofed or enclosed it; what could have become a home is instead just a marker of resources squandered.

Abstract. When I worked on my **dissertation**, I was clear with my **committee** members that even though I was engaged in social science, I wanted to create a work of literary nonfiction. I had in mind writers like Paul Goodman and Joan Didion, writers who could draw powerful meaning from the everyday circumstances around us. I wanted my work to be read rather than merely shelved. (That's why I had a novelist on my dissertation committee.)

The day after my successful dissertation **defense**, one of the associate **deans** came to me to finalize paperwork for submitting the dissertation to University Microfilms International, the American standard repository for dissertations and **masters' theses**. He asked me to revise my abstract to include findings. The very thought repulsed me. How could I possibly encapsulate all of these stories, all of these lives, into a paragraph? And why would I give away the end of the story before a reader ever had a chance to engage it? It was like the ultimate spoiler.

I didn't understand the nature of the abstract as a literary genre, a paratext that only some would read. An abstract of an academic article or book is a brief guide to whether or not a particular academic reader would find it worthwhile to download or ask her **library** to order. Academics are swamped with text, usually text that isn't any fun to read. Rather than slog through the whole landscape, they use an article's abstract to help them decide whether to slog through one particular acre of it. Here's a broad paint-by-numbers guide to constructing an abstract.

In [my subfield], [some phenomenon] is well understood, but it is not yet clear [some adjacent phenomenon]. This study employed [some **method**] in order to better understand [a component of the unclear phenomenon]. As a result, [particularly interesting, important, or counterintuitive findings]. These results offer [implications for further research or external applicability].

As an example, here's an abstract you might see for this very book.

In higher education, considerable attention has been paid to the typical sequences of graduate school and faculty careers, but this attention has not been sufficiently detailed so that prospective community members might truly understand the culture they hope to enter. This book offers a glossary of important, and likely unfamiliar, terms so that prospective doctoral students and faculty members might better understand the daily experience of the path they're considering. As a result, I hope that those students may have a more realistic and empowered sense of their possible futures in higher ed. This work offers resources not only for student readers, but also for experienced faculty and administrators charged with the welfare and progress of doctoral students and early-career faculty.

You should read the abstract of every article that comes to you in seminar, and start to learn the fine points of the genre as it pertains to your field. Academic writing has a thousand elements of form—elements that are rarely taught and must be intuited anew by each generation. Learn to copy from the masters, just as painters and musicians learn by replicating what already exists.[2]

Academic freedom. Whenever some group of people feels that it has the liberty to follow ideas wherever they lead, others will feel that they have the responsibility to temper or channel or restrict those developments for what they perceive to be collective benefit. And whenever the collective wisdom is that some individual has acted irresponsibly or dangerously, the individual responds with claims to freedom and liberty. So it is in all social life, and so it is in academia.

Academic freedom is simple in principle: scholars must not be prohibited from, censured for, or overridden in the findings of their honestly practiced intellectual work. But of course, the concept becomes far more nuanced when applied in any context and practice. When Noam Chomsky writes political analysis, he's speaking from outside his academic basis in linguistics; is that protected academic speech or just civic life? When a teacher

2. One of my favorite higher ed books is Gerald Graff and Cathy Birkenstein's *They Say, I Say: The Moves that Matter in Persuasive Writing*, 3rd edition (New York: W. W. Norton, 2014). It's a series of templates, similar to the one I've offered for building an abstract, that helps novice writers see patterns in the texts around them and make use of those patterns themselves.

offering a course on feminist thought asks that enrollment be limited only to female students, is that an intellectual choice or a discrimination?

Academic freedom is often considered as a bill of rights, though rarely codified on a given campus. Academics are usually considered to have the right to

- manage their classrooms to achieve their intellectual goals for their students;
- freely choose their own topics of research interest;
- submit their scholarly findings for critical review, and publish them if the review warrants; and
- respond to the work of others with honest, reasoned critique.

In the wild, of course, all of these are subject to modification and negotiation. And as Victor Frankl once wrote, the Statue of Liberty on America's East Coast should be balanced by a Statue of Responsibility on the West. In this case, the countering responsibilities might be considered to be

- the awareness of one's own biases in **teaching**, and the creation of an academic environment that is safe and respectful of all participants;
- the creation of courses that take their places within a larger **curriculum**, reflecting both the college's mission and the **discipline**'s or profession's standards;
- the selection and practice of research that is in the public interest, is free from conflict of interest, makes judicious use of resources, and carefully considers its ethical obligations to human and animal participants;
- the generous acknowledgement of the work of others, whether mentored students, **postdoctoral** staff, project collaborators, or prior scholars and their writings; and
- the maintenance of an open record of one's intellectual steps, and the free and public distribution of one's findings.

And in just these two simple lists of clear principles, there is enough ambiguity to disagree about almost any decision.

Rather than get into contextual details of how academic freedom plays out in specific case studies, I want to talk here about how you, as a doctoral student or an early-career faculty member, won't have any.

As a doctoral student, you will follow the research interests and **methods** of your supervising faculty. Sometimes, that's very literal, as in the laboratory sciences: doctoral students are brought in to be part of specific work teams, and some interesting problem is hived off from the larger project and made to be that junior researcher's specialty. In the more interpretive fields, doctoral students typically aren't part of lab teams, but you still have to choose topics for which you can find guidance and supervision from among your faculty. If you're a physical anthropologist in a **department** filled with ethnographers, or if you want to study Arts and Crafts bungalows and your faculty are all involved in digital design fabrication, you're not going to have a happy experience.

The degree of academic freedom that you do have will come through choosing the right program with the right **mentors**, so that your desired goals can be achieved with resources they'll already have and trust. Making that fundamental decision well gets you a long way toward the intellectual leash length to follow your own inklings and desires. But be prepared to be periodically or even frequently overruled. Your faculty advisers will have their own favorite bodies of knowledge and systems of interpretation, and you'll have to incorporate them. If you want to support yourself, you'll need to take on a **research assistantship** or a **teaching assistantship** in which, as in any job, your supervisor's priorities will become your own.

Once you become an early-career faculty member, you will avoid making waves, will attempt to pursue research that attains **indirect cost** support (and good public relations) for the college, and will attempt to **grade** your students' work so that the median across your courses comes out more or less at a B. You will serve on committees that seem to have been scripted by Samuel Beckett, and walk the line between doing what your department **chair** asks and being seen by the others in the department as too closely allied with that chair and his cronies.

The perfect land of intellectual freedom comes near the end of one's career, when all **tenure** and promotion hurdles have been safely crossed— only then does a faculty member truly have the ability to ignore the overt and subtle pressures for conformity. Unfortunately, by that time, most will have been house-trained sufficiently to not seek the open door.

Accreditation. If you want to be a doctor, you have to get a license. So too if you want to be a social worker, an electrician, a barber, a hair stylist, a forester, or a commercial trucker. But the world of higher education, although it may not be visible to the civilian eye, has a lot more in common with fashion modeling than it does to medicine. Just as models become models because some beautiful people see a new beautiful person and say, "She's got it," so too everything about academic life is governed by **peer review**, in which those who are acknowledged to hold some capabilities recognize others as having similar capabilities. There's no licensing exam to become a college **faculty** member—just people in the club who see a particular new person and say, "Welcome in."

It turns out that whole colleges also live and die by peer review, through the process of accreditation. The United States is divided into regions, and each region has an accrediting body for education (extending from kindergarten through doctoral research universities) that periodically reviews each school's practices and prospects and offers an opinion about its continued viability. Some accrediting bodies are known primarily through acronyms (such as SACS) and others by geographic shorthand (like Middle States), but whenever you hear a college **administrator** say that SACS or Middle States "is coming," you can be sure that it's with the same trepidation as a meteorologist tracking a hurricane's likely landfall.

Having been a college's NEASC (New England Association of Schools and Colleges, pronounced "knee-ask") accreditation liaison, supervising the school's review process, and having served on a NEASC visiting team to review another school, I'll use the NEASC practices as an overview; the others, since they're all recognized by the Commission on Higher Education Accreditation (CHEA, pronounced "chia," as in "Chia Pet"), play by pretty similar rules. NEASC asks each of its 243 member colleges in New England—from Yale University to the Woods Hole Oceanographic Institution to Kennebec Valley Community College to the Gordon-Conwell Theological Seminary—to submit an annual report about its operational status. But the big adventure is the cyclical accreditation "visit," a shorthand for the hurricane of events that will disrupt the entire operation of the institution, usually leaving its survivors shaken but standing.

NEASC, under normal circumstances, schedules an accreditation visit for each school in ten-year increments. Work on the visit begins two years or so in advance, with the mobilization of a team responsible for creating what's called a "self-study," a massive report that covers all aspects of institutional operation:[3]

---

3. It's often the case that there are eleven teams of two to five people each, assigned to write the eleven sections of the self-study—a practice I can't advise against strongly enough. Far better, for both writing consistency and schedule maintenance, is to have

1. mission and purposes
2. planning and evaluation
3. organization and governance
4. academic program
5. faculty
6. students
7. library and information resources
8. physical and technological resources
9. financial resources
10. public disclosure
11. integrity

The self-study is a promotional tool of careful literary craft, through which an institution seeks to describe itself in the most advantageous terms available to it. A college with steadily declining enrollment will focus on its coming new programs that are better aligned with the realities of the changing economics of its region; a school that's lost money for five straight years will crow about its restructured **development** office and the stream of income sure to follow; a college that has a faculty that's 80 percent adjuncts will talk about the importance of teachers with active professional lives. Once the self-study is prepared by the underlings, it's usually marked up and massaged by the **provost** and **president** for optimal public-relations impact before final submittal.

Once the self-study is submitted, usually in the summer prior to the accreditation year, NEASC chooses a visiting team made up of five or six faculty members and administrators from other NEASC schools. The visiting team members get the self-study a couple of months before the visit, as well as assignments for which of the eleven standards they'll each focus on most specifically.

When the team descends upon the school for its actual visit, the school puts forth its best hospitality: nice restaurants, a goody bag, flowers in the hotel rooms, and an army of impromptu concierges ready to escort a team member or locate a resource at the least hint of need. The team operates from a "team room," a locked space to which only the team has access, fully supplied with computers, printers, the school's most comfortable chairs, records specific to each of the eleven standards, and snacks and sodas galore.

---

a single coordinator receiving information from all eleven groups and being solely responsible for coordinating and writing it all herself.

Before the team leaves, after three days and dozens of interviews, they offer a summary of their observations, but aren't allowed to give the secret nod that a school has or has not passed accreditation; the decision isn't theirs to make. Instead, they'll go home and write an overview of what they've seen pertaining to each standard, and the team chair will write a summary of praise and recommendations. After some back and forth among the team, that report is sent to the NEASC office and to the school under review; the school has the "opportunity" (universally taken) to write a commentary on the report, offering clarifications or politely worded rebuttal. Then the self-study, the report, and the school's commentary all get forwarded to "the commission," a body of two dozen or so volunteers from within and beyond higher ed who meet quarterly to review accreditation packages and make recommendations. The commission can choose to renew a school's accreditation wholeheartedly, to renew it with some focused areas of improvement that will be expected within a certain time frame, or to put a school on probation until significant and wide-ranging improvements are shown. Repeated probation can, in rare cases, result in the commission removing its accreditation altogether; a school might also close or merge with another institution rather than suffer the humiliation of a terminal defeat.

When only a handful of well-to-do families sent their children to a handful of well-to-do colleges, institutional accreditation was simply a marker of perceived quality among one's peers. But today, accreditation by one of these regional bodies opens the door to participation in various federal and state higher-education programs, most especially students' eligibility for financial aid. Given that more than 80 percent of college students receive some federal financial aid,[4] accreditation underpins the entire financial structure of higher education.

There is also a wide range of disciplinary accreditations that pertain only to one **department** on campus: the National Architectural Accreditation Board, the National Association of Schools of Art and Design, the American Chemical Society, and dozens of others. Some of these carry weight with regard to professional licensure of graduates, while others are simply opportunities for recognition and quality control. Find out whether your **discipline** has an accrediting body, and make sure that any institution you're considering for grad school or for employment has had a stable regional accreditation.

4. National Center for Education Statistics, "Fast Facts," accessed December 28, 2014, http://nces.ed.gov/fastfacts/display.asp?id=31.

Acronym. I've been in higher ed for decades, and not a day goes by when I'm with colleagues that I don't hear a new acronym that others seem to recognize and I don't. It's OK; go ahead and ask.

Lots of them will be organizations: AAC&U, SACS, NAICU, NOMAS. Some will be programs or offices: RCR, IRB, REU, GSA. Some will be standard practices: RFP, ITR, FWI. The real trick is to know whether to pronounce the letters (more accurately an "initialism" than an acronym) or try to say it as a word. I've been part of the Council on Undergraduate Research for a long time, and it's pronounced like the dog; it always sounds funny to hear a newbie pronounce it as "see-you-are." NAICU (the National Association of Independent Colleges and Universities) doesn't look like a word, but it's most often pronounced "nye-cue," or sometimes "nay-cue." Even there, of course, there are subtleties: The National Collegiate Athletic Association has always been "N, C, double-A," but the American Association of Colleges and Universities is "A, A, C, and U." If you were to say "Double-A, C, U" in a conversation, I'll bet half of your listeners wouldn't know what the heck you were talking about, even if they'd been AAC&U members for years.

The extensive use of acronyms can act as a field marker to help differentiate **faculty** and **administrators** at a quick glance. Administrators, because of their coordinative roles, tend to work across a lot of different programs. I just received an **e-mail** that employed eight distinct program acronyms in four short paragraphs, each of which was a proxy for months or years of experience and multiple people involved. Faculty members—focused as they are on specific students, specific bodies of research, and specific funding agencies—tend to have a far more constrained acronymic vocabulary.

If you get to start a program, don't torture yourself making its name work out into a cute word. There are too many programs called stuff like Ably Completing Homework with Intellectual Energy and Vigorous Engagement (a highfalutin study hall) or Students Committed to High Outcomes, Learning, And Results (none of whom will finish their refrigeration-repair certificate program). Call it Childress's Law: The more blandly pleasant the acronym word is, the less rigor there'll be in the program's conception and execution.

Adjunct faculty. Also known as contractual faculty, contingent faculty, instructors, or lecturers. Whatever the term, we're referring to people who are paid (badly) by the course to teach, and who typically have no other affiliation with the college, rarely receive benefits beyond their stipend, and have no suggestion of permanence or protection. This group is increasing in both number and proportion in higher education, and is nearing 60 percent of the instructional community nationwide.[5]

As the oversupply of PhDs increases, the competition even for adjunct positions can be high. It's an efficient market in major urban centers, where the abundance of doctoral programs and well educated persons makes "filling a course" pretty easy. In less populous markets (or in professional **disciplines** in which **doctorates** are rare), the bar for entry is lowered, and a master's degree can be sufficient to get a teaching gig.

If you take on an adjunct position, you should insist on knowing several things.

- How much will you be paid for this course, and when will that occur? Will taxes be withheld, or are you on your own?
- Is the stipend all there is, or are there some prorated benefits involved? (There are some schools—usually **unionized**—in which retirement contributions are made on behalf of adjunct as well as permanent faculty.)
- Will you be expected to hold **office hours**? Will you have an office in which to do that?
- What kinds of computing resources will be available to you, and will you have a college e-mail address?
- How many students are likely to be enrolled in this course? If it's a huge class, will you have **teaching assistants**? What happens to your stipend if the course is canceled due to low enrollment?
- Is there a separate stipend for **course development** if you're creating or substantially revising a course? And who owns the course materials that you create?
- If the course goes well, is it likely that you'll be asked to return, or perhaps to take on additional courses?

You should also know that there is only one path available from the adjunct to the permanent faculty, and that is for doctoral students who are teaching at their own or another college in order to support themselves while completing their **dissertations**. Once you have completed your PhD and teach as an adjunct subsequent to your degree, you immediately ac-

---

5. American Association of University Professors, "Figure 1: Trends in Instructional Staff Employment Status, 1975–2009," accessed April 27, 2015, http://www.aaup.org/NR/rdonlyres/7C3039DD-EF79-4E75-A20D-6F75BA01BE84/0/Trends.pdf.

quire the stench of desperation and will be shunned by hiring committees forever.[6] Publishing and being accepted to present at conferences will be more difficult without a faculty affiliation, and of course, you'll pay your own way. Yes, you have to eat, and taking on four or five (or more) courses a semester will at least keep a low rent covered and gas paid from one campus to another; but don't imagine that it's a step in the right direction. Do anything in your power to avoid teaching as an adjunct after completing your **doctorate**. Stay on as a **research assistant** in your lab or research group; get an industry visiting position (ideally term-limited, so that it isn't a "**career** move") and doesn't thus mark you as being disloyal to academia) or scholarly **postdoc**; anything but teaching at some poor college to make a couple thousand dollars.

Remember when you were eleven years old and your dog died? That's the kind of news I'm bringing you here. If you are a doctorate-holding adjunct instructor for more than two years, you must seriously think about a career change. There are ways of making a living that will use some of your intellectual skills and give you livable pay and benefits. Don't be the guy who refuses to leave the casino, thinking that the next hand will be the big turnaround. You gambled, you had a good time, but you lost. Go home. Now.

Administration. Like any industrially sized workplace, a college workforce can be divided roughly into labor and management. Labor—in this case, the faculty and graduate students—actively produces the scholarly and teaching work that the institution offers for sale. But as important as that is, it's scarcely enough for most institutions of all but the most boutique scale to operate.

Some of the administrative functions a college requires are relatively obvious. Somebody needs to pay the bills, so colleges have various forms of accounting and bookkeeping staff. Somebody needs to manage payroll and benefits and labor law compliance, so colleges have human resources departments. Somebody has to fix the plumbing and tend the grounds, so colleges have **facilities management** teams. Somebody has to be in charge, so colleges have **presidents**. But that's only a couple of dozen people—so

6. Yes, of course this is an overstatement, but only just. It is crucial to understand that getting an adjunct position in a desirable department will not in any way position you for a subsequent faculty line there or elsewhere, and may work against you by labeling you as "merely" a teacher, one whose scholarship is increasingly stale.

why are most colleges at or near a 1:1 ratio of labor and management?[7] (Seventy percent of the positions posted in *Higher Ed Jobs* during 2014 were administrative rather than faculty.)[8]

Well, a few things have happened. One is that public colleges used to be very low-cost for in-state residents, because we used to believe in paying taxes for public goods (and also believed that a generally well educated populace was, self-evidently, a public good). But over the past forty years, college has largely come to be seen not as a public good provided inexpensively, but rather as a consumer good purchased for individual benefit. What that means is that for most families, college had once been a relatively spartan public service: huge dormitories with gang bathrooms, lunch-lady-style food service, a gym with a half-sized pool and a half-baked weight room, inconvenient parking if any at all. But now, colleges have to compete against one another in the quality of their amenities, and we're all choosy consumers—so a vast system of student life administration (and associated facilities, upkeep, and other overhead) is now the norm for most colleges.

We also acknowledge that learning happens outside classrooms, a surprisingly recent idea. So some mix of offices of community engagement, **undergraduate research**, international travel, and other co-curricular supports have arisen in most colleges. In addition, we've finally figured out that being smart is not sufficient to make someone a good teacher, so lots of schools now have permanent faculty development teams to put on workshops and do coaching for teachers. Whenever you see a "center for **teaching** and learning," which you might naively think is just a synonym for "college," what you've found is the faculty teaching-support service. And there are endless requirements for **assessment** of outcomes, comparisons with peer groups, participation in consortia; each of those requires personnel and **travel** and meetings.

Another phenomenon is that, as a society, we've developed a stronger sense of social justice; we care about issues and people that we used to not care about (a care which often takes the form of regulation). There are equal opportunity offices, and resources for mental health and drug intervention

7. Or worse . . . public research universities collectively have a FTE faculty to FTE administration ratio of 0.55; that is, just about half as many FT faculty as FT administrators. Jenny Rogers, "3 to 1: That's the Best Ratio of Tenure-Track Faculty to Administrators, a Study Concludes," *Chronicle of Higher Education* (November 12, 2012).
8. Higher Ed Jobs, "Higher Education Employment Report, Fourth Quarter and Annual, 2014," accessed April 27, 2015, http://www.higheredjobs.com/documents/HEJ_Employment_Report_2014_Q4.pdf.

and learning disabilities and child care and student employment support. The informal image of higher ed prior to recent years was that all students were white, all were straight, most were male, all were between the ages of eighteen and twenty-two, single and childless and in good physical health, financially and emotionally supported by their parents, native English speakers and readers, prone to too much beer but not much else. Now that we know better and intend better, we offer more resources in support of a more diverse community.

Technology has also inflated administrative size. Aside from a few schools with elite engineering and computer science programs, colleges didn't have "information technology" departments when I first went to school. The relevant forms of information technology were typewriters, adding machines, index card files, and carbon paper, and they came from the same operations office as the pens and envelopes. Now there's a substantial division on any campus whose job is to maintain desktops and laptops and servers, to update software and work out bugs between older and newer versions, to extract reports from immense databases, to manage electronic **learning management systems**, and to conduct data backups and post-disaster reinstallations. (Make friends with these people, soon.)

Finally, and likely most immediate to your concerns, higher education is following the role of most other industries and centralizing its decision making at the managerial level, minimizing the role of labor through both number and power. The proportion of instruction carried out by contract labor is increasing, and the proportion of tenure-track faculty assumed to have a permanent relationship with their schools is plummeting. The operation of the school, historically a divided form of government between the executive branch and the legislative (faculty senate) branch, is increasingly skewing toward the "strong executive" model in which administrations are larger and more empowered. There *are* some good things about this: radical democracy of the kind that occurs in faculty-driven schools tends to slow organizational change and privilege historic practices. And it's a truism, nonetheless too often true, that the people least capable in teaching and research will be the ones most interested in running the faculty senate; faculty governance is noted for its oversupply of small-minded curmudgeons and nitpickers.

But the change toward the administrative university has a couple of important negative ramifications for your life. One is that there will be fewer permanent faculty positions, which means more competition as you enter the market. And the other is that you'll often run into unexpected obstacles when you want to take on a project, because some college office or another will want to have a say in how your project is organized and operated. As in any bureaucracy, whether Comcast or Michigan State University, there will be rules and procedures you will never have imagined.

Find an organizational chart of your prospective institution, and have an experienced member of the college community walk you through it. Don't gloss over it; expect to spend at least a couple of hours on your study. It's crucial that you know how the institution works, who the players are, and how your work might be both supported and hindered.

Administrative assistant. Every institution of moderate to large size operates through the unseen and unrecognized work of many, many secretaries and clerks. These are the people who make sure you have a room to teach in, who conduct your travel bookings, who make sure that you're reimbursed when you come back from a **conference** and there's food at your reception and the guest speaker is paid and the course evaluations are distributed and the accrediting team is happy with their accommodations.

Whenever you have some basic question with the root "How do I . . . ?", you'll ask an administrative assistant, who will either know the answer or will know whom to ask. Please be kind to them; acknowledge them as crucial allies in the work. Don't do rote things like bring candy or a card on Administrative Professionals Day; find out who they are, what they like. Treat them the same way you do any of your friends at work. They're good people, often educated far beyond the nature of their job description: in my last office, two of the four administrative assistants had master's degrees, and one of the others was an active professional musician. The musician's predecessor was, oddly enough, an internationally sought-after choreographer of marching bands. Just because someone prints your letters onto letterhead and orders sandwiches for meetings doesn't mean that's all he has to offer.

You may, like me, carry the particular mental disability of hating to ask people for help. I don't want to add burdens onto already burdened workers. So let me recommend a few hints to help both you and your admin assistant feel better about things:

- Try to give lead time. Don't ask for work that needs a ten-minute turnaround; if you can ask for something with a **deadline** three or four days from now, that's far more welcomed.
- Don't be fussy about things that don't warrant fussiness. If you're sending a letter to the president of the American Association of

Colleges and Universities, you want the printer to align the paper exactly right; if you're sending your receipts to Accounting for reimbursement, it doesn't matter much if it's printed two degrees askew. Don't ask for four iterations of your itinerary planning in order to save twenty minutes in layover time. "Easygoing" is a re- markably endearing adjective when it comes to one's colleagues.

- Don't confuse organizational hierarchy with power. You're not "her boss." Your department's administrative assistant is probably super- vised by a senior administrative manager; you don't get to decide when she comes in or goes home or how she does her job or when she takes lunch. You're asking for assistance, and if you're a gener- ous, friendly person, you'll get it more quickly and amiably than that jerk down the hall who's always threatening to get her fired.

The administrative assistants around you are, like all groups, people of mixed talent and mixed intention. In my experience, the mix is more posi- tive among admins than it is among almost any other group on campus.

Administrator. Most colleges have predictable hierarchies of administrative roles on the academic side. We don't wear epaulets or stripes on our sleeves, but they're understood to be there. **Chairs** take care of individual **depart- ments**, and **deans** take care of a number of chairs. **Provosts** (also referred to as academic vice presidents or the like) corral the entirety of the deans, and argue on behalf of their educational needs to the **president** (who is also beset by other vice-presidential arguments related to finance, **facilities**, athletics, student services, and fund-raising). If the **faculty** members are the enlisted troops who range from private to sergeant, the administrators are the commissioned officers from lieutenants to generals. And as in military hierarchy, each of the two communities claims that the other is ignorant of reality.

One of my good friends is a faculty member who launched a new gradu- ate program at her school and had taken a three-year leave of absence from her department to chair this new entity. Her faculty colleagues felt aban- doned; her administrative colleagues treated her as an interloper. Another friend was recently strong-armed by his college president to leave his own faculty position to become the school's provost. He'd been a faculty member there for a dozen years, but at the first faculty meeting he attended in his new position, he found longtime colleagues saying—*in his presence*—things like "Well, the provost wants . . ." or "The provost needs to advocate for . . . ."

Without any change in his larger identity, my friend was no longer their colleague William P. Goodguy; he had in their eyes gone over to the dark side, and become the [nameless] provost.

So why are administrators the natural enemies of the faculty? (I was going to make some analogy to cats and dogs, but I'm sure those on each side see themselves as the pack-oriented, amiable, and good-natured canines, and their opposites as the scheming, fussy, and disloyal felines, so I gave it up.) Think about the two roles. Faculty members are paid to be teachers, scholars, and department members. All of those are focal tasks. The relationships and allegiances are close at hand, the topical material that got them interested in higher education still makes up much of their everyday lives, and their attention is constantly drawn to the detailed and esoteric world of their **disciplines**. Administrators, on the other hand, typically have no direct students and rarely an active scholarly agenda. They're called upon to engage the overall health of the institution, to look beyond the relationships and allegiances they formed as teachers and scholars in order to take the measure of the whole. Instead of dealing with six faculty colleagues and fifty students in the major, a dean might have responsibility for 106 faculty and 1,500 students. Administrators are at much more immediate mercy of the mercurial desires of the college's **president**, and thus have less predictability in their work from year to year (or in particularly bad cases, from day to day) than faculty members, who know more or less what they'll teach and what they'll research well into the future. The two communities have different sets of responsibilities and different parties to whom they're immediately responsible.

In most cases, administrators have to prioritize from among far too many good possibilities. Colleges are filled with smart people, after all, and smart people come up with smart projects. And we academics have been patted on our heads since childhood for being clever, so we do tend to personalize a rejection, even when that rejection is based not on the quality of our work but rather on some larger institutional agenda, much of which we can't see. So if a faculty member's project isn't funded, or their **curriculum** has to change, or they have to add a course to their **teaching load** for a semester, there are only a handful of possible meanings they can imagine:

1. You don't think my work is good enough.
2. You don't understand my work well enough.
3. You don't like me.
4. You're vile and cruel.

And it could be that none of these are true; a well-intentioned chair or dean may recognize that the work is smart and important, and may think highly of the faculty member who's doing it, but may have to respond to a budget or a piece of legislation or an **accreditation** requirement or a presidential fantasy in ways that cause other projects to take precedence.

In the late 1960s, Laurence Peter and his coauthor Raymond Hull developed the idea of the Peter Principle: that people who are good at what they do are promoted into jobs that require different kinds of skills, and continue to be promoted until finally they reach jobs they're no good at. The oft-quoted summary of their work is: "Every employee tends to rise to his level of incompetence." Colleges are no different than any other organization in this regard; in fact, Laurence Peter himself was a faculty member and administrator at the University of Southern California. In any mature organization, higher-level positions are often held by people with little training or experience in that form of work. Just as faculty members who got their jobs through stellar research find themselves as untrained teachers and proposal writers, deans and provosts who got their jobs through successfully leading intellectual work find themselves dealing with organizational budgets in the millions of dollars and the political climate of public policy and private donors. It's a miracle that the enterprise works even a little bit, but it does, and we should all cut each other a little slack.

Age. Nobody wants to acknowledge this, of course, but many characteristics unrelated to your suitability for intellectual service will work in your favor or work against you as you enter the academic **job market**. That's why you dress well for an interview, and why you don't use a typeface like 𝔏ucíδía 𝔅𝔩𝔞𝔠𝔨𝔩𝔢𝔱𝔱𝔢𝔯 for your **CV** (even if you're applying for a position in 𝔥𝔢𝔞𝔳𝔶 𝔪𝔢𝔱𝔞𝔩 𝔰𝔱𝔲δí𝔢𝔰).

So we all know those things that mom and dad taught us: wash behind your ears, sit up straight, smile, firm handshake. There are, however, some other things that you can't control, and that your hiring committee will notice: for instance, your height, your weight, your complexion, your general physical attractiveness. As always, it's likely that being physically attractive will work to your advantage if you're male, since it's thought that men can be both beautiful *and* capable. And as always, it's likely that being physically attractive will work against you if you're female, since it's too often thought that women can only be beautiful *or* capable.

You can disguise your physical appearance somewhat, with the help of talented tailors and stylists. And you should absolutely do your best to manage the appearance of your age as well. You're shooting for twenty-eight to thirty-three as a starting **assistant professor**. Younger than that, and you're a little too close in age to the undergrads; older than that, and you're not going to reward the hiring committee with a three-decade colleague. But really, those reasons are just me trying to rationalize a bias; the fact is that if you're not in that window, you don't fit the image the hiring committee has of a new faculty member, and that image is powerful.

This is another example of the ways in which class works in higher education. In a 2008 article for *Inside Higher Ed*, a doctoral student named Sterling Fluharty discussed his statistical findings that older candidates get less prestigious jobs, if any.

> If you have the resources and privilege to attend a highly selective institution for your bachelor's degree, start graduate school as soon as you earn your bachelor's degree, and then work continuously on your degree without having to stop to earn money, then you will probably go far in this profession . . . If you were raised without these resources and privilege, if you took a few years off between your bachelor's and graduate programs, or if you received your doctorate in your mid- to late 30s, then you might as well as admit that your doctorate will likely get you little more than a low-paying or adjunct position.[9]

I was actually advised of this directly by my undergraduate **mentor**, a brilliant and kind man who occasionally opened the curtains of higher ed for me. I had gone back to college late, and was finishing up my undergrad at age thirty-one. I told him that I wanted to go on to grad school, and he said, "well, let's see, that would make you thirty-five or thirty-six when you get your PhD . . . that's not *too* old." But, although I was warned explicitly, I worked in an architectural research firm for two years to save some money; even though I powered through my doctoral program in five years, I got my PhD when I was thirty-eight. I didn't know it, but I was about to be remaindered to the dollar store with all the other expired groceries.

Again, a statistical trend doesn't predict a specific instance. If you're going to finish your PhD program at age fifty-two, as one of my fellow students did, and it really matters to you that you're doing it, you have to live

---

9. Scott Jaschik, "Bias against Older Candidates." *Inside Higher Ed* (December 17, 2008), accessed April 27, 2015, http://www.insidehighered.com/news/2008/12/17/age.

your life the way you see fit.[10] But it would be irresponsible of me to not put the trends on the table.

Alt-careers. With the university **faculty** economy in shambles, there's been a lot of talk in recent years about alternative **career** paths, the word *alternative* usually intended as a synonym for *emergency backup*. But the fact is that you're almost certainly going to have an alt-career, given that higher ed hiring has become so gruesome.

The problem is that there aren't many careers aside from college **teaching** that either require or take advantage of the critical skills that doctoral life brings.[11] If you attempt to do "research" within the professions, you'll quickly discover the concept of the billable hour; there just isn't scope within most professional budgets for risky thinking and the inevitable pondering and confusion that precedes it, nor do most clients want to hear something other than a finely detailed and workable version of what they were already planning. You'll hear the word "overqualified" relatively often, as you compete with baccalaureate holders for jobs as a financial analyst or state government administrator.

The physical sciences have the best track record of employment outside academia; the University of Pennsylvania's PhD alumni questionnaire, for instance, shows the vast majority of their nonfaculty alumni in healthcare/medicine and biotech/pharmaceuticals.[12] Lab life is lab life, regardless of venue. But if your **doctorate** is in history or anthropology, the alt-careers are neither as evident nor as uniform. As generations of families have said to their kids, "Literature? What are you gonna do with a degree in literature?"[13]

10. He already had a faculty position on the basis of having a terminal degree (M. Arch) in his field; for him, the PhD was both an intellectual journey and the possibility of promotion. He wasn't starting out on the market at age fifty-two, which would have been foolhardy.

11. Certainly not K–12 teaching, which not only will ignore your PhD in favor of required state certification (yay, *another* few years of schooling to go through!), but also has curricula that are much more tightly constrained by state departments of education. There just isn't much room for intellectual life in a high-stakes-testing, quantitative-outcomes school structure.

12. University of Pennsylvania, Division of Vice Provost for University Life, "8–13 Year Out PhD Alumni Survey," accessed March 21, 2015, http://www.vpul.upenn.edu/career services/8–13yearphdsurvey.php#Question3.1.

13. To which the best answer, I think, is, "I can keep studying literature, because I love doing it."

Most good graduate programs will have a career services department, but it'll be dealing with the entirety of the university population, from undergrads to **postdocs**. Check to see if they have specific resources for doctoral students and postdocs, and how they help their clients prepare for lives both within and outside faculty careers.

The moment of your (successfully passed) **comprehensive exams** makes a terrific moment for career examination. You've done the coursework and preliminary projects that give you a pretty good sense of what life in your academic **discipline** will feel like; now have a serious conversation with your broader galaxy of professional friends and family members about what the white-collar world has to offer, and the pleasures of the worlds of business or public administration. Think about how your **dissertation** and its inherent skills might translate to the professional world, and keep your eyes open for unseen paths hidden in the roadside brush.

As we attempt to tell our undergrads all the time, there's no reason that education must invariably be tied to a certain form of employment. Not only is the entire formulation of "I'll do A so that I can get to B" unreliable in a social ecosystem, but more importantly, if doing A doesn't have enough intrinsic motivation to sustain your interest, then doing B is going to be miserable anyway. Get your PhD and be the best educated, most interesting thinker in your warehouse or restaurant, a way of living that has its own rewards. There are good-natured, good-humored colleagues in all sorts of work, and your life is bigger than your job.

Anonymity and confidentiality. These two terms are too often conflated, but they actually mean very different things. "Anonymous" means you don't know whose information you're seeing; "confidential" means that you do know, but aren't going to tell anybody else. Privacy concerns touch all aspects of higher ed, including issues of human resources, job searches, tenure reviews, and hallway gossip. But I'd like to focus on a few specific forms of anonymity and confidentiality that you ought to consider as you enter this culture.

First, if you do social research, you'll often be promising your participants that they won't be identifiable. Anonymity is the strongest form of that promise, useful for things like questionnaires or online commentary. But if you're interviewing or living among your participants, they're relying on your confidence, because you could completely mess with their lives if you're cavalier with their information. When I did my **dissertation** research among the high schoolers of a Northern California community, I used pseudonyms for the towns involved, all the landscape features smaller than the Pacific Ocean, all the roads, and all the people. That worked perfectly fine for the larger academic readership in Omaha and Orlando; but worked not at all in the context of the local community. They all knew who I was, so when the book came out, they naturally knew what towns Curtisville and Union were, and they knew the shop teacher and that one girl who ran the lights for the school play and the boy who was the photographer for the student newspaper. The kids had all seen in my work in advance and knew how I was representing them, and I tried to avoid the salacious or damaging; but I wasn't able to protect them in the way I'd intended.

Another element of anonymity is blind review, which is **peer review** of scholarly work in which the reviewers and **authors** don't know one another's identities. For journals, double-blind review is common, in which author and reviewer don't know one another's identity. In book publishing, single-blind review is more typical: the reviewers know the identity of the writer, but not vice versa. Blind review is intended to reduce social pressures for kindness and collegiality, and to let the work stand solely on its intellectual merits. (While this is *anonymous* for the participants, the **editor** who receives the manuscript and recruits reviewers is in a position of *confidentiality*—she knows everyone involved, and keeps it under her hat.)

Confidentiality is also related to student records, about which you can read more in the entry on **FERPA**, though the short version is, "Just shut up already and don't say anything." But another, less often considered issue has to do with colleagues' **e-mail**. Although everything on your university e-mail account belongs to the school, nobody's going to look through it unless there's some sort of criminal or security concern. And so students or teachers frequently use e-mail as a way of testing ideas with their colleagues, organizing political support or opposition, or just venting about a terrible faculty member or dopey administrative decision. Please, please, be careful with your use of *reply*, *reply all*, and *forward* in your handling of e-mail. If you have any question at all, ask the person involved whether it's okay to make their message public. Terrible embarrassment and career damage can be done with one thoughtless e-mail command, and once a message has gone public, it is never retrievable.[14]

14. This irretrievability has led to a unit of time measurement known as the *ohnosecond*: the tiny moment between hitting "send" and realizing you shouldn't have.

Assessment. Years and years ago, I wrote a piece on why football was a better learning environment than almost anything we do in the classroom.[15] And one of those reasons is a fact shared with music and woodworking and sex and driving and almost any sport: the immediacy of feedback. You have almost instantaneous connections between an action and an assessment, that assessment being "uh-oh" or "oops" or "ohhhhhmygod."

Education, like dieting and exercise and farming and writing and running for political office, is cumulative rather than immediate. We don't really know whether today's class mattered, to ourselves or to our students. We don't know that their lives have been changed, don't know that some connections were revealed or arcana unlocked, don't know whether the quietest student in the seminar today might write us a kind note fifteen years down the line. But we ask our nation, and our students, to spend hundreds of billions of dollars per year on an enterprise with less assured outcomes than that of using our turn signals.

We have always treated education as a presumed good, as a self-evident benefit to both the individual and society. It's only really been in the past decade that assessment has become a regular part of higher-education parlance, mainly because college has gotten both expensive and broadly accessible. When more and more people consume a more and more costly public good, the public looks in to ask whether or not it's money well spent.

Although assessment in higher education has a long, long history, we might date the contemporary ubiquity of assessment concerns to the Spellings Commission of 2005–6, in which the Bush administration and its secretary of education, Margaret Spellings, opened a year-long investigation of the state of higher education. One of the core components of that investigation was related to accountability, the idea that individual schools could be visibly and uniformly able to demonstrate their outcomes and that the consumer public deserved to know whether one school was "doing better" than another.

Higher education faces a dilemma, though: its purveyors and its consumers hold multiple definitions of what "doing better" means. The Spellings Commission was very particular in naming the primary responsibilities of higher education as economic, contributing to America's collective prosperity and the individual student's financial prospects. If we're going to spend on education, the thinking went, we need a return on investment.

15. Herb Childress, "Seventeen Reasons Why Football Is Better Than High School," *Phi Delta Kappan* 79, no. 8 (April 1998): 616–19.

The concepts of an informed citizenry, the self-actualized life, and the aesthetic delights of encountering and navigating new intellectual landscapes were hardly marginalized; they weren't entertained at all.

Return on investment is easier to measure than informed citizenry or self-actualization or aesthetic pleasure, so assessment can easily skew in that fashion. But ROI also fails by being a globalizing measurement; how can we know whether Professor Ernest Musing's existential philosophy class contributed more to a student's lifetime earnings than Professor Jeanne Sequence's upper-division biochemistry course? (If nothing else, we'd have to wait forty years to find the cumulative contribution.) And how would we know that the session on Thursday, November 19, had a greater responsibility for that success than the session on Tuesday, October 27? Or that Dr. Sequence's students were more economically productive than Dr. Anne Syme's students in the same course?

As you embark on your academic career, you'll undoubtedly be drawn into assessment conversations, with some people urging you toward "common metrics" and other people urging you toward resistance to the whole assessment enterprise. But with regard to any individual course, the greatest component of assessment (and the greatest benefit of all this assessment talk) is that you'll be forced to name for yourself what you want your students to understand and accomplish. You can't know if you're reaching your outcomes until you can name the outcomes you want. The simple exercise of stating clearly what this course is for and what students should be able to do immediately lifts education from the bland status of the "presumed good," and lets you understand whether you're accomplishing what you want, which is all assessment can ever do.

Finally, I'd like to advocate for qualitative as well as quantitative assessment—what Elliot Eisner once called "educational connoisseurship."[16] Education is, among other things, an aesthetic experience: it can please us, move us, unsettle our complacency or build our resolve. As such, it shares characteristics with art, literature, fine food and wine; and Eisner argues that a thoughtful critic can exercise her analysis and judgment on any given instance, just as a good reviewer illuminates elements of a book or a film. There ought to be far more opportunities for classrooms to be public events, with public commentary.

Students themselves are pretty capable reviewers, when taken in the ag-

16. Elliot Eisner, "Educational Connoisseurship and Criticism: Their Form and Functions in Educational Evaluation," *Journal of Aesthetic Education* 10, nos. 3–4 (1976): 135–50.

gregate. Several entrepreneurs have developed websites whereby students can offer ratings of their instructors and courses. RateMyProfessors.com (or RMP) is the most well known of these, and it has drawn endless ire from the academic community, who use it to vent the same weary objections to their students' laziness, incapability of critical judgment, and desire to be entertained rather than challenged. Certainly, as a statistical tool, the RMP system falls short of social science norms, but leave the numbers alone and just read the comments. For the most part, they strike me as relatively nuanced, and their authors are actually quite accepting of a hard course if they think that the workload is clear and helpful. And, having looked at the comments students have made about a great number of my friends in higher education, I can say that in almost every case, the person the students describe is the person I know. In the absence of professional education critics publishing in popular media, RMP is the closest thing we have to public connoisseurship of education.

Assistant professor. That most and least fortunate creature of higher education. The assistant professor is blessed among us for having won the doctoral lottery, being among the one-sixth of all new PhD recipients to get a tenure-line job.[17] A two-dollar scratcher from the liquor store has better odds than one in six.

But even with the **offer** letter and excited e-mails and all the negotiations about salaries and moving expenses, the newly hired Dr. Phil Notquite also knows that he has merely been driven to the doors of the mansion, not given its keys. For the next six years, Dr. Notquite will not be able to say "no" to anyone's request for any purpose. The real hurdle, coming in most cases six or so years after first hire, is the **tenure** review. And that review is conducted primarily by his new colleagues, those same people who already cheated the odds to get him in. He wants to keep on their good side.

So he never declines a course assignment, and gets all the worst ones. He invests far more time than is reasonable in his student mentoring and support, because he can't afford to be responsible for a course with poor **grades** or bad evaluations, or for a parent calling the college **president** to complain because their golden child got an F for plagiarizing material that Dr. Notquite found verbatim after ten seconds on Google.

17. "The Disposable Academic: Why Doing a PhD Is Often a Waste of Time." *The Economist*, 12/16/2010, accessed April 27, 2015, http://www.economist.com/node/17723223.

He never declines a committee assignment, and gets all the worst ones. If some crowd wants to get a group together to air their grievances about how the university's expanded core **curriculum** doesn't allow sufficient courses for content knowledge in the major, he'll be asked to serve, even though it's a committee that cannot in any way succeed. And within that committee, he'll be the one who will research curricula at other colleges, who will find the recommendations of the disciplinary societies. He will be the grunt who does the labor so that the elders can fruitlessly opine. His department **chair** ought to be looking out for his development and steering him away from the dead ends, but the chair's a busy guy, too, and may not be paying attention.

He never turns down a lunch date or a party invitation from his departmental colleagues, and gets all the worst ones. The pontificators and conspiracy theorists, having previously worn out the patience of all of their officemates, will focus their attentions on the new guy, looking once again for an understanding audience. He will be expected to be earnest, empathetic, and supportive. He will attend the parties where the only beverage served is the host's undrinkable home-brewed beer, and where conversations are supplanted by awkward games of Pictionary.

He will be asked, frequently, to be a reviewer for minor-league journals. He will dial back his research aspirations in order to publish more frequent and less interesting small studies; the major project holds too much risk, placing all the eggs into a single basket.

Dr. Notquite will, in short, be in a sort of purgatory state, relying on the supplications of others to move on to glory. He will have left behind his funny, snarky grad-school colleagues, even the worst of whom were occasionally energized by the electric pleasure of discovery. He will not yet have joined the ranks of the senior scholars, who still ignore him at conferences just as they did when he was a graduate student. He will be afloat in the dead waters of labor not yet rewarded, waiting for a favorable wind to show direction.

Associate professor. If Dr. Notquite manages to meet his institution's stated and unstated thresholds of achievement for young **faculty**, he will be invited to submit a dossier of evidence to justify his possible promotion from assistant to associate professor. The nature of this dossier will vary by **department** and **discipline**—the stereotype is "the milk crate," a box (sometimes it really *is* a plastic milk crate) containing

- a syllabus, student work samples, and course evaluations from every course taught;
- an offprint (*not* a photocopy or a Word or PDF original) of every **journal** article published;
- letters of **reference** from internal constituencies, related to **teaching** and campus service;
- letters of reference from external constituencies, related to scholarly merit and service to the larger discipline and profession;
- a copy of every **grant proposal** submitted, their funding outcomes, and reviewers' comments.

This milk crate is the subject of a long review session, in which a committee of fellow faculty from Dr. Notquite's home department or academic division ostensibly reads every damn page of it. It's the equivalent of an **accreditation** review visit, focused on a single person.

The home department typically takes a vote on whether to extend the offer of **tenure**, but that vote is only the start of things. After the department vote, the review then goes to the **dean** of the division, and then on to the **provost**. It's relatively rare to have an upper **administrator** overturn the positive judgment of the department, but the dean and provost will carefully study the case of any negative vote because of the potential for lawsuits. High-powered schools are tougher, and senior administrators all the way up to the **president** can and will nix a candidate already approved by a department.

All of this, just like the selection process for a fraternity or the Masonic Temple, is pretty secretive, and data are hard to come by. How many people, really, are denied their tenure application? The California State University system seems to deny tenure to just below 10 percent of its probationary faculty (not including another 5 percent who see the writing on the wall and resign prior to review),[18] whereas the more elite Penn State, denying tenure to more than 40 percent of its applicants, was in the middle of their unnamed comparison group.[19] And the High Ivies? The old joke is that to

18. California State University Office of the Chancellor, Human Resources, "Report on 2011 Faculty Recruitment and Retention Survey," accessed April 27, 2015, http://www .calstate.edu/hr/FacRecSurvRep11.pdf.
19. Penn State University Vice Provost for Academic Affairs and Office of Planning and Institutional Assessment, "Faculty Tenure-Flow Rates: 2009–10 Annual Report" (January 2010), accessed April 27, 2015, http://www.psu.edu/president/pia/planning_research /reports/spring10-tenureflow.pdf. Note that, at least at Penn State, for thirteen years of

get tenure at most schools, you have to have written a book; at Harvard, you have to have had a book written about you.

But let us be optimistic and say that Professor Notquite's application for promotion has been approved, the champagne opened, and tenure securely held. This is the very last final exam he will ever take; he's now closing in on forty years of age, and has only ever known one model of self-validation: preparing for and passing intellectual hurdles of increasing sophistication. He correctly spelled "disciplinarian" in third grade; he won the high school science fair in tenth grade; he defended a dissertation proposal and then a **dissertation**, and later presented it well enough to get a job; and now he's submitted a huge chunk of work and had it deemed worthy.

Now what?

Life is full of transition moments that confuse us, at which a narrative that has served to guide us is no longer workable. Adolescence, young adulthood, divorce, retirement—all of those are moments at which a formerly reliable story becomes newly, surprisingly outdated. So too the moment of being named an associate professor. Our "student" days are now irrevocably ended; there are no more tests. Pair this with an expanded demand for administrative duties—committee service, faculty governance, **professional societies**—and the associate professor is really entering unfamiliar territory, just at the same time as the easy physical youth of their thirties is giving way to the sudden surprises of a body at forty, maybe the rediscovery of a **partner** and kids marginalized during the marathon of new-faculty life, maybe the first hints of menopause. The midlife crisis hits home in vast and unpredictable ways.[20] And with the average retirement age of academics now over seventy, the new associate professor is looking at thirty more years. He's far too young to be the éminence grise, far too old to be the prodigy; he's now just the institution's middle child.

Author/coauthor. When I was a **research assistant** in my doctoral program, I was part of a **research center** funded by a major manufacturer

---

faculty hires through the 2002 entering cohort, tenure came more easily to white males than it did to minorities and women. Your college had better have this data and make it available to its faculty and prospective faculty.

20. See, for example, the research showing that of all TT ranks, associate professors express the least satisfaction with almost every aspect of their higher-ed careers. Scott Jaschik, "Unhappy Associate Professors," *Inside Higher Ed* (June 4, 2012), accessed December 28, 2014, https://www.insidehighered.com/news/2012/06/04/associate-professors -less-satisfied-those-other-ranks-survey-finds.

of building components. We were asked by that patron to develop a **white paper** related to the concept of environmental quality in the workplace. I did about two-thirds of the conceptual work on that paper, and wrote all of its final text. My doctoral student colleague, a fellow research assistant, was responsible for almost all of the rest of its intellectual development. The head of the institute came to a meeting every couple of weeks and reviewed our work. When that white paper was published, the head of the research institute was listed as the primary author, I was second, and my friend, the other RA, was third.

On the other hand, I later worked on an extensive writing program evaluation in which seven or eight of us met every week for months to determine the nature of the **assessment**, the texts we would have our students use in their writing, and the wording of the rubric against which we would review their work. I set up the review event, designed the carefully blind assignment of papers to reviewers, conducted all of the data analysis, and wrote the entirety of the final report except for its introduction. I was ultimately third author on that one, with the **director** and associate director of the program as first and second authors. The others who participated for a year in the devising of the evaluation weren't credited as authors at all, their contributions lost in the "acknowledgments" paragraph.

Oh well. You win some, you lose some.

The concept of "authorship" is different in academia than it is in literature. A literary author is a one-woman shop—the inventor of the concept, its sole developer, its most central **editor**, and its foremost proofreader. Nobody wonders what Joyce Carol Oates did on a particular manuscript; she did all of it. By contrast, an academic author had some unspecified role in conducting an element of the research, of obtaining its funding, of organizing the working team, of doing data analysis, of devising measurement, of writing text, of editing text, or of offering final approval to publish on behalf of the project. The number of coauthors can multiply almost infinitely on major projects, up to (so far) the 2,926 coauthors[21] from 169 institutions on a 2008 article having to do with the ATLAS particle detector at the Large Hadron Collider, perhaps the best use of "et al." in the history of academic publishing.[22]

---

21. Including four Hills, four Zhaos, four Zhous, six Smiths, and six Joneses. "No no, not *that* Smith, the *other* Smith." There's something Pythonesque about all that.

22. G. Aad, et al., "The ATLAS Experiment at the CERN Large Hadron Collider." *Journal of Instrumentation* 3 (August 2008), http://iopscience.iop.org/1748–0221/3/08/S08003/.

As with almost all of academic life, different norms pertain in different **disciplines**; but really, authorship is still the Wild West, in which power and aggression allow the strong to claim territory. In the laboratory sciences, the lab chief is often first author even if she or he had little or nothing to do with the work under review, because it was her resources and her general line of inquiry that facilitated the work. If you're a lowly **postdoc** who conceived of, conducted, analyzed, and wrote the research, are you really in a position to argue?

Even in the face of institutions' and disciplines' attempts to clarify authorship roles, there's enough gray to paint a navy-ful of battleships and ten thousand English skyscapes. Get clear up front about what authorship means in your field, and check that definition against what your colleagues believe authorship means on your specific project. Just raising that question may label you as crass, premature, or grasping. Better those than uncredited.

Bb

Biographical sketch/statement. If you're asked to present at a **conference** or have a **publication** forthcoming, your **publisher** or speaking host may ask you for a biographical sketch. If there are strict guidelines, you'll be told. Otherwise, limit yourself to one hundred words of current employment and position, most recent other employment or projects, degrees, and some significant accomplishment or **research agenda**. Here are the ninety-seven words I'm using next month:

> Herb Childress is the director of metaphor at Teleidoscope Group, a consulting firm offering guidance to clients in higher education and other nonprofit arenas. Prior to launching Teleidoscope, Herb was dean of research and assessment at the Boston Architectural College. He received his BA in architecture from the University of California at Berkeley, and

---

When your last name has to start with *two* A's to come up first alphabetically, you're either in big-science publishing or the Chicago phone book.

his PhD in architecture (environment-behavior studies) from the University of Wisconsin–Milwaukee. His research investigates the ways in which people build emotional relationships with places in their lives, and he has particularly focused on the spatial and emotional lives of teenagers and young adults.

I've learned over the years that if I'm going to be introduced as a speaker, the person introducing me may not have met me before, and will read my bio sketch straight out of the program. So think of this as a statement to be spoken aloud, because it may well be.[23]

Book review. There's a big difference between a book report and a book review. In a book report, that staple of fifth grade, you read the book and provide a synopsis—basically, you're telling your readers what the book was about. But a book review gives you a chance to argue, to dissect the writer's intentions and positions, and sometimes to discuss more than one book at a time and really think through some important topic.

I wouldn't normally bother with such a basic distinction; you know this. But many academic journals in the social sciences and humanities have a section of book reviews, and writing those reviews can be an important first route to scholarly **publication**. Writing strong reviews about important books gives you an excellent chance to show yourself as a scholar to people who care about your field. You make connections with journal **editors**; those editors may become curious about your own research, and they already know that you write well. You get to keep your writing muscles exercised, with **deadlines** and word limits that your **dissertation** may not offer. You get a free copy of the book you've reviewed; in my case, some such books have been surprisingly important additions to my own research library.

Most scholars have an area of their **CV**s for book reviews; it's a common early step on the long path of publication, and you should seriously consider it. Have a look at some of the leading journals in your field, and find out who the book review editors are. Shoot an editor an **e-mail** and let her know you're available for a review now and then. Most review editors are overstocked with publishers' copies of books to review, and if you have decent writing capabilities, those editors will be grateful for your assistance.

---

23. Expect also that they'll mispronounce your name and read parts of your bio incorrectly, since they're even more nervous about public speaking than you are. Be gracious and let it go without correction.

Burnout. I was part of a working group many years ago whose facilitator was talking about having done his graduate studies in management on the topic of burnout. Burnout, he claimed, was not the result of too much work. Instead, he found two primary causes:

1. feeling as though your work is not accomplishing outcomes that matter to you; and
2. feeling as though your work is not recognized by others.

Burnout is not "Gosh, I'm exhausted"; it's "I don't know why I bother with this crap." It's a classic instance of labor alienation, in which a worker can no longer identify the ends or the meaning of her own work. This is often especially surprising and confusing to professionals who have come from working-class backgrounds; we have supposedly entered the privileged land of work that we exercise some control over, unlike the miner and the waitress who are pointed to a pile of work and told to complete it. Working-class labor isn't supposed to be fun or satisfying (or, as we might say after having read Maslow, "self-actualizing"); but we imagine that becoming a professional means making your own decisions and spending your time on your own desired outcomes. We're often surprised and unprepared when we discover trepidation at the prospect of going back for another day at the office.

To avoid burnout, pay careful attention to the reasons why you want to do the work, and steer as closely to those motives as you can when you structure your days. If you love to read and write, or love to camp out in the lab for days on end, try to maximize that and make sure you get enough of it to sustain you. If you're driven by **teaching** and **mentoring** excited young people, try to avoid the most tedious **committee** work and institutional governance, and keep your nose close to the ground of the classroom. Working long hours at the same job for decades isn't a bad thing if the work achieves your goals, is recognized by your students or colleagues, and gives you a chance to grow and improve.

Literary scholar Donald Hall urges his readers to take up an annual exercise of writing what he calls a "professional statement" of what they're engaged in and engaged by, and how that should inform their next steps.[24] You may never share that statement with anyone (though I'd encourage you to

24. Donald Hall, *The Academic Self: An Owner's Manual* (Columbus: Ohio State University Press, 2002).

do so); its primary function is to clarify for yourself what matters most in your professional and personal life, so that those larger goals are visible and present for you as you choose your path through your near future.

Buyout. People talk about getting a buyout for all kinds of reductions in their **teaching load**, but really, the term ought to be reserved for its more literal use. When you're part of a team working on **grant**-supported research, the grant will often pay the college for some or all of your salary in exchange for the college giving you more time to work on the project. Thus, the grant has "bought out" some proportion of your **teaching load**, because the college now has to go hire an **adjunct** to teach the course(s) you've been freed from.[25]

There are lots of other reasons that you might get a course reduction, but most of them aren't technically "buyouts," since the college is still supporting them. If you become a department **chair**, you'll teach fewer courses while you're managing the **department's** affairs. If you're asked to lead a major curricular revision or an **assessment** effort, or to manage an upcoming **accreditation** visit, you'll often get a reduced **teaching load** during those duties. People refer to all of these as buyouts, so don't be surprised when you hear the term.

Another use of the term comes much later in one's career, when a school asks a tenured **professor** to depart before she or he might like. This might be personal; in particularly bad cases, someone who's just a roaring pain in the ass but who hasn't stepped over the line to dismissible conduct might be offered an early retirement option. But more often, it's used as a tool of institutional management. At the departmental level, enrollments may have dropped in a particular program such that its department is no longer viable. And whole institutions can become oversupplied with full professors who are still ten or even twenty years away from retirement. They're expensive, and they take up **faculty** lines that a school might prefer to spend on more cutting-edge scholarly ideas. The buyout is a college's device to offer senior faculty an enticingly soft landing. Varieties of incentives include a certain number of years of continued income, temporary pay raises for new retirees, and extra contributions to one's retirement account. If the institu-

25. And because you have the specialized knowledge you do, and are leading upper-division students and grad students through their specialized courses, the course that you'll be freed from is the intro course—the one in which young students need the absolute best instruction, and the one we think we can find just anybody to cover.

tion is doing this at a large scale, they'll send out a mass mailing to faculty telling everyone beyond a certain threshold (such as *age + years of service* ≥ *80*) that they're eligible.[26] If your **dean** or **provost** is doing it at a personal scale, you'll hear about it when the dean comes to you in the hallway and says "Hey, George, stop by my office sometime today, would you?"

Cc

Candidate. At one school I worked at, students were asked to name themselves immediately upon enrollment as "candidate for" whatever degree they had embarked upon. That was intended to combat the rapid attrition among first- and second-year students, a problem shared by less selective colleges nationwide, by getting them to focus on their ultimate destinations.

Noble motives aside, though, you are not a "candidate" for anything just because you're paying tuition and taking classes. In design schools, for instance, there are often midcourse thresholds that students pass through by submitting **portfolios** of prior work; those students only become "candidates for the Bachelor of Interior Design" once they've entered the final segment of their **curriculum**, having demonstrated their likely capability for acceptable completion of a comprehensive design project and degree. Doctoral programs are the same; you become a "doctoral candidate" only after having completed all of your coursework, having passed your **comprehensive exams** (or "comps"), and having an approved **dissertation** proposal. Prior to that, you're a "doctoral student," which is the more encompassing term that applies from first enrollment through graduation.

The term "doctoral candidate" is synonymous with the more formal "dissertator" and the more colloquial "**ABD**," or "all but dissertation." At every level of education, candidacy is a condition of having passed through

---

26. I have a friend at one of the smaller University of Wisconsin schools who was helping to organize a spring 2015 buyout offer to hundreds of his colleagues, in the face of a statewide slashing of higher education funding.

several thresholds of judgment on your work, and being seen as likely to complete your endeavors.

You can remain a doctoral candidate for years and years, paying your small continuation tuition to remain on active status. Doctoral programs often have time limits—ten years from first enrollment to completion, for instance, or six years as a dissertator—after which you have to petition **the graduate school** for permission to continue, permission which is almost always granted. There are many ghosts who wander the landscapes of doctoral programs, neither quitting nor completing nor being dismissed; they merely scrape their chains across the ceilings of seminar rooms periodically to remind others of their liminal existence. "Candidate . . . ," you hear them groan like a chill wind. "A . . . B . . . D . . . ."

But not you. On that glorious sunny day when you're called to the stage at commencement, you and your group will be introduced by the host. "Madame President, it is my privilege to present to you the *candidates* for the degree of Doctor of Philosophy." Candidacy is a specifically bounded time, from passed comps on one hand to the conferral of the degree on the other. Set yourself a time period for your candidacy status, and stick to it as best you possibly can. The curriculum is of a knowable length; make your candidacy a known quantity as well.[27]

Career. As Søren Kierkegaard wrote, "Life can only be understood backwards, but it must be lived forwards." *Career* is the word we choose for the selective, retrospective narration of decades of surprises and productive mistakes.

The notion of the ballistic life, in which one takes aim at a desired target from a great distance, is both unlikely and dreary: unlikely because it discounts all possibility of contextual change, and dreary because it discounts all possibility of personal growth. But it is such a pernicious myth that huge bookshelves are dedicated to career strategy and career planning.

I often tell my architecture students that people don't want buildings. What their clients will want are profitable businesses, smart students, happy families, aesthetic pleasure, rapid patient recovery, and satisfied staff—and

---

27. When I was about to move across the continent for grad school, I came across an article in the *San Francisco Chronicle* about the length of time needed for doctoral programs. Engineers, it said, were fastest, at an average of five and-a-half years; English majors were the worst, at over eleven. The overall average was just over eight years. I literally tore that page out of the paper so that my then-wife wouldn't see it, and told her I'd finish in five years. And I did, too: five years and three months.

they'll buy a building because they believe it might get them those things. I think the same is true of careers. People don't really want careers; what they want is interesting work, financial security, enjoyable colleagues, respect, prestige, and a sense of challenge and growth.

There is a "career ladder" in higher education, which has rungs labeled "PhD recipient," "assistant professor," "associate professor," "chair," "full professor," "dean," "provost," "president." Each rung is restrictive, with fewer occupants above than below. But if we imagine ourselves to be on the ladder, we take too much of our self-definition from being the winner of every more difficult challenge, imagining ourselves drawing the sword from the stone. And if we "stall" at some point up the climb, we write ourselves narratives of ineffectiveness and incapability.

My ex-wife's mother was a terrible traveling companion. She spent all of her time on a trip narrating the guidebook's explanation of what we were about to see, evaluating the guidebook's recommendations on where we should go, or recording (in precise Gregg shorthand) where we had been. She almost never experienced where she was. People who privilege the career ladder are often just as pinched and unpleasant, never savoring what they do in the moment. I was listening to an National Public Radio interview with the musician Elvis Costello, by that time a senior statesman in rock music. He said that worried parents often asked him if their children should pursue a career in music. "Make sure it's actually music that they're pursuing, and not fame," Costello explained. "Because fame as its own end is liable to be disappointing, but music is very rarely disappointing."[28] The same holds true of all human endeavor; if you love what you do, you will have happy days—and a succession of happy days turns out to be a successful career.

Chair. Not something to sit in, but a person. Formerly chairman, sometimes (rarely, awkwardly) chairperson, now mostly just chair. In this context, we'll talk specifically about the role of the **department** chair, who is a **faculty** member elected by her peers or asked by the **dean** to be the liaison between the departmental faculty and the college **administration** for a set period of time. The chair has several responsibilities, which usually include setting the coming year's budget, advocating with the dean on behalf of the

28. Elvis Costello with Scott Simon, "Elvis Costello Gets a Little Bluegrass." National Public Radio, *Weekend Edition Saturday*, December 12, 2012; audio file accessed April 27, 2015, http://www.npr.org/templates/story/story.php?storyId=105326845.

department, reviewing and ensuring course coverage within her faculty's teaching-load limits, and managing requests for resources (faculty and student travel, leaves, and so on). In exchange for taking on these administrative tasks, a chair usually has a reduction of course load during her term, and may periodically be allowed to step away from research or scholarly productivity as well.

It is certainly the case that junior faculty may be asked to serve as department chairs, but I'd recommend against it. It's political work at a time when you just want to make friends; it pulls you away from teaching and scholarship at a time when you need to demonstrate excellence in both. The probabilities are small upside and large downside.[29]

If you successfully endure **tenure** review, becoming department chair may be a useful and relatively low-risk way of testing the waters of whether you'd ultimately be interested in an **administrative** position. You have the safety net of your faculty line, you have the protection of tenure, and you can treat the chair as a sort of visiting position from which you can always return home. It's critical to note that the department chair is the *only* administrative role on campus that holds this safety net. If you decide to move on from your department chair experience into a further administrative role, such as an associate deanship, it is highly likely that your promotion will come with the loss of your tenured faculty line. You'll get more money, a little more power (whatever that might mean), more college-wide oversight, and the possibility of being put onto the sidewalk at a moment's notice. You'll be free-climbing: faster ascent, no safety ropes.

The term "chair" is used in other senses. There's the chair of a **committee**, who usually is the only person actually doing the work while having to seem receptive to the grousing of the less productive members. And there's the endowed chair, who holds a faculty position directly paid for from a named **endowment** fund rather than from the college's standard operating budget. Avoid the first one unless you really care about the outcomes that the committee might have and believe that its recommendations might carry force, and don't worry about the second one, which is usually available only to faculty at mid- and later-career points.

---

29. A friend who's a provost at a small college read this entry and said, "I would make this much, much stronger. An untenured faculty member should never be chair. If they do the job well, they will certainly piss off some colleagues. If they want to stay friends with everyone, then they won't do the job well and piss off the dean."

Chancellor. In the University of California and University of Wisconsin systems, the head of an individual campus is the chancellor, and the head of the entire consortium is the president. In the State University of New York and University of Texas systems, the head of a campus is the president, and the head of the entire consortium is the chancellor. Don't try to figure it out . . . just learn the local parlance, and know that others will be different.

Children.

> I want to stress the importance of being young and technical. Young people are just smarter. Why are most chess masters under 30? I don't know. Young people just have simpler lives. We may not own a car. We may not have family. Simplicity in life allows you to focus on what's important. — Mark Zuckerberg, CEO, Facebook (age twenty-two when he said this in 2007).[30]

Simplicity in life allows you to focus on what's important. That is, on work. Boyfriends, girlfriends . . . expendable. Choice of location . . . hey, if the job's in Minot, that's where you go.[31] Family relations . . . that's why you have siblings, to live near home and take care of your parents.

Babies are a whole order of magnitude higher than any of these on the list of **career** disruption, which is one of the reasons why young women often have a higher hurdle in getting that **assistant professorship**.[32] They might (gasp) have a baby. To become an assistant professor, you have to be *young enough* to have a baby—higher ed doesn't want any new PhDs in their late forties, either—but you certainly ought to have the sense not to do it.[33]

30. Andrew S. Ross, "In Silicon Valley, Age Can Be a Curse." SFGate (August 18, 2013), accessed April 27, 2015, http://www.sfgate.com/business/bottomline/article/In-Silicon -Valley-age-can-be-a-curse-4742365.php.

31. Everyone has their own personal "no-fly zone," an area of the country where they can't imagine themselves living. Mine is any state or region that is significantly "red" or has flat and treeless topography. In the world of the faculty search, those considerations are off the table, and you follow the work. Period.

32. See some specific data under the entry on minority preference.

33. This is borne out by a study showing that, though women are underrepresented in academic hiring, single women without children were 16 percent *more* likely to get jobs than unmarried childless men. It's the women with young children who are closed out. " . . . women suffer at the beginning of their academic careers because they marry and have children, not because they are women." Nicholas H. Wolflinger, Mary Ann Mason,

You think I exaggerate? One of my wife's former colleagues had submitted a **tenure** packet of strong **course evaluations**, powerful references, ample and significant service, and a record of research **grants** and **publications**. Her department **chair** was unimpressed, and said, "It's a good thing your first kid died of SIDS, or you'd have been even less productive."[34]

If you're a woman of childbearing age, be prepared for unspoken discrimination based on the "tenure clock." The basic conceit of the clock is that you have six to eight post-college years of nonstop labor to get your PhD, years in which you can allow no distractions whatsoever, and then you get a **faculty** position with six years of even more unrelenting labor to achieve tenure. Assuming you start grad school at twenty-five, this takes you to near forty before it's safe to have a kid (at which point, if you do, you'll be accused of "mommying out" or becoming unproductive dead weight, but at least you'll have tenure).

Guys? Forget I mentioned any of this. Go ahead and have kids whenever you want; the assumption will be that your wife will take care of them while you "focus on what's important." Or better yet, that you'll get divorced (which happens a lot in doctoral programs), and your wife will take the kids off your hands so that you can "focus on what's important."

Chronicle of Higher Education. Subscribe and read. Period.

There are lots of periodicals having to do with higher education, many of which are pretty good. But *The Chronicle of Higher Education* is the *New York Times* of collegiate reading: politically astute, on top of breaking trends, willing to investigate new issues and to revisit an older story. It also has terrific editorial content by engaging staff and guest writers, akin to the various magazine segments of a major daily newspaper, and a great website.

Most centrally, the *Chron*[35] is the most thorough and reliable source of **job postings** in higher ed. It takes a little training to read the want ads. The text-only announcements that thread their way across dozens of pages are alphabetical by **discipline**, so that you can quickly find "geography" or "statistics." But there are also display ads from colleges with multiple

and Marc Goulden, "Problems in the Pipeline: Gender, Marriage, and Fertility in the Ivory Tower," *Journal of Higher Education* 79, no. 4 (2008): 388–405.
34. This was in 1985, and we hope things have changed. Probably what's changed is that now she wouldn't say that out loud, but would just think it.
35. If you say "the *Chron*" in San Francisco, you'll be referring to the *San Francisco Chronicle*, one of my favorite daily papers. Everywhere else in the country, though, your colleagues in higher ed will immediately know you mean *The Chronicle of Higher Education*.

positions to fill, and a display ad with a job in your discipline can be any place in the employment section. So look first for the possibilities among the alphabetized, position-specific ads, and then browse more slowly across the display ads.

Citational power. Chess players have rankings: master, grandmaster, and so on. But those named ranks are actually based on a numerical rating system originally devised by the chess enthusiast and Marquette physics professor Arpad Elo. A player's rating changes after every match, based not only on winning or losing the game but also on the differences in rating between the two players. A strong player winning against a weak player gains a handful of points, and the loser loses a handful of points; a weak player beating a stronger player, though, results in a much greater shift of ratings.[36]

It turns out that academics have attempted to develop their own research ranking system, based on one's **publications**. The expectations for publication are so strong that pretty much everyone coming up for **tenure** has publications on their record. Is someone with twenty publications "doing better" than someone with five? It's the same principle as chess; winning twenty times against little kids is not as impressive as winning five games at the US Open.

Journals are assigned "impact factors," based on the average number of times their articles are cited in other academic bibliographies. Thus, if the *Journal of Setting Things on Fire* publishes six hundred papers over the course of its first two years, and those papers are cited a total of nine hundred times, the *JSTF* has an impact factor of 1.5.[37] The *Journal of Watching People Do Things* may have published only sixty papers over that same period, but have those papers cited three hundred times, for a *JWPDT* impact rating of 5.0. There are other forms of citational-power ratings having to do with how immediately a journal's papers are cited, or how selective the journal might be from among its submitted manuscripts. These ratings are intended only

36. Other sports, notably table tennis and competitive Scrabble, also use a variant of these ratings, at which an internationally competitive master player has a rating of 2,000 or so. The wonderful book *Word Freak*, by sportswriter Stefan Fatsis (Penguin, 2001) is about the year he spent and the characters he encountered on his quest to achieve a 1,700 rating in tournament Scrabble.
37. Of course, four hundred of those citations were probably of three particularly important articles, so "average" is kind of meaningless. The median might be a better measure but, as in most aspects of higher education administration, we forget everything we learned in statistics.

to compare one journal against another within a **discipline**, but they often work by proxy to judge one academic against another: Who's publishing in the high-impact journals?

There are, in fact, attempts to have ranking systems for individual scholars. For instance, there's the *h-index* proposed by Jorge Hirsch, which is the highest number of papers an individual has published that have received at least that many citations. If you publish one article and it's cited by someone else, your h-index is 1. If you publish ten articles that have each been cited at least ten times, your h-index is 10, even if you've also published fifty other articles that individually were cited only nine or fewer times.[38] This obviously describes a geometric function of influence, since someone with an h-index of 10 has been cited at least one hundred times (ten articles with at least ten citations each), compared against someone with an h-index of 5 (five articles with at least five citations each) who may only have been cited twenty-five times.

But all of this strikes me as misplaced precision. If you're in some high-powered research lab in the bench sciences, you'd better be setting something on fire and writing about it on a monthly basis; whereas if you're teaching a four courses a semester in literature in a small liberal-arts college and you publish two major papers on feminist readings of eighteenth-century German poetry during your **assistant professor** years, that's a big deal. And none of this takes into account the excellence of your conference **presentations**, the quality of your teaching, the degree of your service, and the generosity and collegiality with which you make your way in the world. Someone, somewhere, is hard at work on quantifying those as well.

Citational system / style guide. Every **discipline** has its own way of organizing bibliographic material, which is a huge pain in the ass if you're attempting an **interdisciplinary** life. And individual **journals** within a discipline will sometimes have small "refinements," because of course everybody wants to be special. If you employ a bibliographic management software system like EndNote or Nota Bene, it will organize your materials into

38. Hersch's approximate threshold for tenure in physics at a major research university is an h-index of twelve. My own h-index is six, which would be embarrassingly small in the physical sciences but isn't bad in the odd intersection of the social sciences and humanities that I occupy. You can calculate your own h-index using *Google Scholar*, if you're a civilian, or *ISI World of Science*, if your college has access to it. It's kind of like knowing your own IQ, though: it's really only good for humiliating yourself if it's low or annoying people if it's high.

Table 1. Differences in citation across academic communities

Style guide	Body note	Bibliography
Chicago Manual of Style, 16th edition (2010)	Numbered footnote, with full citation in that footnote on first appearance and an abbreviated version for subsequent appearances.	Childress, Herb. "Kinder Ethnographic Writing." *Qualitative Inquiry* 4, no. 2 (1998): 249–64.
MLA Style Manual and Guide to Scholarly Publishing, 3rd edition (2008)	Parenthetical note in text, with last name and page number of quote, such as (Childress 255)	Childress, Herb. "Kinder Ethnographic Writing." *Qualitative Inquiry* 4.2 (1998): 249–264. Print.
ACS Style Guide: Effective Communication of Scientific Information, 3rd edition (2006)	Numbered reference to bibliography entry	Childress H. Kinder Ethnographic Writing. *Qual. Inq.* 1998, 4, 249–264.
Publication Manual of the American Psychological Association, 6th edition (2009)	Parenthetical note in text, with last name and year of publication, such as (Childress 1998)	Childress, H. (1998). Kinder Ethnographic Writing. *Qualitative Inquiry, 4*(2), 249–264.

the appropriate citational sequence for more than five thousand different journals. But in the end, just as with automakers or accounting firms, you're probably going to be dealing with some variant of one of the big four: Chicago/Turabian, Modern Language Association (MLA), American Chemical Society (ACS), or American Psychological Association (APA).[39] Every journal will have a statement in its call for manuscripts that explains exactly what system they use and which edition of the style guide is pertinent.

Let's take the example of the simplest case: a single-**author** journal article. See table 1 for a summary of how each of these four systems would treat it. Note that ACS and APA, seeing themselves as "scientific," attempt to convey the objectivity of knowledge by reducing the author to an initialed identifier rather than a person, and privilege the year of publication since

---

39. Of course, there are specialized citational methods for specialized fields. Philosophers need to know the Bekker number for citing Aristotle, musicologists need to know the Köchel number of Mozart's works, legal scholars need to know how to cite case law, and so on.

knowledge changes rapidly and you'd better be citing current scholarship. On the other hand, the more humanistic Chicago and MLA allow me to go by my full name, since they acknowledge that a specific person actually thought this stuff up; and they bury the year of publication somewhat, since it's still productive to cite intelligent people from long ago. The MLA body note format, and its use of the page number in particular, shows us one crucial difference between citation in the humanities and the sciences: you almost never *quote* people in science, but simply report their findings, whereas humanists often quote particularly revealing or elegant phrasing, and expect that you may want to track down that exact quote yourself and will need its page number. The citational styles reveal the values of their communities, if you look carefully.

Your **library** will have most of these style manuals, but it's worth buying the one you'll use most and having it near your computer. The manuals cover far more than just citational format, and offer guidance on issues of preferred grammar and punctuation (quick . . . one space after a period, or two?), how to deal with tables and figures and equations, how to cite new kinds of media, and how to do page layout. There's no reason to have a manuscript returned without commentary because you ignored the publication conventions of your field. Knowing the basics of your appropriate style marks you as someone who takes seriously the forms and rituals of your tribe.

Cohort. When entering an elite college, the incoming freshmen are stamped with not their year of entry, but rather with the year of expected degree, like an expiration date on a can of tuna. Students arriving at the dorm with their luggage and their high school jerseys (which they'll soon learn not to wear at college) in late August 2015 are immediately stamped as "the Class of '19." The expectation is that they'll walk through the program together, graduate together in four years exactly, and continue to be part of the Class of '19 in the alumni organization.

Your life in grad school will be somewhat different than that. You'll come into your doctoral program together, as a clump of five or ten, and you'll take all of your core courses together. But then you'll get started on your own research, and one of you will be a **research assistant** on this project while another is a **teaching assistant** for that instructor, and your paths will diverge. You'll possibly take your comprehensive exams more or less together, since they're often linked to the end of the core **curriculum**, but you'll propose and conduct and defend your **dissertation** at your own pace.

Likewise, you'll be part of a cohort if you get an academic job. Your college will hire a few new assistant professors each year, if for no other reason than to replace the retirements and departures, and the new hires will go through the various orientations together. But after that, you'll have no reason to encounter one another ever again, even though you'll all come up for **tenure** review at roughly the same time.

I would like to encourage you to think more like those freshmen at Duke and Stanford who immediately label themselves the Class of 2019. If you imagine yourself as a free agent, as an independent scholar who will live or die solely on your own merits and labors, you enter the field of battle defenseless, unable to predict the unexpected dangers that arise. If, on the other hand, you imagine yourself as part of a collective, you can share reports of threatening weather, and bring news of opportunities discovered. You can commiserate in times of injury, and celebrate in times of victory. Humans band together for reasons both logistical and emotional, and there's no reason to leave that behind just because you're in grad school or on the faculty.

I'd love to see more enlightened **provosts** consider their incoming **faculty** each year as a cohort—they're all on the same six-year tenure clock, after all—and provide consistent professional development to each group as they move toward their tenure review. By doing so, they would ease the paths of each junior faculty member, build a sense of whole-college allegiance rather than departmental isolation, and foster a culture of collective care.

Committees. You can look at the separate entry on **dissertation committees** for that specific variant of the species. This is the more general discussion of any group of people charged to think about a problem.

The world of business humor uses the committee meeting as one of its most common tropes, standing in for ineffectiveness, inefficiency, and political maneuvering. And committees can often be exactly that. But committees can also be empowering and exciting places where collaborative thought really does generate exciting and unexpected ideas.

One major difference is that between the standing committee that is seen to be an eternal element of the organization, and the task force or ad hoc committee that arises in response to a particular issue. Eternal committees

are absolutely the place where ideas go to die; there's no urgency, no need
for consensus, nothing that has to get done today. It's only important that
the minutes from the last meeting are reviewed, minutes of the current
meeting are kept, and the chair maintains adherence to *Robert's Rules of
Order* (which, being based in a system of governance that is permanent,
rigid, and oppositional, almost guarantees that its adherents will become
permanent, rigid, and oppositional).

The task force, on the other hand, is usually appointed by an authority
to figure out what to do about some circumstance. It's time-sensitive, it has
an end point, and the **administration** has asked it to do the work; and thus
it is more likely to consider its findings. Getting yourself onto a task force
can be an enormously rewarding and pleasant form of committee service.
Avoid being placed on large standing committees, which will not merely
annoy you but will in fact cause you to become the bitter, scheming, petty,
backbiting senior **faculty** you now use in cautionary tales. You will see your
colleagues at their worst, and you will become worse yourself.[40]

Organizations of all kinds misuse the opportunities they have to bring
people together, and spend a lot of money doing it. **Presidents** gather all
of their school leaders together on a regular basis just for the pleasure they
take in being able to command obedience, and then proceed to talk at them
for an hour. This is work that could have been accomplished by **e-mail**, or
through a podcast; but that wouldn't satisfy the real reason for the meeting,
which is the instillation of fear and public shaming.

People have limited amounts of time to work. Every meeting I go to is
time not spent at my desk getting things done. If we use the standard round-
ing of the two-thousand-hour working year, each hour of meetings costs
one-two-thousandth of my annual salary and benefits.[41] Bring forty **admin-**

---

40. A simple way to gauge whether a standing committee might be a productive use of
your time is to listen to the people who are asking you to be part of it. If they describe
it in the same terms as would be used to describe it in an organizational manual, just
naming its functions, don't go. If, though, they talk about it being exciting work or a
great opportunity to learn new practices while supporting students, it holds promise.
41. Of course, the notion of a salaried position makes that two-thousand-hour year a
total fiction. Our vaunted national "gains in productivity" are based in no small part
on the conversion of lots of jobs from wage-based to salary-based, and the subsequent
ramping up of expectations for those salaried positions to fifty-, sixty-, and seventy-
hour weeks. If a supervisor had to actually spend $30 per hour per person to bring people
to a meeting, she'd think twice; hell, she won't even buy coffee and doughnuts for the
meeting, because that's $25 against her budget. But because the personnel expense of

istrators together for an hour with the president, and she has invested two to three thousand dollars for the pleasure of telling us that the budget will be tight again this year and implying that it's our fault.

Because meetings are expensive, we need to think carefully about what they're for. You can't write policy in a room with thirty people, changing words and reordering paragraphs. And you can't change the institution by sitting alone in your **office** writing a manifesto. Let me put forth some rules of thumb about what differently-sized groups are good for.

One person, maybe two, can do production work: writing, graphic layout, scheduling, budgeting. If you pretend that you're doing a writing task with a larger group, you're still going to put one person to work on finalizing that text, which will be vetted once again anyway.

Three to six people can conceive of large changes to organizational practice—especially if they represent different areas of the college, they have enough breadth of knowledge to understand their area's needs and desires, and understand the likely implications of any changes for their own practices. If you want to change a **curriculum** or plan a conference, a task force of six is perfect: small enough so that everyone can be heard, large enough to be representative of broad constituencies, and including enough hands to carry the load.

Ten or twenty people can review an idea in the works, can offer subtle revisions that the working group may not have considered, can raise the voice of a constituency not originally at the table.

More than twenty people or so, and it's just a lecture. Lectures can be wonderful, inspiring, thought-provoking events. People go to church every week to hear lectures; they watch a billion TED videos to see smart lectures. But don't pretend that you're doing something in that room that you can't do.

If you have a choice about committees, always choose the one that has an outcome to achieve. If you don't have a choice and get placed onto a standing committee, don't try to make that rickety structure support more than it will bear; attend and be active while you're there, and leave it alone between meetings as much as you can.

Comprehensive exams / comps. There are several stages to doctoral progress, but we can really think of the stages as "student" and "scholar," with a knuckle in the middle. As a student, you'll be taking some amount of added

---

meetings is just an integrated ingredient of the infinitely expandable workload casserole, she can be pretty cavalier about demanding her staff's presence.

course work to learn the history and controversies and major **methods** of your field, and to expand your intellectual vocabulary and practices. As a scholar, you'll propose, conduct, and defend your **dissertation**, and go on (we hope) to a great intellectual **career**.

That knuckle in the middle is the hardest test you'll ever take in your life.

Different kinds of programs conduct different formats of comprehensive exams (often shortened to "comps"), but the key word is indeed "comprehensive." The intention is to evaluate a student's mastery of a **discipline**'s concepts, methods, and major thinkers. The student's work is usually reviewed by several senior members of the doctoral **faculty**.

Some programs, like my doctoral program at the University of Wisconsin–Milwaukee, have a written examination that requires the creation of one or more brief, rapid research papers on areas that lie outside your proposed dissertation topic. In my case, there were four such papers, each for one of the pillars of the program: disciplinary history and major issues, social and intellectual theory, statistics and research design, and professional application of research findings. My **cohort** argued that we'd prefer an integrative question, since by virtue of having passed each of the four courses, we'd already demonstrated sufficient mastery of each. The program committee agreed, in part ... and gave us five questions, the original four *plus* the integrative question.

A more quantitative program may have the world's worst math test, which could last a full day.[42] Still other programs may require the dreaded oral exam, which could also go for a full day.[43] In some cases there will be an official reading list, and examinees must be prepared to address the gross and detailed arguments of each of dozens, or hundreds, of major works. I've seen some of these reading lists, and they might as well say "everything."[44]

42. There are gruesome museums of these quantitative exams available online. See, for example, Stanford University Department of Economics, "Comprehensive Exam Archive," accessed April 27, 2015, http://economics.stanford.edu/graduate/current -phd-student-resources/comprehensive-exam-archive. Each of the archived examples represents a six-hour test—probably given in a cinder-block room, under a bare bulb.
43. One of my friends from a noted architectural history program had a six-hour oral exam. His dissertation chair, by way of pre-test advice, told him to bring a towel and fresh shirt, so that he could clean up at lunch and be ready for the afternoon.
44. Here, for example, is a fraction of a topic list, from the Marquette University Department of Philosophy, "Ph.D. Comprehensive Exam Information and Reading List," accessed April 27, 2015, http://www.marquette.edu/phil/documents/phdcomps.pdf. Just look at the list of topics one should be prepared to discuss under the subsection on ethics:

In other cases, the examining committee basically just makes sure you have access to the library and calls it good.

So, with all that, why was my comprehensive exam one of the most satisfying parts of my intellectual life? One reason was that my cohort did it as a cohort, with the five of us spending a full week—Sunday noon to Sunday noon—camped out in the doctoral student office. Each of us had checked out our maximum complement of seventy-five books from the university's library, and had thus amassed 375 books that we believed would be most useful to us—plus, of course, file cabinets full of the papers we'd read and photocopied over the first two years of the program. We had piles of junk food, jugs of coffee and water, and a week's freedom from expectations related to grooming and social life.

We played by the rules. For each of the four content areas, we were given a choice of two questions to address, so we spent the first half hour reading the exam and discussing which of the questions each of us was going to write about; but after that, we didn't offer each other any suggestions or read one another's drafts. The only conversations that went on were things like "Who's got the Altman and Low book?" or "Anybody got an extra disc?" or "I think I have to go home for a while." But the fact of working together, sitting at adjacent computers until three or four in the morning for days in a row, fostered a great bond among us, and gave us confidence that we could actually all do this.

In my case, the comps rewarded my best abilities: reading, synthesizing, and rewriting at a fast pace. If I'd had an oral exam instead, it would have been more difficult for me; my first words are often not my right words.

Most importantly, I left that week believing that, when necessary, I could rapidly develop a lecture or a course on almost any topic that might pertain to my field. I got through a vast amount of literature quickly, organized it neatly, and explained why my framework and argument were sensible. And

---

"psychological and rational egoism; realism and relativism; deontology; consequentialism; utilitarianism; natural law theory; virtue theory; issues in business ethics; bioethics; nuclear deterrence theory; abortion; euthanasia; affirmative action; the principle of double effect and various applications of it; environmental ethics; sexual ethics; the ethics of war and peace; methods of justification in ethics, e.g., coherentism and foundationalism." Sounds like a great dinner party, but imagine being prepared to discuss all of these, plus eight other equally dense topical categories, based on three thousand years of literature, at the potential cost of being dismissed from school. It's like being on *Jeopardy* with the losers being taken out back and shot.

I knew that I could do it again, on demand, with not much more than some text resources and a little open time.

Your job, as always, is to find out how your school organizes things, and to ask prior generations about their experiences. Think of the preparation for your comps as being like physical training. As George Patton once said, "The more you sweat in peace, the less you bleed in war." The study can be a lot of fun on its own terms, and you'll walk into the exam with anticipation rather than desperation.

Conference. I remember the first time I went to an academic conference. It was the Environmental Design Research Association (EDRA) conference of 1992, in Boulder. I went with seven or eight fellow doctoral students, all first- and second-year. We rented an Oldsmobile Silhouette minivan and drove across the plains from Milwaukee to Colorado, more than one thousand nonstop miles achieved by alternating drivers.

Once at the conference, we banded together somewhat for protection. After all, we were the only people we knew, surrounded by several hundred anonymous others. If we'd been at a Super Bowl or Academy Awards pre-party, we could have been star-struck: "Oh, look, Jennifer Garner! Tom Brady!" But since all of our new stars were known to us only through the brilliant lines of text we'd read in seminar, we had no tabloid images to link to the people streaming by, and no red carpet or camera line to imply their importance. "Oh, look! It's Mike Brill! And there's Linda Schneekloth!"

We didn't know what conferences were for; we only knew that we ought to go, because that's what people in our field did. We attended the sessions by the writers of our beloved seminar papers, and found them to be varied people of varied thinking. We discovered the wilderness of the **poster session**: research projects not deemed suitable for live sessions, displayed instead on four-by-three-foot foamcore boards in a reception hall filled with rows of easels, each poster with its author standing nearby, and stacks of photocopied full papers awaiting distribution to eager readers who never materialized.

Having been to dozens of conferences, I've since learned what they're for. They're for seeing old friends and making new ones. They're for auditioning ideas before they're published, finding collaborators for new projects, and sharing gossip and insider information. They're places to harvest that one brilliant idea that inspires your next steps. They're places to see young talent before it's recognized, and to strike other young scholars off your list. They're places for the conference-hosting organization to fill its task forces, and places at which individual faculty members can let it be quietly known that their allegiances might be bought with a better **offer**. They are your **discipline's** bazaars, sites of both commerce and intrigue.

Conferences are intellectually unnecessary; scholarship is a paper-based lifeform. What conferences do that paper cannot is the human work that underlies scholarship: to connect, to inspire, to **network**, to renew, to brainstorm, to laugh and drink and remember why this was once so very much fun. A good conference experience leaves us with a refreshed commitment to our work, new ways of thinking about it, and new colleagues with whom to practice it.

My inaugural conference came during the middle of my second doctoral semester, while I was working through our "Theories in Environment-Behavior Studies" course and had become enamored of the ideas of phenomenology. I had a rudimentary understanding and was burrowed deeply into translated Heidegger, attempting to hack my way through the problems of being-in-the-world, and the concepts struck me as true ways of experiencing exciting and unfamiliar landscapes. Because I wanted to know more, I went to the conference meeting of the EDRA Environmental and Architectural Phenomenology Network, where I struck up friendships that would shape the next decade of my life and ultimately result in the **publication** of my first book.

You have to learn how to go to a conference. As at any party, if you hang out only with the people you came with, you might as well have stayed home. Ask your teachers to introduce you to a few people you especially want to meet. Keep your eyes open, as you read the program, for key words in the **abstracts** of the sessions—not just content words, but theoretical and **methodological** hints of kindred spirits. Make sure you get contact information for the people you want to talk with further,[45] and then send them messages shortly after you get home telling them what a great time you had talking with them. The parallels with dating are many and obvious; the difference is that with conference contacts, promiscuity is welcomed.

45. It's far from a uniform practice, but your university really ought to issue business cards to its doctoral students. If they don't, make up your own and get a hundred printed for ten bucks. Don't use the college logos or other copyrighted images; text-only is fine. You just need a way to exchange info quickly and professionally without writing your e-mail address on a torn-off corner of the program.

Conference interview. You've applied for a serious position in your field. You won't know until much later, if ever, how many other applicants there were, but let's be conservative and say one hundred. Let's also say that half of them are immediate rejects—not yet finished with **dissertation** research, in the wrong **disciplines**, or having misunderstood the basic instructions. So now there are fifty, and the hiring committee can't deal with fifty applicants, so they raise the bar a little and get themselves to a dozen who might be interesting.[46]

The college can't afford to bring twelve people to campus for interviews; they need a way to winnow the number down to at most five.[47] So what better than to ask the semifinalists to pay for their own interview **travel** and lodging? Thus the origin of the conference interview.

It's hard to know just how many disciplines feature screening interviews as a normal part of their annual conferences. Like much in higher education, it's not about secrecy, but rather the simple expectation that *everyone who could possibly matter* already knows all of this. The conferences most noted for interviews are those of the Modern Language Association (MLA) and the American Historical Association (AHA); big scientific conferences often have career fairs at which governmental labs and industrial recruiters meet new researchers.

There's lots of advice online about how to prepare yourself for a conference interview: what to wear, how to build your **elevator speech**, how to get the search committee members to talk about themselves or their **department**. That's all just Job Search 101, and you can study that anywhere. But since I'm an architectural researcher, I'd like to have you think about the fact that conference interviews very often take place in the hotel room of one of the search committee members.

Being invited to come to someone's room, a room equipped with beds, carries an inevitable awkwardness, especially for female candidates; there's just a *squick* factor about it. Now that there are more and more suites in hotels, it's possible that the hotel room might actually have chairs and couches,

46. If you're one of those dozen, by the way, good job. Making that major cut is a big deal, and you should be congratulated on how your paper materials have represented you.
47. The more I write about academic job search sequences, the more it feels like I'm describing *America's Top Model*. Everybody on the show is attractive, but every week, a new challenge allows the judges to dismiss yet another participant from consideration. Maybe some department of media studies somewhere will actually do their faculty search on live TV, with weekly challenges and weepy off-stage interviews; if so, I want the executive producer credit and 20-percent royalties: *ProfSearch* ©2013 Herb Childress.

and particularly well-heeled schools may rent a more public hospitality suite, but you should absolutely be prepared to perch on the edge of one of the two queen beds in room 1708 while the committee sits on the facing edge of the other. There had better be more than one interviewer, ideally across gender lines; if not, gauge your comfort level, trust your gut, and do not hesitate to leave if anything feels off. The job is not that important.

Let's think about three crucial ways in which the physical structure of the hotel room interview is different from that of the classic employment interview. We'll call them *posture*, *preparation*, and *protection*.

Posture. In an office or seminar room setting, you'll be in a chair with a hard seat and a hard back, and you'll sit up more or less straight. On a couch, in an armchair, or on the edge of a bed, the posture is just more relaxed, more reclined, and, unless you're doing a lot of Pilates, you'll have a tendency to slouch. Any effort to remain upright can make you appear stiff; and in fact you *will* be sitting artificially upright, given the equipment's design. There is no way to be good at anything without practice, and I would advise you and your fellow grad students to practice looking professional while sitting on nonprofessional furniture. Body language is always a big deal—eye contact, firm handshake, slight forward lean to express interest, all of that—but body language is supported or hindered by context, and you need to practice in context.

Preparation. When you're being interviewed at a conference table, you've got a place to put your hands, you can bring a legal pad or tablet computer and take notes, and you can lay out additional copies of your **CV** and business cards. When you're perched on the edge of a low-quality couch or on the corner of a bed, you have none of that work space available to you. I advise bringing a nice nonleaking pen[48] and a small notepad; the classic black Moleskine softcover 3×5 journal makes you look literary and serious, both of which are good. Take a few notes when you ask questions, and make eye contact when you're answering them.

Bring your (clean, single-dark-colored, nonvinyl, rectangular) briefcase, and set it on the floor next to your feet. Clean it out so that there's nothing in there except your business cards and extra CVs, so you can get to them efficiently. Don't rummage; don't pull your keys and the leftover half-sandwich out onto the bed while you're looking for your cards. If your briefcase has organizing pockets, use them and know where things are. Even inside your

---

48. Please don't bring a fountain pen. Just don't. Why risk even a 1-percent chance of such a memorable disaster?

briefcase, keep your CVs in a file folder, to protect their edges; you want to hand over a sharp document, not some tattered, wrinkled disaster that looks like a C-minus freshman comp essay.

Protection. At a table, the others who are watching you for any sign of weakness can only see one-third of your body. In a club chair or on the edge of the bed, your entire self is open for examination. This puts greater importance on your shoes, the cuffs of your pants, or the hem of your dress. Your legs will be considered, as will your socks and an untied shoelace. If you fidget below the table, rocking your feet back and forth or tapping the floor, this becomes a visible tic in a conference interview. Shielding your body from view is one of the unconsidered benefits of tables.[49]

How do your clothes look when you're sitting? Guys, when you go to the tailor and buy a suit, he checks you for fit while you stand in front of the three-sided mirror, rotating pleasingly like a Maserati at the auto show. Sit down in a slouchy chair and that suit can go to hell in a hurry. Unbutton your jacket, flip your coattails back, and consider wearing a tie bar so that your tie doesn't slide distractingly sideways across your stomach as you lean on one arm of the chair. And a skirt that wasn't all that short while you were standing gets shorter now that you're sitting directly across from three fifty-year-olds, doesn't it? That's something you don't want to be thinking about when you have half an hour to convince senior faculty members that you're one of them, and that you should be invited to move from the dozen to the four.

If your body meets cultural norms, being on display can of course work to your advantage; if you're heavy, it will count against you. When a short man sits in a chair at a table, his reduced stature is less visible; when he sits back in a couch or deep lounge chair and his feet don't quite reach flat to the floor, it will count against him. Sacrifice your comfort for thirty minutes, sit forward with your knees together and both feet on the floor, and remember that you're on display physically as well as intellectually.

Contracts: nine-, ten-, and twelve-month. When I was young, my family went camping every summer at Silver Lake State Park, on the broad white dunes of Lake Michigan. I loved cars and car racing, and finally one summer

---

49. Furniture makers know this, too. If you go into an office and see an employee facing you directly, that desk will have what's called a "modesty panel" to keep her legs from being on display to everybody who walks by. The conference interview removes that modesty, so you have to figure out how to re-create it through clothing and posture.

persuaded Dad to take us to Mac Wood's Dune Rides, so we could go tearing around the sand hills on what turned out to be a hot-rodded, open-air tour bus.

It was every bit as much fun as it looked like on the billboards, and I loved it. But the reason I recount it here is that I remember one of the adult passengers talking to the driver, and the driver saying that he drove for Mac Wood every summer, but that during the rest of the year he was a high school teacher. I was quite surprised by that. I thought everybody just had one job, like my dad's job at the Continental Motors factory or my mom's job at General Telephone and Electric. Your job was such a huge part of your identity that I couldn't imagine having two of them; it would be like being Superman *and* Clark Kent at once.

But the larger revelation was that high school teachers might need to make some extra money to make ends meet. They were smart people, they wore ties; they *must* have been doing well. I had no idea that teachers had the summers off just as I did, and that many of them took summer jobs just as I would once I made it to high school myself.

Higher-education employment is not so different from high school employment. The historic expectation has been that you'd teach during the fall and spring semesters, your days filled with seminars and grading and advising and **committees**, and that your summers would be the time when you conduct your own scholarly life. You could **travel** to the archives in Germany, you could return to the field camp in the Serengeti, or you could just sit in your lab or your home office with a bottle of iced tea and no interruptions and get your writing done. This is all no great surprise, but what surprised me was that a lot of faculty contracts are structured to reflect this experience. A great number of schools offer their faculty nine-month or ten-month contracts, which means that your annual salary is paid out in nine or ten chunks (September through May or June), and that you have to float without institutional income for the summer.

There's a way in which, you know, so what? If they're paying you $60,000 plus benefits (and your benefits will carry through the summer, regardless of your contract type—you're still permanently employed by the college), who cares if that comes out as twelve times $5,000 or ten times $6,000 or nine times $6,667? You're a grown-up, so you can budget to hold some of that money to pay rent and groceries over the summer, right?

Well, as it turns out, there is an advantage to a nine-month or ten-month contract. If you have a nine-month contract and can get small **grants** for your summer research, you can build in a stipend for your off-months that equals your monthly contracted salary. So instead of driving a dune buggy for Mac Wood's, you can do your own research *and* get an extra month or three worth of overload. Sweet!

The other advantage to a nine-month or ten-month contract is that the college is explicitly saying that they have no claim on your time during those off months. If the school gives you a twelve-month contract, that almost always means that you'll have some **teaching** or **administrative** duties year-round, a regularly scheduled component of "normal work" that will keep you from the classic research summer that higher ed relies upon.

The general civilian population, knowing as much about college teachers as I once did, will use the nine-month contract as another way of blaming you for having a cushy life: "You make all that money, you only teach ten hours a week, and you get your summers off." It may or may not be worth trying to explain how multifaceted and laden a faculty member's life is. If the complaints are coming from your uncle, he'll probably at least listen to you; plus you'll see him again at Christmas, and it's good to keep peace in the family. If they're coming from the guy who's come to clean the septic tank in mid-July, it's probably not worth arguing. His job *is* harder and nastier than yours, after all.

Course development. Putting together a high-quality course is a significant academic exercise, equivalent at least to writing a good academic paper. Let's think about all of the individual components that go into course development.

Most centrally, there's the content and its organization. For example, say you're **teaching** a course on our common concepts of life stages. Do you want to frame the weeks chronologically around the historical development of life-stage concepts (the invention of adolescence in the early twentieth century, for instance)? Do you want to frame the weeks around each of the contemporary differentiations (infant/toddler/early childhood/ early adolescence/mid-adolescence/ late adolescence/young adulthood/ mature adulthood/menopausal-andropausal adulthood/senior citizenry/ elderly/frail elderly)? Or do you want to frame the whole thing around an understanding of the different developmental-psych frames, the Freudian or Piagetian or Vygotskyan or Kohlbergian or Gilliganian understandings of human intellectual and emotional growth? These are not trivial distinctions, since each choice privileges a particular kind of understanding; that frame is the hidden curriculum of the course.

Once you know what the course is about, you have to decide what student success would look like. What is it that you want students to accomplish through having taken this course? What should they know, what should they understand, what should they be able to do? Having named that, you can then develop the readings, assignments, or tests that will enable students to reach the destination you've set.

How will the course be structured? Will you lecture, or create a seminar environment? Will there be laboratories or other apprentice-master opportunities for experiencing the conduct of the work? This has a lot to do with your own skills as a teacher; every instrument has its own repertoire, and you may fall more naturally into some teaching practices than others. You should be constantly working to expand your repertoire, of course, but you should also acknowledge that it exists, and play from your strengths.

How many class sessions are there, and how long is each one? The fifteen-week semester can be forty-five sessions of an hour each, or thirty sessions of ninety minutes each, or fifteen sessions of three hours each. You can't think of your course as a continuous forty-five-hour podcast that can be interrupted and restarted as necessary; each class session is its own theatrical event, with prelude, staging, climax and denouement.

There's the development of the syllabus as an object, which can be an integral part of the experience of the course; it's the physical representation of the work, and the physical representation of you as an instructor. There's work with the **library** to put books and articles on reserve, interaction with the writing center or its like to develop student supports, and the development of a course structure within your **learning management** software.

Once you know what room you'll be in, you should visit it to make sure that you know how to use it to its greatest advantage. It may have technology installed, or you may have to work with your media office to have projectors and computers and TV/DVD carts brought to class. Does the room have a blackboard, a whiteboard, a projection screen, a lectern, pin-up walls, wireless access?

All of this and more goes into developing a single course. If you're an adjunct instructor, you may just be handed a standardized syllabus, with many of these decisions taken out of your hands. It doesn't mean that you can't still subvert the course design in useful ways, but if you're given the course, you won't get any added stipend for course development. If you get to create the course structure, see if the school will offer you a one-time course-development payment; it's possible, and never hurts to ask. And also ask about the **intellectual property** ownership related to course development; what rights are you keeping, and what rights are you surrendering to your temporary employer?

If you're a permanent member of the **faculty**, you'll probably have a predictable mix of courses that you're regularly assigned to teach. Think about revising one of them every year, so that in the space of three or four years they'll all be on a cycle of refreshed thinking and attention. As one of my colleagues used to remind us, "If you're still teaching the same thing after five years, either your field is dead or you are."

Course/teaching evaluation. I was once asked by a colleague from biology to review some data that had come from a questionnaire of university administrators. The questionnaire, designed by faculty and administrators from the physical sciences, was a shambles: overlapping and nonexclusive answers, forced rankings of fifteen options (as if anybody could seriously distinguish their own preferences between their eighth and ninth most preferred option), a set of responses that were category mismatches (such as a sentence stem "If you were hosting a formal dinner, you'd choose . . . ," followed by the options "roast duck," "George Clooney," and "your best china"). It was abysmal. I was like: "I wouldn't come into your lab and try to set up your centrifuge! Keep your hands off the questionnaires!"

But in our age of SurveyMonkey and Qualtrics, pretty much anybody thinks they can design a questionnaire, and evidence of this abounds in university course evaluations, which are designed by **committees**, rife with level-of-measurement error, administered in uncontrolled settings with wildly varying field instructions, and yet treated as though they had substantial revelatory power. Ugh.[50]

But this is not the place for methodological discussions. This is a tactical rather than an intellectual conversation, and the tactical knowledge you

---

50. I have a colleague in chemistry who works very hard on his teaching. His most recent intro chem class resulted in a minuscule 10-percent failure rate on his department's standardized end-of-semester lab exam, in a department where 40-percent failure on that test is unsurprising. That success, though, came at the cost of relatively poor course evaluations, in which students complained bitterly about his "flipped-classroom" methods of off-site reading and on-site problem sets, in contrast to the lecture-and-homework methods they were more familiar with. The course demonstrably worked, but for the students it was painful and unfamiliar, and he was mildly reprimanded by his department chair for those evaluation results rather than praised for the student learning outcomes.

must acquire concerns what your college does with the results of course evaluations. In some schools, copies are given to the instructor, and the originals are stuck in a file cabinet and never seen again. This is actually quite a good outcome, because it allows the instructor to learn something from her students, especially if there are significant open-response sections where the students are asked to write about their experiences. Low stakes, high opportunity for growth.

In other schools, evaluations are seen only by the relevant faculty member and her department **chair**, and the chair looks them over for areas of significant concern in order to have coaching conversations as needed. This was true at both of the schools in which I've taught; it can also be a helpful strategy, but among overworked administrators, the tendency may be to focus on the difficulties rather than to congratulate people on their strengths.

But there are schools in which the numerical rankings that come from course evaluations are used as part of the data set that determines contract renewal, tenure, merit pay, and teaching awards. The fact that the data are gigantically flawed is probably outside your control, but if you teach in a school where quantitative course evaluations carry high stakes, then friend, you had better find out what those evaluation forms are asking, and think carefully about how your teaching and curricular practices will support those criteria.

It's also likely that the stakes will be higher for **adjunct** and contingent faculty than for those on the **tenure track**. Promotion and tenure is a complex, multivariate calculation, whereas adjuncts are ignored until contract renewal time, are rarely observed in the classroom, and have neither oversight nor assistance unless specific student complaints arise. The course evaluations may be the single data point an **administrator** has to make the decision about renewal.

Course evaluations are among the most politicized aspects of higher education, and they reveal the subtle differences among our various conceptions of what college is for. They can be designed as customer-satisfaction surveys; as final marks, like **grades** or ice-skating scores; as tools of institutional management and supervision; as facilitators of instructor reflection. Each of those motives would lead us to develop a different kind of tool, but when those motives are not named, too many evaluations are a clumsy blend of all of them. The college's administration and faculty senate will fight over every line, and then, exhausted and bloodied, not touch the evaluation rubric again for years.

And I know it's probably too much to ask, but please, have some respect for disciplinary expertise, and stand back while the social scientists design your instrumentation. You wouldn't make suggestions to your plumber.

Cover letter. When you apply for acceptance into a graduate program, and again when you apply for an academic position, you're most often sending them two paper pieces: your **CV** and your cover letter. Both are crucially important, but they're fulfilling two very different functions. The CV is a factual retrospective: *This is what I have accomplished.* The cover letter is persuasive and prospective: *This is what I intend to accomplish.* Think of your cover letter as a form of proposal:

1. This is what I would like to do.
2. This is how I'd structure it.
3. This is why I'm the right person to do it.
4. This is why you'll benefit from partnering with me in order to do it.

This persuasive function of the cover letter is why you absolutely must craft an individual letter for every job to which you apply. You may be personally committed to a specific **research agenda** that won't change no matter where you find yourself. But in order for you to be considered for any particular position, your scholarly intentions have to fit the capabilities, resources, and interests of your host institution. Your work has to support the larger work of the **department** and the college, which means that you have to do some research about the specific departments and colleges to which you apply, and make the case directly that your proposed work and your capabilities are good for them.

This is not a simple task. You'll need to get on the college's website, read every single **bio** of every single **faculty** member in the department, and build yourself a profile of what that department is interested in. Don't trust the homepage boilerplate about what the department wants you to think they're good at; that's marketing, crafted by people whose primary intellectual goal was search engine optimization. Look at the **research** and **teaching** interests of the departmental faculty, and be prepared to write about how your work enhances an existing strength or fills a crucial gap. Don't mention names, saying that you're especially looking forward to working with Dr. Hugh Jeego or Dr. Elle Koholic, unless you're in the lab sciences and are applying specifically to work in that person's lab. In the social sciences and humanities, you'll just trigger land mines that you have no way of perceiving from your current vantage point.[51]

Have a look around the college's website as a whole, noting particular features of its **library**, laboratories, or other resources that you can take advantage of. If the library has an archive related to your interests, mention it as another reason why you and the college can build a productive relationship.

Do not use the cover letter to make demands or complicate issues. The cover letter is a place to make the hiring committee excited about you as an opportunity, not a place to talk about your need for a spousal hire, or your need for specific experimental equipment, or your need to use the family tuition discount to get your seven kids through college. And don't talk about your desire to live in the college's particular city or region, unless you can make it germane to the work of teaching and scholarship that you propose. Wanting to *live* in Oakland because you're tired of winter or because you have family in the Bay Area will be seen as trivial; wanting to *work* in Oakland because of your intellectual and social commitment to urban public education will be seen as relevant and important.

A specific cover letter immediately sets you apart from all the candidates who have submitted generic, all-purpose letters. A forward-looking cover letter sets you apart from all the candidates who've just restated their CVs in different terms. A beautifully formatted cover letter sets you apart from all the candidates who've needed new ink cartridges in their printers and still use Courier as their default typeface. Your cover letter is one of the only two pitches you get to make in the qualifying round; make it terrific.

Curriculum. There exists a general consensus that a college degree should take roughly four years, a **master's degree** should take two more, and a **doctorate** should have another two years or so of coursework before the **dissertation**. But no matter the **discipline** in which one embarks or the level of degree to which one aspires, there is far more to be known or con-

---

51. I applied to one grad school saying that I was especially excited to work with a particular faculty member. What I didn't know is that this particular faculty member had suddenly died at a very young age between the time I researched the department and the time they read the letter. If that proposed relationship had been the primary motive I'd offered for choosing their department, I'd have never been accepted. Fortunately, he was one among many. I do wish I'd gotten to work with him, though; his work really did seem terrific.

sidered than can be covered in a limited period of time. And in any **department** of reasonable size, there will be divergent opinions about what is essential and what is merely interesting; about how students should move from "basic" to "advanced," and what the basis of the field really is.

We each care about how our field is conceived, and about how new initiates are brought into the community. Like Talmudic scholars, we hold nuanced views of the articles of faith, and those nuances can reinforce our depth of commitment or can rend us forever.

The graduate curricula are difficult enough, but they have the advantage of containing their arguments largely within a departmental denomination. Even more difficult are the problems of designing the undergraduate curriculum, which is ecumenical by its intentions. We want students to have the broad general education that helps them consider their roles in the world in new ways; we want the undecided and uncertain to have the chance to discover a side of themselves that they'd never considered. There is a degree of inefficiency by design in all good undergraduate curricula, and one of my great joys is when a student tells me that she's changing majors, that she's discovered a line of thinking that feels both natural and uniquely challenging.

Add to these local conversations the fact that our population is highly mobile, and a vast number of students enter our colleges at some midpoint along the curricular stream.[52] Contemporary college is less like a theatrical performance where we are taken chronologically through a compelling sequence of experiences, and more like an evening in front of the TV, scrolling around with the remote. The credits a student has bought at College A are expected to be legal tender at Colleges B through Z, and state and federal agencies attempt to enforce that fluidity in the reasonable service of individual students' timely and cost-effective completion of a degree. Curriculum designers are asked to permit more and more exceptions to the careful choreography of their learning. A diner menu may specify "Sorry, no substitutions," but a college never can.

Finally, accrediting bodies weigh in, telling us what our students should experience and be able to do. An undergraduate curriculum should have a

52. About a third of all undergrad degree recipients from the 2006 starting cohort transferred at least once, and 15 percent attended a college *in a state* different from the one where they graduated. Don Hossler et al., "Transfer and Mobility: A National View of Pre-Degree Student Movement in Postsecondary Institutions," National Student Clearinghouse Research Center (February 2012), accessed April 28, 2015, http://nscresearchcenter.org/wp-content/uploads/NSC_Signature_Report_2.pdf.

minimum of forty-five general-education credits, says one; the major must be at least thirty-six credits, says another; all students must have the opportunity to have a fifteen-credit minor along with their major and their general education, says a third. Every professional organization's accrediting body will tell you that it's not mandating the contents of the curriculum, even as it also tells you exactly what every graduate must have experienced and accomplished in order for a degree to bear its imprimatur. In architecture, **accreditation** is defined in part by students having demonstrated capability in twenty-six different SPCs (student performance criteria), each of which has its own advocates behind the scenes.

Jill Ker Conway, the former **president** of Smith College, once wrote that the curriculum is the battleground upon which academic wars are fought.

> Academic institutions may present a calm front to the outside world, and even persuade their new initiates into scholarly life that curricular discussions are based on strictly academic criteria—such as the potential interests of the fictive "student," the hours she or he can devote to study in a given week, the level of preparation she or he may bring to college-level work, new fields versus "core" subjects—but in reality, these academic concerns are merely props, a backdrop or part of the set for the stage on which individuals and groups contend for power. Sometimes the contest is polite and open, sometimes devious and ugly. It may subside for a period of uneasy truce, like some guerrilla war in an unsettled territory, but it is always smoldering, with the contenders ready to snatch up their weapons and begin a fresh assault on some battle-scarred, body-strewn curricular territory.[53]

But as bad as those fights could be, she was referring only to the factions that existed within her faculty in the 1960s and '70s. The wars are much more complex now; like a rebel conflict in Central America, local struggles are manipulated and fed by the great powers, who see each small nation merely as an instrument applied to their own goals.

All of that having been said, if you have the opportunity as an early-career faculty to become involved in curricular discussions, you should step forward. You'll never have a better view of how your colleagues understand the nature of your field, or the divisions within it, than when they attempt to bring that understanding into the structure of a degree program. You'll

53. Jill Ker Conway, *True North: A Memoir* (New York: Vintage, 1994): 154.

be forced to articulate your own partially formed thoughts about what you find most important, and those thoughts will be more fully shaped through friction with others.[54] The years of curriculum deliberation act like a rock polisher, with the constant, tumbling abrasion refining your thoughts from beach roughness to a fine high sheen. It's frustrating and difficult, and if you go into it thinking that you have to "win," you'll be angry and bitter the entire time; but if you can imagine that you're exerting your own small pressure on the direction of your department or college culture, you can do good work for the school and its students, and become wiser yourself.

Curriculum vitae, or CV. A singular mark of the scholarly enterprise is the overreliance on Latin, a holdover from two earlier conditions: that the academy was largely humanistic, and that the reading of Ovid was part of the early schooling of every one of the tiny cohort of privileged children who were aimed at Yale from birth. Now that higher education contains a much broader array of intellectual and professional fields and an expanded cultural community, the continued embrace of Latin is simply one of the secret handshakes that divides insiders from outsiders. We could refer to the CV as an extended or expanded or full résumé, but that wouldn't be nearly as impressive.[55]

A CV is a full listing of all of the qualifications you have obtained and work you have done that pertain to your professional and intellectual life. (The key words in that sentence are "all" and "pertain," and we'll come back to them in a minute.) Like a résumé, a CV includes educational history, work history, and high accomplishments; unlike a résumé, it goes into significant detail about **publications, presentations, committee** work, **professional society** memberships, and academic service. A typical CV might have section headings as follows:

- education (from highest to lowest degree)
- professional employment/experience (in reverse chronology)

54. One of my favorite colleagues at my last college was a man with whom I agreed on almost nothing having to do with architecture. We wanted very different things, not merely for our students but for our profession and for the physical world, that our profession could bring about. We may have argued about one course or another, but underlying that was a fundamental disagreement about the definition of good buildings and good cities. We had, for four years of our weekly mutual participation in curricular revision, a generous disagreement that left both of us smarter and broader.
55. A tavern occasioned only by academics might be referred to as a CV joint.

- publications (each section in reverse chronology)
  - **peer-reviewed**
  - professional
  - other
- **presentations** (again, most current first)
  - academic **conferences**
  - professional conferences
  - other
- teaching history
  - courses you have personally developed or reconstructed
  - other courses you have taught (and the student level of each: lower-division undergrad, advanced undergrad, masters, or doctoral)
  - **thesis** or **dissertation** committees you've served on
- awards
  - funded projects
  - recognition or honors without compensation
- service
  - to your college
    - mission-related (curricular, research, or hiring committees)
    - other (as new-student ambassador, in LGBT outreach)
  - to other colleges or associations
    - elected offices held in disciplinary or professional organizations
    - **committee** or board work in disciplinary or professional organizations
    - paid or volunteer consulting within higher education
  - to the nonacademic community
- other (notable nonacademic achievements, languages and proficiencies, specific academic software skills such as SPSS, and so on)

The norms in your **discipline** might differ slightly, but table 2 offers a decent template to start with. Let's loop back to that key word "pertain." What exactly is pertinent material for your CV? This is a question that can only be answered with precision within your discipline, and you should regularly review your CV with more senior academic colleagues. But see table 2 for some guidelines for developing your first draft. Remember, your CV is not a summary, and it's not a place to be humble. And that brings us back to the second key word, "all." If you've done it, if you're proud of it, and if it

Table 2. Pertinent entries in each CV category

CV subdivision	Pertinent	Possible	Irrelevant
Education	PhD master's bachelor's You can name honors if you were summa cum laude or something, but *never* include your GPA.	professional certificates related to your field (for instance, LEED certification for architects)	one-off continuing ed courses associate's degrees certification unrelated to your field (for instance, being a real estate agent)
Experience/employment	academic positions (including postdocs and assistantships) professional positions related to your disciplinary work	professional work not related to your field (for instance, if you were a banker before your life in geology)	two summers as a dishwasher during college
Publications	peer-reviewed scholarship invited contributions to scholarly work (book chapters, for instance)	book reviews, especially for academic journals professional or general-public publications, *if* the articles are related to your work or your field	syllabi and course handouts items for the church newsletter
Presentations	presentations at academic and professional conferences guest lectures at other institutions	public venues (being an invited expert on a TV or radio news program, for instance) panel discussions on larger issues that your field touches on	speeches made to the Rotary Club calls in to a National Public Radio show
Teaching	all courses taught in higher education (including those taught as a teaching assistant, though make sure you note that) thesis or dissertation committee memberships undergraduate researchers supervised or mentored	grade-school or high-school teaching, especially if related to your academic discipline professional society training you have offered	experience as a Pop Warner Football coach
Awards	funded grants professional society awards significant private awards (e.g., Fulbright or Rhodes scholarships)	merit scholarships and academic awards during student life, *if* they were particularly good *and* if they relate to what you're doing now	third place (drums) ribbon at band camp "most improved" award in your bowling league

Table 2. (*continued*)

CV subdivision	Pertinent	Possible	Irrelevant
Service	significant college or departmental committees (both standing and ad hoc) professional society committee or board memberships, conference planning, etc. reviews for academic journals or conferences	committee or board membership in civic or volunteer organizations other service to nonprofits *if* it's an enduring commitment, *if* you can relate it to your field, or *if* it's heartwarming (e.g., four years as a Big Sister, providing post-earthquake engineering services)	service as church usher polka band visits to a senior home
Other	languages and fluency particular software skills important to your field current memberships in professional/academic societies	hobbies and avocations that you've taken to high competency (BCA-recognized billiards instructor, for instance): less likely if you're applying to a research-centered position, more likely if you're applying to a liberal arts college.	likes kittens makes beer

relates to your academic life, it goes into your CV and stays there. The only things that might go stale are the lesser awards and service; if you won a departmental research award as an undergrad, or if you served on the campus Earth Day planning committee as a master's student, those might go away by the time you finish your PhD and apply for academic jobs.

As you can imagine, CVs can get to be pretty long documents. At the beginning of your graduate-school **career**, yours might be two or three pages. Mine right now is at twelve. I've seen a forty-two-page CV from a senior member of my field, and heard of an eighty-five produced near the end of a fifty-year career in economics. Don't worry about how long your current CV is compared against those of others. Your CV needs to be complete, accurate, and pertinent, rather than merely extensive.

The busier you are, the more frequently you should update your CV. You'll forget stuff if you wait a year; I'd recommend setting a calendar update to review your vita every three months.

I have to say in closing, however, that there's something kind of sad about a culture all of whose members must maintain documents listing their every single accomplishment, both major and minor. It's as though we're keeping our own notes for some imagined posthumous biographer, a laser-printed proclamation that our work *really has mattered*. There's no other profession in which a résumé goes on for more than a page or two, even for senior executives. But academics are often greatly afflicted by the fraternal twins of vanity and insecurity, and the rabbit's foot of a growing and well-tuned CV is a comfort in an uncertain world.

Dd

Deadline. In the late 1990s I worked for a company that submitted a lot of proposals for government work, some of which were allowed to be submitted by fax. The fax machine, normally as reliable as a door hinge, sometimes balked (or was misfed by a panicky operator) at unhelpful moments. The sign above it read: "This machine can sense fear."

There are two kinds of deadlines in the academic world: institutional and project-based. Institutional deadlines—things like submittal dates for **grant proposals** and other forms of applications, getting your **dissertation** in to the **graduate school** in time for your inclusion in this semester's commencement—are sharp and incontrovertible. If your grant proposal goes to the National Science Foundation forty minutes late, it might as well have never existed. It will not be read, and there will be no grace period. It's like a half-court shot after the buzzer has sounded; it might be pretty, but sorry, game's already over. Get used to meeting those deadlines with hours, or days, to spare; something will *always* go wrong on your first attempt to upload a form or get a document back from Kinko's.

Project-based deadlines slide by harmlessly, like the bullets passing all around Neo in *The Matrix*. Once we recognize that they have no reality, we can ignore them without risk.

OK, maybe that's a bit of an overstatement. But projects that don't have externally mandated deadlines are always being weighed against the innumerable priorities of every other participant, and won't always rise to the top. If the registrar's office needs your syllabus by Friday and you get it to them the following Monday, you'll be ahead of half of the faculty anyway.

We always have too many good things to do, all of which are on some sort of schedule, and those schedules are more fluid than we often realize.

If you owe someone else a product by a deadline, and you know you'll be late, **e-mail** him with an apologetic note that includes a real deadline that you *know* you can meet. If you have routine institutional paperwork (annual workload reports, syllabi, an updated **CV**, etc.) to submit, try to meet the deadline, but as much as a week beyond it will still be useful.

If you're setting the deadline, set it artificially early by a week or so. Send a reminder to your project colleagues a week prior to your fake deadline. Send another reminder to those who haven't responded on the day of the fake deadline. Call the two or three people who haven't sent you anything within a couple of days after that.

Dealing with project deadlines in a spirit of good faith will win you many friends. But always remember that institutional deadlines recognize no such intent, and the letter of the law will be adhered to precisely.

Dean. I have a friend, Jim, who was recently named dean of enrollment and student financial services at his college. When his promotion came through, I asked if I could call him James, Dean.[56]

Dean Martin, Dean Jones, Howard Dean, Jimmy Dean, Dizzy Dean: those I get. How the hell did "dean" get to mean some character who runs a college? Blame it on the Latin again; *decanus* is someone responsible for a group of ten people. That role was part of the bureaucratic structure of big monasteries and the colleges that grew out of them. So a dean's work is something akin to that of a military captain in charge of a group of sergeants, each of whom is in charge of a small company of soldiers.

In small colleges with only a single academic unit, the dean may be the chief academic officer, but in larger institutions, a dean supervises one of the several core academic divisions or functions. Duke University, for instance, has two major undergraduate divisions—the Trinity College of Arts and Sciences, and the Pratt School of Engineering—each with its own dean, and with a few lesser deans in Trinity responsible for humanities, natural science, social sciences, and academic affairs. The graduate schools—the Fuqua School of Business, the Nicholas School of the Environment, the San-

---

56. See, this is the kind of working-class wordplay that gets you in trouble in higher ed, where "dean" is a title far more commonly than it's a person's name. I also have a drawing of a famous *Looney Tunes* character wearing a cap and gown instead of his more traditional hunting hat and shotgun, whom I call Elmer PhD. The more stuffily educated just sigh, roll their eyes slightly, and go on to more important things.

ford School of Public Policy, the Divinity School, the Law School, and the **graduate school** as a whole—also each have a dean. The Medical Center, with its med school and nursing school, has its own structure, with deans all over the place. Add the words "assistant" or "associate" or "deputy" to dean and you get a palette of hierarchy as rich as any clergy or military structure. And trust me, everybody knows exactly where they are on that hierarchy, and recognizes what every minuscule variant implies.[57]

In the most general terms, it works like this. There's a department— let's say biology—with fifteen faculty. One of those faculty members is appointed to be the **chair** for a while, but is still primarily a faculty member while she also handles some administrative duties. But the biology department has sibling departments—let's say geology, chemistry, physics, sometimes mathematics, sometimes psychology, maybe nursing, maybe computer science—that are organized together into a college of natural sciences. That college has a dean who is a permanent **administrator** rather than primarily a faculty member. In fact, if one of those departments' faculty members is internally promoted to become the dean, that department will usually get a replacement faculty hire as compensation for giving up a faculty member to the administrative team.

There are also deans who serve in ways not related to a particular departmental structure. These could include a dean of students, who's responsible for student life and student discipline; my former role as dean of research and assessment, responsible for the entire institution's **accreditation** and academic data analysis; or the dean of the faculty, responsible for organizational management of recruitment, **tenure**, and promotion issues.

The deans (captains) of the multiple colleges and academic program areas each report to the **provost** (think colonel or major), who is responsible for the entirety of academic and scholarly affairs on campus. The provost is one of several members of the leadership team of the **president** (the general), along with the heads of finance, **facilities**, fund-raising, enrollment management, public affairs, or other major functional areas.

Almost no one goes into graduate school or early faculty life aspiring to be an administrator. Scholars make their way by attending to one thing in precision; administrators attend to the intersection of all things. Faculty members are paid to focus; administrators are paid to be interrupted. We

57. I have a friend who was recently named her college's "interim associate vice provost for high-impact practices," which holds my personal record for longest job title with least clarity. The only unambiguous word in that whole string is "interim."

talk easily about scholarly productivity, but how does a dean assess her effectiveness? Deans have stopped accomplishing any sort of productive work of their own in ways that are easily measurable, and their labors are entirely managerial. Deans organize processes, coach their junior administrators, resolve interpersonal difficulties, advocate for resources, plan events, and review the work of others. They have ceased to be moving parts of the engine, and have volunteered for service as lubricants.

Trust me, lubricants are a crucial component of any machine; they reduce friction and allow the power train to function without conflict. But in any engine, you replace the oil a lot more often than you replace an intake valve or a piston ring. Faculty, up to and including the chairs, are expected to be permanent fixtures of the institution, whereas deans and above are more mobile. They're more likely to change schools than faculty are, and more likely to see themselves on an upward track through the officers' hierarchy. To do well, deans have to focus on the work of the whole institution more centrally than on any of its component endeavors; they have to lubricate all of the parts sufficiently, and none of them in excess. In doing so, they absorb and dissipate all the heat, and are likely to burn out.

Defense. Such a funny term, the *dissertation defense*. It portrays a sort of gladiatorial moment in which you, standing alone on the floor of the Colosseum armed only with your wits and the shield of your scholarship, are set upon by the old lions of the **department**, with your committee of emperors waiting to raise or lower their thumbs in verdict.

Really, it won't be like that. If your research is sound, your **dissertation** defense is more likely to be a victory lap. You've done innovative and important work, and you've used intelligent **methods** to do it. So you talk about some of the most interesting parts for half an hour, and then your committee asks you questions (or tells you how impressed they were with some part of it or another) for another hour, and then any guests have the chance to ask you questions. Then you part company with your committee for a little while, and they decide whether to just pass you or to award a commendation. Then they rejoin you, tell you the verdict, and it's pink hearts and kittens all around.[58]

Your committee members, especially your dissertation chair, do not

---

58. Check this with your own graduate school; but typically, you can receive one dissenting vote from among your committee members and still graduate. So if you've got one curmudgeon, you're still OK.

want to be embarrassed among their colleagues by portraying their own leadership of your scholarly work as haphazard or ill-informed. They will not let you schedule your defense until they believe that your work is competent and complete. This is another reason to work with the most capable scholars in your department; you want dissertation committee members who really know their material, and who insist that you do as well.

A defense can go awry—I've seen at least two pretty awful ones[59]—but almost never so badly as to fail. At worst, you may be asked to submit changes, which you will work on in subsequent weeks with the committee chair. But if you've been allowed to move forward with a defense, it means that your committee is satisfied and ready to move you through. (In some rare cases, it may mean that they think there's nothing more they can do with you and they're just giving up—but you chose a better program than that, didn't you?)

In order to bring yourself some degree of comfort, you should attend every dissertation defense in your department while you're in residence. Most schools make the dissertation defense a public event, though the meaning of "public" varies; almost always, though, at least fellow doctoral students are allowed in. My defense had about fifty people in attendance; I've been part of a dissertation committee in which only we, the **candidate**, and a couple of other students were present. You'll begin to internalize the choreography, you'll start to understand the format, and you'll learn the culture of critique, so that when your time comes, you'll perform with greater ease.

As with every **presentation**, you should master the room and its technology in advance. PowerPoint has the huge advantage of not allowing one to load slides upside down or backward, but you want to make sure you choose a simple, portable typeface and colors that contrast on a projector in a too-bright room and not just on your monitor in a dark office at 3 a.m. Don't rely on technological magic for this performance; don't put a web link or a video into your presentation unless you've made it work flawlessly

59. In both cases the students had done somewhat interesting research, but had employed statistical methods they didn't fully understand. This led them to develop "findings" that they couldn't really explain except by pointing helplessly back at the numbers. In the worst case, a student had found a negative correlation between two phenomena, which was entirely possible but seemed counterintuitive. A faculty guest said, "Really, there's an inverse relationship between A and B? Why do you think that is?" And the student replied, "The r is −0.421." "Yes, I see that, but why do you think those things are inversely related?" "Because the correlation is −0.421."

ten straight times. You want to walk into that space and own it; not cocky, but ready.

If you're proud of your work—if you believe that it's *good* rather than *good enough*—you'll be fine. More often, you'll be the one who's hesitant, and your committee will be telling you (usually repeatedly) that you've done enough, that you don't have to add another component to your analysis, that it's okay to leave some work for the rest of your career. Trust them, and walk into the defense with pleasure and pride.

Department. Academic departments are the locally specific outposts of intellectual **disciplines**, kind of like individual Starbucks outlets in remote towns. As with all chain stores, college departments offer broadly understood products with mild local amendments; a history **curriculum** from one college will be recognized by historians from other colleges nationwide, even while one might have a greater emphasis in military history and another a focus on Asian history. Disciplinary hiring and **accreditation** practices and their associated **professional societies** ensure that nobody gets too far off script.[60]

The department is the fundamental academic unit of any campus's **faculty**. The six teachers that the college has hired to teach chemistry will collectively be the chemistry department, responsible for setting and revising the chemistry **curriculum**, for teaching courses designed for majors as well as "service courses" designed for nonmajors to fill their general education requirements, and for advising undergraduate and graduate chemistry students toward degree progress. One of those faculty members will temporarily be named the department chair, responsible for budgeting and course coverage and for various forms of interface with the larger university **administration**. But the chair is more like the team captain than the head coach—still one of the crew.

For our purposes, the thing to know about your department is that it constitutes the small number of people with whom you will work most closely during your time at the school. When you're a grad student, your department's faculty represents your innermost ring of intellectual advice and your professional network. When you're an early faculty member, your department's faculty represents your closest colleagues, the people you will

60. This is a crucial element of why doctoral graduates of interdisciplinary degree programs struggle so mightily to get hired. They've prepared to run a boutique, but what's hiring are Burger King and Forever 21 outlets around the country.

see in hallways and meetings more often than you see your family. In either role, they will become your strongest allies or your most dangerous critics. Every department stands as the first line of defense over academia's three most treasured goods: the issuance of the **doctorate**, the **offer** of the **tenure-track** position, and the recommendation for **tenure**. You want them to be your champions, to look forward to their interaction with you, to look for reasons to say yes.

You can't make people like you. You can't make people respect you. But if you go out of your way to treat your departmental colleagues with respect and kindness, to ask their advice rather than make pronouncements, your odds will be a lot better than if you play it alone, or if you treat every interaction as an opportunity to vent.

Development/advancement. Both of these are synonyms for "fundraising." A development office or an office of institutional advancement is where contacts are being made and relationships formed, in the hope that someone will think kindly enough of the college to donate.

Not all donations are equal, and the differences are not merely in size. There are donations that the college can put to general use (called unrestricted donations), and other donations that establish particular pools for **grants** or for tuition support, for endowed chairs and for travel programs. Most often, these gifts are not spent directly; they are invested, often after bundling with the gifts of many others, and the interest is harvested for use while the principal remains. It's like a farmer with one hundred dollars; he can buy a lot of apples with the money, but they'll be gone in two months. Instead, he can buy an apple tree with the hundred dollars, and with some patience he'll be able to take apples off it every fall for decades.

Colleges often receive donations with strings attached. For instance, the University of Colorado at Boulder received a million dollars to fund a "visiting scholar in conservative thought and policy."[61] A member of the Saudi royal family gave Harvard twenty million dollars to fund the Prince Alwaleed Bin Talal Islamic Studies Program.[62] Yale once gave back twenty

61. Syndi Dunn, "U. of Colorado at Boulder Names Steven Hayward its First 'Visiting Scholar in Conservative Thought,'" *Chronicle of Higher Education*, March 13, 2013, accessed April 28, 2015, http://chronicle.com/article/U-of-Colorado-at-Boulder/137895/.
62. "A Saudi Prince's Controversial Gift." *Harvard Magazine*, March–April 2006, accessed on April 28, 2015, http://harvardmagazine.com/2006/03/a-saudi-princes-controve.html.

million dollars because the donor wanted the right to approve faculty. [63] I worked for a research institute whose corporate donor hoped the institute would provide ideas that the company could develop into new products and services. There's a fine line between funding an investigation into an interesting question and funding a hoped-for outcome to that investigation; the tensions between **academic freedom** and economic interest are always in play.

The newspaper industry has historically had the same concerns. Journalistic practice declares that there is a "wall between editorial and advertising," so that the newsroom can write critical stories about labor and safety practices at the local big-box retailer, even though that retailer buys 10 percent of the advertising in the Sunday paper. But now, with the advent of merged words like *infotainment*, *infomercial*, and *advertorial*, it's hard to say that there's an impermeable wall between those two rooms. Higher education may be installing a screen door as well, with the increasing use of concepts such as collaborative research between industry and the university, the "professor of the practice," technology transfer, and **intellectual property** development. Perhaps higher education will soon have its own merged vocabulary: the *donorversity*, perhaps, or the *laborriculum*.

Director. Directors are the kudzu of higher education, once imported in small numbers for particular projects but now overrunning the forest. Back in the day, all of the core academic functions of universities were held within **departments** or colleges. But now there are innumerable scholarly supports that run across the entirety of the school: writing across the curriculum, information literacy, **undergraduate research**, first-year experience, writing or tutoring centers, honors programs, faculty development, academic computing, service learning, and an endless number of academic services that don't live in any particular academic home. Rather than being striped, the pattern of higher education is now plaid, with the vertical columns of department structure being overlaid with a nearly equal number of horizontal rows that represent "cross-cutting" academic initiatives.

Each of those lateral initiatives will be supervised by a director rather than a **chair** or a **dean**. Directors typically don't have a **faculty** line unless their directorship is some sort of an overload or **buyout** from their regular

63. Ryan E. Smith, "The Bass Grant: Why Yale Gave $20 Million Back," *Yale Herald*, March 24, 1995, accessed April 28, 2015, http://www.yaleherald.com/archive/xix/3.24 .95/news/bass.html.

faculty duties; they're twelve-month **administrators**, often invisible until you examine the ecosystem closely. They have none of the protections of **tenure**, being hired either on a contractual or an at-will basis, and they can find themselves exiled quickly if they displease a senior administrator.

The rise of the directorate system serves to absorb some of the overproduction of PhDs, and helps to mollify the reserve army of the unemployed, giving jobs to people like me who'll support the work of the institution without requiring the commitment of tenure or the messiness of establishing permanent lines. And because director-run projects serve a broad array of students and faculty, they can be a useful landing spot for folks from **interdisciplinary** PhD programs who know how to operate across borders. But it's not the same as the **teaching** and **research** we aspired to. I had a good run as a director and then as a dean, but it was always a little like living next door to your old girlfriend: you got to see her every day, but you were constantly reminded of the life you'd never have.

Discipline. The title of my first book, which was drawn from my **dissertation**, is *Landscapes of Betrayal, Landscapes of Joy: Curtisville in the Lives of its Teenagers*.[64] It's a study of the ways that schools, homes, and community places held meaning for teens. I conducted it as a doctoral student in architecture, but could just as easily have done it in eight or a dozen other **departments** on the same campus. I took doctoral courses in the UW–Milwaukee Departments of Architecture, History, Anthropology, Geography, and English. My committee members were an architectural historian and designer, an urban geographer, and an environmental psychologist; my two outside readers were an art historian and a novelist.

When I converted the manuscript from dissertation to book, my **editor** was a geographer teaching in a school of architecture; when the academic press published it, the shelving instructions indicated that it should reside in "cultural studies / sociology," and I was asked to find a sociologist who would nominate it for the American Sociological Association book of the year award (as it turns out, I didn't know a sociologist anywhere, having never taken a sociology course, though of course it should have won anyway). The Library of Congress designation group for the book is HQ, which indicates materials on the family, marriage, women, and sexuality—none of which are the book's focus, though it touches occasionally on all of them.

---

64. Herb Childress, *Landscapes of Betrayal, Landscapes of Joy: Curtisville in the Lives of its Teenagers* (Albany, NY: SUNY Press, 2000).

All of this is to say that interesting research lives within an intellectual ecosystem, with general zones rather than strict political boundaries.[65] Who knows where sociology ends and anthropology starts, where physics ends and climatology begins? And really, although we know that the general regions exist, why should it matter that some specific research—or worse, some specific person—is placed firmly behind the brand name of a particular discipline?

But we are not here today to speak of philosophical questions about the existence of disciplines. We are here to get you into graduate school and into a **faculty** job. And in order to do that, we need to be clear that your odds are vastly increased when you declare yourself firmly within the boundaries of a known, named, stable, recognized discipline that every college in America offers. I mean, you'd have to be *insane* to take your PhD in architecture (environment-behavior studies) when you could do exactly the same **dissertation** research in anthropology.

Oops.

Once again, the data are scarce; it's far more difficult to determine how many colleges in the United States have anthropology departments than to determine how many field NCAA Division I men's lacrosse teams. However, it doesn't take much intuition to know that most colleges have anthroplogy departments, and that far fewer have Asian American studies departments; and that thus there will be proportionally more faculty jobs in anthropology than in Asian American studies. Admittedly, there'll also be a lot more doctoral **candidates** and PhDs in anthropology, but at least you'll have a playing field to compete on.

You'll be faced with two competing desires as a pending doctoral student. You can choose to surround yourself with faculty and fellow students who've all chosen to focus on the same fascinating region of ideas rather than on a discipline. You'll be well supported in your dissertation research by senior scholars who know the specifics of people, literature, **methods**, and **publication** venues for your small area. You'll have a great time, but will struggle to identify yourself quickly to the outside world in ways as obvious as "historian" or "sociologist."

Conversely, you can enter a more general department in one of the established disciplines. You'll gain breadth within your field as you work with colleagues who are researching far-flung phenomena quite unrelated to

---

65. Please refer to the entry on "interdisciplinary" for an important paired discussion of this issue.

your own; but most of your faculty members are likely to be almost as amateur as you in the specifics of your own research question. They're likely to
want to help re-mold your interests to match their own—not simply out
of ego or rigidity, but because then they'll know how best to be helpful.
At the completion of your program, though, you can don one of the primary colors of the known disciplines, proudly declaring yourself as orange
or brown rather than "kind of like puce but maybe with a little more red,
sort of?"

In **career** terms, you should consider a primary Crayola degree rather
than a custom Pantone formulation. Let yourself have the advantages of the
more recognizable brand name, and then surprise people with the versatil-
ity of your own interests within that.

Dissertation. As a person with innumerable interests, I've always admired
obsessions. The decision to forsake all other hobbies and interests in order
to pursue one track has an almost spiritual purity about it. There's a reason
why religious orders speak of one's calling: one is thought to be spoken to
by God, urged to follow a path (and often to follow it in the face of one's
great reservations). And in the end, one puts aside everything else to do
that work.

As a doctoral student, you have one advantage over everyone else in
higher education: you have permission to be obsessive. You get to select an
area of research and follow the trail wherever it leads; you get to exercise
your powerful curiosity without reserve. You are engaged in one of the very
few contemporary venues of action that expects, and rewards, singular attention. Your head is completely filled with the day's treasures: the auction
records that reveal ownership histories of a painting, the surprising blip in
the data that might be an anomaly or might be the emergence of a larger
pattern, the story from one of your participants that suddenly clarifies the
meaning of a dozen other observations.

You become insufferable to others. You become a trivia fountain, a repository of what others see as mere brain lint. And it *is* brain lint for them,
because there's no organized system that each trivia point fits into, whereas
you find more and more opportunities to categorize, to connect. You see
the pattern where others only see dots.

You will know the locations of every bowling alley in Milwaukee in 1910
and 1930 and 1950 and 1970, and how that ties into suburban development
and national patterns of immigration. You will know how and why the
townships of Iowa consolidated their school districts by 90 percent in the

1950s and 60s. You will know how to assess the chemosensory responses of *Physella* (freshwater snails) to predator fish. You will know the name of the county clerk who oversaw the 1984 elections in Washo County, Oregon.

Your enthusiasms are out of reach to others; you sink ever further into your own world of murky conspiracies. You move away, "into the field," and build relationships that have little to do with your academic colleagues. You go native. You live in dark places—archives, laboratories, library carrels—and emerge, blinking into the light, only in dire necessity. You eat and bathe and sleep on different cycles than those of your family and neighbors.

You are Adam in the garden, naming the beasts that no one before has ever seen. It is a magical time.

You will simultaneously worry every day that you will bring nothing back. Henry Glassie, in the introduction to his masterwork *Passing the Time in Ballymenone*, wrote of his first trip to Ireland: "Tomorrow I would return to the States with twenty-four reels of tape, 2,192 photographs, 2,387 pages of notes, and my problems unsolved."[66] But you will persist, through the sleepless nights and the hypercaffeinated days, through confusion and despair and into joy and delight. The work itself is the pleasure.

Much of what I discuss in this book is the culture and politics of higher education, strategic knowledge that you absolutely must have in order to thrive in this community. But your dissertation has the opportunity for a clarity and purity of vision that transcends the vessel that contains it. It will be the most difficult—and the most worthy—project of your life. Do it thoroughly, do it with your whole self, and it will make you a better person forever.

Dissertation chair/committee. You will have a number of teachers through your early doctoral career. In my case, since I had come to my PhD program straight from undergrad, I had eighteen courses to take, and those were taught by fifteen different faculty. Over the course of that time, a few of the **faculty** came to feel like allies: people who shared my interests, who supported my enthusiasms and chastised my weaknesses, and whose advice and recommendations I begin to trust. You needn't (and shouldn't) choose a dissertation committee and chairperson until you've developed that contextual understanding.

Your dissertation chair is the person most responsible for your timely

---

66. Henry Glassie, *Passing the Time in Ballymenone: Culture and History of an Ulster Community* (Philadelphia: University of Pennsylvania Press, 1982), 27.

movement through the progress of researching and writing your work. During that time, the ideal chair will play a great number of roles.

She will lead you through the thickets of institutional procedure. She will know when dissertation manuscripts are due in **the graduate school**, remind you to submit your protocols to the **IRB** or **IACUC** early enough to deal with the inevitable snags, and ensure that the right paperwork is filed so that you can continue in dissertator status with library and web access at greatly reduced tuition.

She will read far too many early and middle drafts of your notes (too early still to call them a dissertation). She will caution you against early conclusions, spot connections between phenomena you believe to be separate, warn you of your own biases. She will toss in a key reading at the right moment, help you reorganize chapters to make a better argument, nag you about your grammar.

She will help to set the stage for your adult doctoral life. She will advocate behind the scenes for your brilliance among her colleagues, she will alert you to pending **job openings**, she will tell you who she knows at those schools and what they value. She will think with you about **publication** venues, and think with you about how your dissertation work might be separated into several interesting and useful articles as well as a full monograph.

She will have a sense of the yardstick by which early-career scholarship is measured, and will know where you stand in comparison. Because of that, she will tell you that you're not yet done when you think you are. And in the end, she will tell you that you're ready when you think you aren't.

In many fields, your early reputation, before others know your work in detail, will come through the borrowed glory of your dissertation chair. In the sciences, it's common to see that a PhD was completed under the supervision of, say, Dr. Lou Manari. But even outside the lab sciences, people in the know still recognize that the students of one scholar are likely to be strong, independent thinkers, whereas the students of another will be drudges who carry out minuscule refinements of the same old research.

The rest of your committee is just as important, because you need different kinds of support. You need reputation. You need a hard-ass who won't let you get away with anything sloppy. You need an enthusiast who can see the possibilities that you're starting to unearth. You need an array of content knowledge. You need strategic advice and a broad **network**. You need people you can stand to be around, and who are collegial with one another. It's like arranging the seating chart at a wedding; you have to avoid the feuds and the ex-spouses, keep the drunks away from the teetotalers, and make introductions among people who might like each other.[67]

One final component of your committee is the group of "outside readers," persons who come to your work cold at the point of the **defense**. You get to choose them; you may well know them or may have even taken courses with them, but they can't have had any involvement in the work leading to the dissertation. Some schools insist that the readers be from different departments, or perhaps even from different universities altogether. They are the **peer review** guarantors of your work, offering unbiased but well-informed opinions of your completed manuscript and your public defense. Typically, their votes are equal to those of the standing committee members when the defense is complete and judgment is rendered.

All the members of your committee, including outside readers, will need to be designated as "graduate faculty" by your institution. Typically, this is only a formality; every tenure-track **faculty** member with an earned research **doctorate** will automatically and permanently be a member of the graduate faculty, since it is assumed that the holders of the PhD are appropriately experienced to review the scholarly work of doctoral students. But schools differ on whether others can be graduate faculty. Some allow people with degrees other than the PhD, such as a **terminal master's** like an MFA, or another doctorate, like the EdD. Some allow **assistant professors** to serve on dissertation committees, but not to be dissertation chairs. If you have a guest reader from outside your university, that person may have to be given reciprocal rights by your school. Contact your **graduate school** and find out early; all of these things are typically formalities, but you don't want to discover a month before your defense that some vital member of your committee has suddenly been disqualified.

Doctorate. The "Doctor" in PhD is another Latinate term, originally referring to a religious teacher or scholar. The usage for medicine came after the usage for the person holding the highest possible academic degree, but the physicians have stolen it irretrievably away. Don't refer to yourself as Dr. Smithers in a general public setting, unless you want the universal assumption to be that you're in medicine.

Throughout this book, I'm using "doctorate" and "PhD" synonymously,

---

67. My own dissertation committee spawned a marriage. Not my intention, of course, but the world moves in mysterious ways.

which is the colloquial norm but isn't quite accurate. There are fifty or more different kinds of doctorates offered in American higher ed, clustered into two major flavors: research and professional.

A *research* doctorate, of which the PhD is by far the most commonly conferred, indicates a person who has contributed original scholarship to her intellectual **discipline**(s). The **dissertation** is intended to investigate previously unknown phenomena, to extend the body of knowledge of her field; it must be of **peer-review** quality, and must be judged so by members of the scholarly community beyond her own **committee** members. A *professional* doctorate is a credentialing tool that certifies a person to have sufficient knowledge and skill to legally engage in medicine, dentistry, law, and other "learned professions." The dissertation, if there is one at all, is intended to be a work of applied knowledge or strategy, akin to a **white paper**.

Doctorates proliferate as professions attempt to ratchet up their expectations (and to limit the numbers of newly licensed young competitors). Architecture, for instance, has had long-standing debates about whether its professional degree should become a D. Arch rather than the current M. Arch (or, in some states, B. Arch); this is only partially about presumed increases in knowledge or expectation of scholarship, and more an attempt to bridge the perceived "prestige gap" between architects and physicians or lawyers.

The PhD is the degree that will allow you to pass through the gates of academia unquestioned. Any other, and you'll be asked for documents, have your luggage searched, go through the supplemental screening.

Dress code. Oh, yes there is. It's not written down at most schools, but you can start to intuit it quickly. It will vary by **department**, with the business **faculty** in suits and the field biologists wearing shorts and river shoes. Learning the code is just a matter of observation, but the basic rules are twofold:

1. Even in a relaxed workplace, you're at work.
2. You are a faculty member or an aspiring faculty member, not a student.

So, shirts with buttons, not ones that you pull over your head. Shirts without words or artwork on them. Nothing torn, revealing, or edgy. The cooler the clubs you go to, the less you want to wear those clothes to work.

When you're teaching, those rules are amended and tightened. Your clothing is just as much a part of students' experience of the course as are your syllabus and your handouts and your attitude. You're trying to calibrate authority and collegiality; you run the room, but you're not imperious about it. When I did a lot of teaching, I had a very specific sequential strategy about what I wore. I started the semester in a button-down Oxford shirt and a tie, because I was teaching freshmen and I wanted them to have the reassuring experience of having a grown-up in charge. That went on for about three weeks, until they understood both that I knew a lot about the topic and also that I was friendly and that there weren't any predetermined right answers to the questions we had at seminar. Then the tie came off and the collar button was undone, and class went on for another seven or eight weeks in that way. The last few weeks were usually dedicated to production and review, and I started to (literally) roll up my sleeves and occasionally wear nice jeans to class.

Your clothes are not about you. They're about you in context. Have a look for faculty members similar to you in age on your current campus, and see if you can determine tendencies in what they're wearing. Start from there in your new doctoral program, or in your new faculty life.

Ee

Edited volume. It's a common practice in the humanities and social sciences, where books are often valued more strongly than single papers, to combine a bunch of papers into a thematic book edited by a leading scholar in the field. The editor gets credit almost authorial in influence without having to lift the entire weight of the manuscript, and the individual chapter **authors** each get a plus mark in their **CV** for another **publication**. It sounds like a winner all around. Let me then tell you why it's unlikely that I'll ever contribute to such a book again.

First off, it's much harder for other scholars to find your work in an edited volume than in a **journal**, which is indexed, or as a whole book, which is catalogued. It can be found, certainly, but its presence in an edited volume adds steps, and the work doesn't come up quickly when you're doing a search. My most cited works are all in journals, and in my sole-authored academic book. One of my very best pieces is buried in an edited volume, cited only twice in the past fourteen years. So your work in an edited book does less good in the world.

Second, you have no control over the other content in an edited volume, and run the risk of being the best house in a bad neighborhood, which never sells.

Third, you have no control over the pace of the editor or the other authors, which means that even if you finish your requested chapter in the allotted six months, your work might sit in the can for years, awaiting completion of the rest of the book. You'd never send your paper to a journal with a two-year turnaround, but that's a common fate of the writer for an edited book. I lost one publication because it sat for nearly a *decade* awaiting other people to decide whether the whole book project was worth their while; it's now a stale chapter, and I have to figure out whether it can be refreshed.[68]

Finally, you never know what the editors of a volume are going to consider common property. I once wrote an extensive chapter for a small handbook, and the lead editor wrote back to say that she thought it was terrific, but that she'd actually just wanted the case studies rather than the theoretical material. So I dutifully revised it down to focus on the case studies. Once the book was published and I got my contributor's copy—the first time I'd seen my work in its context—I discovered that the book's introductory chapter, under the byline of the book's editors, framed the whole book by using the first three pages of my theoretical framework verbatim, without any acknowledgement that it was mine.

There are a couple of upsides to publication in an edited book. The first is that you usually have a little more freedom as a writer to structure your argument; you can be more conversational, more wide-ranging than you can in most journal papers. And the second is that your work might be lifted in stature by being adjacent to chapters written by leading lights in the field. But the downsides are much greater, and it's unlikely that I'd do it again.

If you're invited to contribute to an edited book, you owe it to yourself to ask sharp questions. Who else has committed to write for the book? You don't want to be the most famous person in the table of contents. Who's the **publisher**? If it's an internal monograph to be published by a university or **department**, don't bother; you get far more **career** credit for work supported by a legitimate publisher. (If there is no publisher yet and the

---

68. I've used it in my teaching, so at least my students have found it useful in their own work; but the CV line is lost.

editor is working on spec, big red flags should be flying clearly.) Will the publisher insist on **peer review** of each chapter? You should hope so, since that will act as a marker of quality for your work. Is the publisher going to stand firm on **deadlines**? Again, you should hope so, since that means they're serious about the project. Any wrong answers to that list and you should graciously but firmly decline, and prepare your work on your own.

The other end of the workflow—being the editor of a compilation—isn't any more attractive. A scholar who proposes an edited volume has to locate a sufficient number of interesting contributors; has to hold them to some degree of thematic consistency and gently rein in their impulses toward lateral thinking; has to wait and wait and wait for the final chapter or two to appear;[69] has to inform all her contributors that there's yet another publication delay and the book won't be out until 2017; has to inform one of her contributors that the external reviewers thought his chapter was superfluous/irrelevant/dopey even as they thought highly of the book as a whole. Yuck. A line on the CV just isn't worth that kind of pain.

Editor. Anything you publish will go through the hands of an editor, and perhaps more than one. The **journal** you want to publish in has an editor, a fellow academic (and usually a volunteer) who coordinates the reviews of the papers, but also makes fundamental decisions about whether a submitted piece fits the mission of the journal. If you hope to publish a book or scholarly monograph, the publishing house will have a paid professional editor who responds to (and, ideally, acquires) your work. The section of the magazine or newspaper you write for will have its own editor, who is also a paid staff member of the **publisher**.[70]

There are two fundamental things to remember about any editor. The first is that she gets a lot more submissions than she'll be able to attend to carefully, much less publish. The second thing, which is somewhat related, is that her allegiance is to the publisher, not to you. That means not that she'll be hostile to you—far from it, in my experience—but simply that her mission is to locate and help re-craft written work that advances the standing of her publisher. So she'll be excited by your good ideas, but won't be a pushover for any random side thought that comes to mind as you're

---

69. If you're on the tenure clock, you cannot afford to wait for your prospective authors. If you're thinking about coordinating an edited volume, maybe post-tenure might be a good time for that.

70. All three of these publications may work with copy editors as well, making red-pen markups for syntax, spelling, punctuation, and adherence to the relevant style guides.

writing your first draft.[71] Your editor is an invaluable partner, working with you to make a gem out of a nice rock.

For **peer-reviewed** journals, it's acceptable to send an **e-mail** query to the editor asking whether your paper on a particular topic suits their needs; editors often receive manuscripts from authors who either don't understand what the journal is about or are desperate after a number of prior **rejections**. There are lots and lots of places to publish your ideas; you might as well send them to someone who's looking forward to them because she thinks the central theme is a useful addition to her publication. And this is what links us back around to the first characteristic of the editor, the overworked part. If you can help her make the connection between your brilliant idea and the needs of her journal or press, you've made her life easier; and then you'll have an ally rather than a gatekeeper.

Elevator/airplane talk. You unexpectedly run into a senior person in your field at a **conference**; the person next to you in the taxi line happens to be a department **chair** at a major college; you find yourself at a graduate-student lunch sitting next to the **dean** of your division. Now's your chance to make an impression.

Always, and I mean *always*, try to be the person who asks about the other person's experiences and interests first. It's generous; it starts the conversation on more comfortable footing for you because they're talking about themselves; it gives you a sense of what they're interested in. But then it'll be your turn to talk about your work and your interests, and you haven't got all day to do it. This is where the elevator speech comes in.

Your elevator talk is the compression of your interests into the amount of time you'd be on an elevator with someone in a moderately-sized building; maybe twenty or thirty seconds. If you have an average speech rate of 150 words per minute or so, that means you're allotted considerably fewer than a hundred words. The elevator talk serves the same function as the **abstract** of an academic paper, giving a prospective listener a chance to decide if he'd like to know more. Here's what I say about my current work when I meet someone in higher ed for the first time.

---

71. And there will be a lot of random side thoughts, for every writer. (Perhaps you've noticed.) We all dream of submitting a piece and getting a phone call from an editor saying, "It's perfect, every word!" In fact, that's not what we should want at all. What we *should* want is a phone call from an editor saying, "I love it. Now let's get to work."

I run a small consulting company that works with colleges on faculty de-velopment, curriculum design, and assessment and accreditation man-agement. We also work with commercial and government clients to do facilities work like needs assessments and master planning, and we've done quite a lot of consumer behavior and attitude research.

I don't have that fifty words exactly scripted, of course, but something of this density is a twenty-second intro. It offers the opportunity for my con-versation partner to ask for examples or to discuss the problems they're having on their site; it has conversational Velcro, with lots of points of attachment. If I were talking to a businessperson instead of an academic **administrator**, I'd change the terms a little.

I run a small consulting company that works with clients to do strategic planning and project management. We do facilities work like needs as-sessments and master planning, we do consumer behavior and attitude research, and we do professional development around goal-setting and evaluation.

Same company, same projects; different ordering, different language.

The airplane speech is the same genre, but it presumes that, instead of a twenty-second elevator ride, you now have five minutes or so on the plane with a new seatmate while you're getting settled in, pulling out your laptop, and tucking your water bottle into the elastic pocket. The airplane speech is a second vital tool, because it's how you'll start every interview when you're on the market. When the search committee chair says, "Tell us a little about your background and your research interests," you've got three or four minutes to be interesting and engaging.

Your **dissertation** goes on for a long time, and it took you years to write it. Social interaction is much more abbreviated, and you have to persuade a new person quickly that your work is interesting and important. Use lan-guage slightly less specific than your field's most specialized jargon, offer key terms and a quick example, and let conversation take its course.

The counterpart to the elevator and airplane talks, of course, is the busi-ness card. You should keep a small pack of business cards in a convenient pocket every day, so that you don't have to rummage around in your brief-case to find one when the elevator door is opening. There are lots of card sleeves and card cases available that will keep ten of yours available while you also accept one from your new colleague. The short talks are the introduction that you can follow up at a later time, but you have to have the contact info to do it.

E-mail. Concentration and focus are the engines of academic life. Research and reading and thinking require unbroken time, uninterrupted space. You need time to be lazy, to let the ideas spin around in your head without conscious direction so that patterns can emerge. The constant drive to be productive can keep you from being productive; the same computer that allows you to write also brings you e-mail.

E-mail (and its vile twin, texting) is a force akin to nuclear energy in its simultaneous power for good and evil. E-mail allows people from around the campus and around the planet to keep in contact instantly, and that ease is terribly abused. Most faculty members receive dozens of e-mails per day; **administrators** often a hundred or more. As with the paper that comes in your mailbox, some of it is advertising that can be immediately jettisoned, and some of it is news and magazines that you can read later if you ever get a minute, but a lot of it—more than you can adequately deal with—is from people you know who need your assistance.

Because e-mail is so easy to send, and because you receive it so quickly, it presumes equally instantaneous response. But just because some idea came into someone's head doesn't mean that you'll be (a) interested or (b) able to respond this second. As a recipient of e-mail, you're always prioritizing. There are requests from important people; those go to the top. There are requests from colleagues who quickly need information that only you have; those go to the top. There are links to funny dog videos; those go to the top. Everything else sinks, and the bottom can be a long way down.

Schedule your e-mail the same way you schedule a meeting; give yourself half an hour in the morning to write responses, and another half an hour at the end of the day. Check at lunch to see if something urgent is going on that needs a quick response. (Anything more urgent than a half-day turnaround is going to result in a phone call anyway, so don't sweat it.) The rest of the day, keep your e-mail utility turned off. That ping of every new message will break your concentration, and you'll feel more and more harried. An increasing body of research seems to indicate that people don't multitask well; that those who think they multitask well are worse at it than everybody else; and that habitually attempting to multitask gradually reduces your capability to focus. I know that after years as an **administrator**,

I was much less able to read a long, dense argument, and it's taken some recovery time and specific exercises to allow me to regain my concentration.

As a sender of e-mail, there are ways that you can keep from contributing to this deluge. Reduce the number of "reply all" messages; decide whether your request is immediate or can wait until you happen across someone in the hall; pick up the phone. If you're involved in a **committee**, resist the urge to conduct business or continue deliberations via e-mail between sessions; just put your idea on the agenda for the next meeting. And if you've sent something and it feels like you're being ignored, go ahead and call; it's probably not true that your recipient doesn't like you, and more likely that your request or idea simply hasn't risen to the top of his urgency list yet.

Given that you've made it through an undergraduate program, this next idea probably doesn't need to be said, but I'll say it anyway because I've seen it too often missed in practice. The writing conventions of e-mail are still linked to physical mail, not texting.[72] So when composing e-mail, you need to employ a salutation, a body (with paragraphs), the appropriately mixed use of upper- and lower-case letters, the minimization of abbreviations and acronyms, and a pleasant closing. "Hey Nora. When's our homework due? TTYL" is not an e-mail, and will mark you as an oaf rather than a colleague. Slow down and write a real note.

Emotional balance. Jean-Paul Sartre once wrote that our emotions are a response not to present conditions, but rather to our vision of the likely future.[73] Grief is a response to knowing we're forced to live on without a particular person or pet or place; anger is knowing what we want but seeing something blocking our path; shame is about knowing that we will go through life as diminished, unworthy persons.

Given that this book is about your endeavors to capture a particular future as a doctoral student or as a member of a college **faculty**, we have to honestly address the issues of emotional management. You will be writing

---

72. I have a colleague who, because she has two teenage sons, sends far more messages by text than by e-mail. I have an old cell phone with just the number keypad, so when I want to return a text from her, I begin by typing, "Hi, Jenny." Which on my phone means thirty keystrokes: 44_444_111111_5_33_66_66_999_1. I once told her that, and she laughingly replied that in a text I didn't need to write, "Hi, Jenny." In an e-mail, you do—including the comma (that's what the 111111 is).

73. Jean-Paul Sartre, *The Emotions: Outline of a Theory*, trans. Bernard Frechtman (Secaucus, NJ: Citadel, 1975)

and rewriting tentative stories of your coming life, and you have to work constantly to remind yourself that both the high and low stories are fictions.

An example: You go online to New England HERC (the Higher Education Recruitment Consortium, at http://www.hercjobs.org/new_england/) to look for **job postings**. You do it with a mixed sense of foreboding and resentment, because there hasn't been much there for your field in the past four months. The search has become a meaningless tic that you conduct without conscious thought. You put in your search terms and discover — miracle of miracles! — there's a new posting for a tenure-track **assistant professorship** in American studies, specializing in nineteenth-century visual and material culture, at Middlebury College. The pleasure of finding a plausible job to apply for almost matches the pleasure of getting it, so you have a little *frisson* of premature achievement. Which, frankly, you've earned. You've done a **dissertation** that makes you expert in a particular area, and now you see that your area is valued enough within higher education that someone wants to hire for it.

You excitedly read and reread the posting, thinking about how you'll frame your **cover letter** and who you'll ask to write **recommendations** for you. Later that day, you casually open Realtor.com and look to see what houses are like in Middlebury, Vermont. That Dutch colonial on Elm Street looks professorial, doesn't it? Lots of odd angles, a welcoming porch, a stone wall along the drive … and only $239,000. What's an assistant professorship pay at Middlebury, anyway? A few more keystrokes in Google … about $78,000, on average. American studies is probably below the average, but still, even at $60,000, you could afford that house. Wow, a job in your field, a real grown-up's salary, a house and not a plywood apartment. You think about your first party at the house with your new department colleagues, all standing in the warm kitchen with cocktails and witty repartee ….

Fast-forward to the spring. You didn't get it. You're a loser, again. The **rejection letter** congratulated you for being among the very strong pool of 209 applicants, and wished you well as you continue your endless, futile search. But you're never going to get a job. Your dad was right when he kept asking you why the hell you were spending all your time looking at the differences between European and American tableware from the Westward Expansion. Who gives a crap about that? Study something people *want*, like your sister the accountant did. She's younger than you and she's had a house for ten years, and she can afford a real car, not like that shitbox you're driving around.

You're near tears. Should you keep the letter filed away or crumple it up immediately and fling it into the recycle bag? And the rest of the day, the rest of the week, the rest of your career is ruined. Why bother sending your article manuscript to *The American Quarterly* as you'd planned to do next week? You're a fraud, you've got nothing to say, everybody knows, everybody knows, everybody knows . . . .

The house was not real. Neither was the salary, nor the cocktail party, nor the charming little stone wall. But the end of your career is likewise not real. Your family, though they don't understand what you do exactly, will understand what not getting a job means, and will rally 'round. The **editor** of *The American Quarterly* will still give your paper a fair reading, and no, she hasn't gotten a fax from Middlebury with your picture partially obscured by the international "no" sign.

Holding a sense of emotional balance requires that we always understand the future as fantasy, whether delightful or disastrous. We do not know what is coming; we *cannot* know what is coming. We can only do the work we're presented in the moment we're presented with it. It may be that excellent work is not rewarded in the way we imagine that it ought; the world is neither just nor efficient. But excellent work will usually open some avenue for additional work; someone will notice it and ask for more. And if we focus on the work to be done, we'll occasionally glance back at that mountain of work we've accomplished and call it a life well lived.

Endowment. Almost all colleges, including public universities, have a few big savings accounts that they use to generate some additional income. They don't burn up the principal; they make use of some of the interest to augment the income they make from tuition, from state subsidies, from research funding, and from merchandising agreements.

The school with the largest endowment in America is, of course, Harvard University, with a set of long-term accounts worth about thirty-six billion dollars.[74] Things drop rapidly from there, but all of the top twenty have endowments of five billion dollars and more.

Back in the full-speed early 2000s, big university endowments were making huge returns, 20 percent or more per year. But we all know what

74. "Harvard University endowment delivers 15.4% return for fiscal year 2014." *Harvard Gazette*, September 23, 2014, accessed April 28, 2015, http://news.harvard.edu/gazette /story/2014/09/harvard-university-endowment-delivers-15-4-return-for-fiscal-year -2014/.

happened in 2008, don't we—the fastest drivers hit the wall hardest, and Harvard alone lost about ten billion dollars all at once. Many endowment managers are now a little cautioned by that experience.

Where does the money come from for the endowment? The first big chunk comes from alumni or alumni families. That's why the alumni magazine exists, and travel opportunities for alumni, and special alumni ticket packages to the college's sporting events: the school wants to retain a warm glow in the hearts of its increasingly successful and comfortable graduates. The other big chunk comes through investment income as the endowment becomes self-generating, like compost. Here's a common endowment distribution formula: take the average investment income rate for the three most recent years, and divide by two. So, for instance, if the fund made 10, 8, and 3 percent over the past three years, you'd average that to get 7 percent, and divide by two to get 3.5 percent for your harvest this year. The fund managers calculate the rolling average to smooth out bumps, and then take only part of the income so that they can leave the rest in the bank as added principal for further income.

The part that's harvested allows the college to take on projects, or to fund lower-income students whom they couldn't otherwise afford to accept. They can also use it for a sense of graciousness and ease in general daily operations: more support staff, nicer food at the catered events. The photocopier is just always magically full, and a faculty member never has to tear a new ream open and reload the tray in the ten-minute rush before class. A friend once told me about his daughter's experience of working for Disney's cruise lines. Disney has a reputation for flawlessness, for never showing any of the everyday problems that are part of any business endeavor. She said that they made just as many mistakes as anyone else, but that they just had enough money and people to throw at a problem to fix it before it was noticed. The big-endowment universities are like that as well; there's always a little money that they can use like spackle to cover a small crack.[75]

75. Just before the parent weekends at Duke, the grounds crews laid out fresh mulch and replaced tired plants with fresh nursery specimens, so that visiting parents would encounter an immaculate landscape. They'd have mulched with ground-up dollar bills if they'd thought that would help. The goal was to make those comfortable families feel good about the school, because their feeling *good* then would lead to their feeling *generous* later.

Ff

Facilities. Not merely a polite term for the toilet room, but rather a collective designator for every single building, tree, and parking meter owned by the university. We often take for granted that we work in buildings, the alternative being pretty unlikely for us bookish types, but your campus and its facilities are hardly a taken-for-granted element of the operation of the business. Even a relatively small college might have several hundred thousand square feet of buildings and acres of grounds that would be worth hundreds of millions or even billions of dollars on the open real estate market.[76]

Thus, your school will have a facilities management office, which is a combination of custodian, maintenance contractor, space planning design team, civil engineer, and real estate management firm. The facilities team replaces broken glass, and designs the campus master plan so that new buildings can be properly sited. The facilities team repairs leaky roofs and plows snow, and also hires architecture and engineering firms for new stadia or lab buildings. The facilities team mows the lawn and plants the flowers, and also files for city and state permits for millions of gallons of stormwater runoff and the removal of hazardous materials during renovations. It may be the most intellectually content-diverse group on campus, working backstage to allow the rest of us to do our jobs.

It's easy to complain about buildings, about being too hot or cold, about a lamp buzzing or a stuck doorknob or a jammed toilet paper dispenser. And yes, those things should work, and now you know who to call to make them work better. But the facilities crew deserves random calls of appreciation just as much as they deserve the specific calls for requests. Buildings and grounds are enormously complex objects, always in the process of failing and being restored, always able to suck up more money than your institu-

76. See, for example, Virginia Tech University, "Campus Buildings: Physical Plant," accessed May 4, 2015, https://www.unirel.vt.edu/history/physical_plant/campus_buildings.html. This remarkably detailed list itemizes the size and original cost of more than a hundred buildings on campus, plus the golf course and the botanical gardens and the ice pond. By this list, Virginia Tech's facilities group manages more than *seven and a half million square feet* of enclosed building space—the equivalent of two Sears Towers (or Willis Towers, in the new ownership) in Chicago—along with their grounds and roads and path systems.

tion can throw their way. A facilities management team are the quarter-master corps of higher education, making sure that the tools we need are always at hand. Say thanks.

Faculty. Faculty is a collective noun. Individuals are members of the faculty, or are more colloquially "on the faculty."

The faculty may or may not be meant to include the entire teaching corps of a college, depending on the context in which it's said. When reporting student-faculty ratios for federal data reports and **accreditation** updates, the **adjunct** instructors are absolutely counted as faculty (at some pro-portional rate, such as three adjuncts equaling one full-time faculty). But when someone casually says she's a faculty member at Safe Harbor College, she means that she has a **tenure-track** appointment, not a semester con-tract.[77] The faculty senate does not include adjuncts. The faculty services office does not serve adjuncts. The faculty dining hall does not welcome adjuncts. If you get the news about someone's faculty appointment, it's not because they got a contingent position. Faculty means that privileged group to whom the college has made at least the provisional offer of permanent membership, who have been presented the gold pin and the secret hand-shake.

Faculty are allocated in "lines," as in budgetary line items, and different **departments** have a different number of faculty lines. A line can be opened when the senior **administration** decides that a department needs to be bol-stered because of increased majors, increased enrollment in its general edu-cation "service courses," refreshed interest in its graduate offerings, or the shifting tides of trends and politics. A line can be closed when a retirement or resignation occurs or when a **tenure** application is denied, and the ad-ministration decides not to fill the emptied line with a new hire. Other than that, faculty lines are as close to permanent features of higher education as buildings and mascots; once they exist, they tend to persist through more than one occupant.

Because of this, it's exceedingly rare to have a faculty member who's

77. Note, however, if someone states in their résumé or cover letter that they're a "fac-ulty member" at Liminal University, warning bells should sound. A real faculty mem-ber will name themselves by rank—assistant professor, associate professor, professor, professor of the practice, and so on—in any formal material they create. Using "fac-ulty member" in written material is the sign of someone attempting to gain credence through borrowing an informal appellation for formal use and hoping we won't notice.

not affiliated with a department, and thus the norms of **disciplines** tend to ossify. Biology departments hire biologists, sociology departments hire sociologists. Senior faculty can do interesting **interdisciplinary** work, safe in the knowledge that they have a home port to return to; junior faculty have to pledge loyalty to the disciplinary faith above all else.

The line between faculty and administration has a fuzzy edge called "chair." Department **chairs**, the most junior level of administrators, are appointed to their chairship for a specific term and never leave the faculty (though they probably have a temporarily reduced **teaching load** during their term as chair). But once a faculty member is asked to be an associate **dean** or a **director** or a vice **provost** or any other more permanent administrative role, their working life is removed from the service of the department and placed in service of the college as a whole, and a new hire will take their faculty line. In the case of a hardship appointment when a faculty member is pressed into emergency administrative service, the line may be held open for their return,[78] but that's a relative rarity.

As the proportion of the teaching force made up of adjunct or contingent instructors rises nationwide, the proportion of permanent faculty decreases. According to the American Association of University Professors, tenured and tenure-eligible faculty made up 45 percent of all college instructors in 1975, and has dropped to 26 percent in 2013; nonpermanent instructors have increased over that same time from 34 to 60 percent.[79] (Graduate student instructors make up the rest of the pool.) The permanent faculty, oddly enough, are often loath to advocate on behalf of their adjunct colleagues, instead taking a "there but for the grace of God go I" stance toward their leprous neighbors. One would hope that the **academic freedom** that accompanies tenure would free the faculty to push back against the increased use of temp workers; as the saying goes, "Whaddaya gonna do? Fire me?" But instead, the faculty seem willing to be complicit in the

---

78. I have a friend who was more or less strong-armed to become the provost on his campus. As part of his agreement to serve in that role, he insisted both that his department be able to hire a new faculty member and that his own faculty line be retained. But I can assure you that for the four years of his provost service, the faculty did not consider him faculty.

79. John Barnishaw and Samuel Dunietz, "Busting the Myths: The Annual Report on the Economic Status of the Profession, 2014–15." *Academe* 101, no. 2 (March–April 2015): 4–19, accessed April 28, 2015, http://www.aaup.org/reports-publications/2014--15salary survey.

p4ort minimal

restructuring of contemporary higher education, comfortable in their own protections. I would remind them to reread Martin Niemöller.[80]

Faculty handbook. *Handbook* is such a cheery word, isn't it? It suggests friendly guidance, avuncular tone, helpful hints. Kind of like what you're reading now, eh?

Well, wipe that moony smile off your face this instant! The faculty handbook at your college is a component of your employment **contract**. It's as serious and foundational as anything you might sign to buy a house or qualify for health insurance; it sets the terms of engagement between you and your employer forever. Any college you might be considering for your first employment will have a faculty handbook, and it will almost always be available online. Get one and read it, now.

The faculty handbook will start out with some pleasant boilerplate about the history and mission of the institution. But soon you'll get down to work. The faculty handbook will tell you how promotions and **tenure** work, and whether there's tenure at all; it'll tell you what kinds of annual personnel reports you'll have to file and what they'll include. The handbook will lay out the standard **teaching load**, advising load and service expectations; it'll tell you how you schedule classes and what office hours you must offer. The handbook will tell you what accommodations you offer to students with disabilities, and lay out expectations for student and faculty conduct in class and outside class (and in small towns, off campus as well). The handbook will tell you how to avoid conflicts of interest, and whether you can date a student.[81]

The faculty handbook is a legal document, vetted by university counsel, signed off on by the **president** and/or trustees, and relied upon whenever conflicts arise. Treat it with the seriousness it deserves, and keep a copy near your desk for ready reference.

80. Niemöller himself crafted many versions of his famous statement; let's use this one: "When the Nazis came for the communists, I remained silent; I was not a communist. When they locked up the social democrats, I remained silent; I was not a social democrat. When they came for the trade unionists, I did not speak out; I was not a trade unionist. When they came for the Jews, I remained silent; I wasn't a Jew. When they came for me, there was no one left to speak out."
81. Usually there'll be lots of hemming and hawing and qualifying about this, but come on. No, you can't. Just … no. I know that Professor Humbert, now aged seventy-three, met his forty-seven-year old wife when she was a student in his Transgressive Fictions class in 1984, but that doesn't mean it was defensible then, and it isn't now.

Failed search. A search for a new permanent colleague, whether at the **faculty** or at the administrative level, is a resource-rich affair. First, the **department** or division has to make the case for adding a new person to the budget, which usually also entails forming a **committee** to spend several months writing the job description and requirements. Once a **dean** or **provost** is convinced of that need, the position gets written into the subsequent year's budget, and the search is posted in all the usual places (*Chronicle of Higher Education*, *Inside Higher Ed*, diversejobs.net, appropriate **professional society** newsletters, and so on), ideally in the fall prior to the year of appointment. The November **deadline** provides dozens or hundreds of applications for the search committee to read over Thanksgiving; the committee's deliberations lead to phone interviews in January.

Once the committee has met and calibrated their reviews with the **chair** or **dean**, three or four finalists are selected for **on-campus** interviews in March; each visit entails airfare, lodging, meals, and the organization of many opportunities for faculty and staff to meet each candidate. Finally, in April, a finalist is chosen and a background check conducted, often including references beyond those offered by the candidate, as well as extensive web searches, occasional criminal background checks, and sometimes even credit reports. (You signed a million waiver and permission forms already, didn't you, because you were so desperate to be seen as agreeable . . . .)

Presuming the background is clear, an **offer** is made in late April for a start date of August 1. By this time, at least a couple dozen people—the search committee, department chair, dean, fellow faculty in the relevant department, **administrative assistants**, and human resources and accounting specialists—have had their hands on this project. Not to mention the hundreds of applicants, each of whose agony is multiplied for every day a decision is not made.

What a tragedy, then, when it all goes awry.

A search can fail for a small number of reasons. One that you might imagine is that the right candidate did not materialize; although the finalists were all good, none of them represented exactly what the department wanted, and the search committee believed that their odds would improve by waiting for another year's pool. Although no one will ever have precise data on failed searches, I believe that this is a relatively unlikely circumstance. The fear of losing the budget allocation, combined with a genuine interest by the faculty in one or two of the final candidates, will almost certainly override the details of a job description written almost two years prior.

More likely is that there was one unanimously favored candidate who for some reason was no longer available once the offer was made. That person had done so well, had met expectations so perfectly, that she had become a holy grail for the search committee, the chosen one whose luster made all of the other finalists pale and deeply flawed. Searches can also fail if the most desirable candidate makes demands that are greater than the institution can bear—spousal hires, particularly expensive scientific equipment, and so on—but the deliberations draw out long enough that the other finalists are no longer interested or available.

Searches can more often fail if the college's budget projections didn't materialize, or resources were reallocated at the last minute, so that the position no longer had a funding stream available. Now that the number of incoming undergraduates is no longer an infinitely expandable resource, less selective schools worry every fall if they're going to make their numbers; that projected budget that seemed so ironclad in April 2014 might look a lot less certain after the Fall 2015 enrollment figures are a disappointment.

The one good thing about a failed search is that the **rejection letter** received by all of the candidates will actually be informative; it will almost always say directly that the position wasn't funded or filled. This is vastly superior to the legally vapid "thanks anyway" letter generated after successful searches, placing the onus clearly on the institution and not on any presumed failure on your part.

FERPA. At the end of my first quarter in college, I went to the Michigan Tech business department to learn my final grade in statistics. Taped to the professor's **office** door was a list of the thirty or so students in our class, with the final course grade for each student handwritten next to his or her name. I scanned down to *Childress, Herb*, found my B, and checked while I was there to see how many of my fellow students had done better. Yeah, Betsy got an A ... no surprise, she'd aced every quiz all semester.

That was November 1976. Now, almost forty years later, that list taped to the door, as well as my knowing what Betsy had gotten on her quizzes, would be a violation of federal law; specifically, the Family Educational Rights and Privacy Act, or FERPA.[82] The fundamental idea behind FERPA is that an individual student's academic records should be accessible to no

82. It was illegal then as well, since FERPA had been signed into law by Gerald Ford in 1974. Word probably hadn't gotten that far north yet. The only TV station we got at Michigan Tech was from Thunder Bay, Ontario, in good weather.

one other than that student. Their **grades** for individual courses and their overall grade point average, the fact of which courses they're in now or which courses they've taken in the past, their adequate progress or their probation—all of that is privileged information, available only to that student and to your colleagues as needed for daily educational and business functions.

Just as the word "juvenile" is most often followed by the word "delinquent," "FERPA" is most often followed by the word "violation." FERPA violations are everywhere. If you leave a course roster on your desk and another student drops by for office hours, that's a FERPA violation. If the registrar's office leaves a notice of a student withdrawing from your course in your faculty mailbox in the department office, that's a FERPA violation. If the gradebook on your computer monitor is visible from the corridor, or to a guest in your office, that's a FERPA violation. Even if you're coaching a current student and tell her that she should ask Bethany about her work in the class last semester because Bethany did such a great job, that's a FERPA violation.

And yet we're putting up drunk selfies on Instagram. We've lost our minds.

As a **TA** or as a **faculty** member, you have access to educational information that no one else should know. Keep your papers filed away, keep your monitor shielded, and don't talk about one student to another. Once the student is eighteen, by the way, that student himself is the eligible recipient of his educational records, *not* his parents. If Mr. or Mrs. Helicopter calls to find out how their son Carlos is doing in your class, you absolutely cannot tell them. They might inform you that Carlos has filed a FERPA waiver that allows them to see his grades, and that may in fact be true, but only the registrar's office can verify that, not Dad on the phone. If there's any question about any student record, call the registrar's office first; they represent the guardians of student privacy at your school.

The only outside parties who can have access to an individual student's records are accrediting bodies, lending agencies who are issuing that student financial aid, those whom the student has directly authorized (by, for instance, requesting a transcript for grad school or transfer to be sent to another college), someone with a subpoena, and someone who is intervening in a serious legal or health emergency. Even within the school, you shouldn't casually chat about a student with other faculty or TAs unless they have a specific educational or administrative function to fulfill. Let the registrar decide, not you.

First generation. I am a son of a factory machinist and a telephone operator with one high school diploma between them. Mom always wanted me
to go to college, at least in part to fulfill her own fantasy, which had been
disrupted by her marrying my father when she was eighteen. But nobody
around me had college. Our neighbors were factory workers and phone
linemen and bank tellers and septic tank installers; being successful in my
community meant owning the family's car dealership or beer distribution
franchise.

I did OK in high school, and applied to three public colleges: the University of Michigan, Michigan State University, and Michigan Technological
University. I was accepted to all three (mostly on the basis of SAT scores
rather than having shown any empirical promise, high school being then
just as dull as it is now), and had no way of choosing from among them.
They were all just "college." Two were huge and one was not; two were
within an hour's drive of a family member and one was not. I chose the
one that was neither huge nor close, at least in part because the brother of
the girl I desperately wished was my girlfriend went to the small distant
school, and I thought perhaps she might come to visit sometime or at least
think well of me because of my choice.

That didn't happen. Lots of good things did happen, though. Beer, and
a state legal age of eighteen. A roommate with a remarkable stereo and a
shared taste in music. Pinochle. Bowling. Table tennis, and international
players who took it seriously. Miracle of all miracles, sex. I did fine at school,
I had a bland three-point-something-something, I understood derivative
calculus but not integrals, I killed a lot of fruit flies in bio lab, and I never
once took a course on purpose. I went where people pointed me, did what
people told me to do, did it all adequately, and dropped out after two years.

There was no narrative to tie the daily facts into. I was on a path that
didn't have a visible or desirable end. I had capability, but nothing I wanted
to be capable at.

I went back to college after seven years away, for reasons I no longer remember except probably boredom with work, still not understanding the
difference between one school and another. I started with three semesters
of community college at Laney College in Oakland, California, to get some
prerequisites fulfilled, and then transferred to the University of California
at Berkeley, this time based both on **grades** and test scores. Even then, at
twenty-seven, I didn't know it was *Berkeley!* It was just the state school up
the road that had an architecture program. If I'd lived closer to Cal Poly
Pomona, I'd have been perfectly happy going there, too.

I got lucky; it really *was* Berkeley, and it lived up to the reputation I wasn't aware it had. I was surrounded by remarkable scholars: Paul Groth, David Littlejohn, Clare Cooper Marcus, Spiro Kostof, Ed Arens, Gail Brager, Dell Upton. Everywhere I turned, I saw people who cared about ideas, who cared about words, who did their jobs with elegance and precision. My fellow students pushed me, and I pushed them, and we did things we didn't imagine ourselves capable of.

I graduated with my undergraduate degree in 1989, at the **age** of thirty-one. Had I come from a college family, I'd have finished my PhD by the time I was thirty-one; had I come from an *academic* family, I'd have had half a chance at being **tenured** at thirty-one. But it was OK. I had a bachelor's degree in architecture, and a deep longing to be adopted into the community of scholars. I knew what the holy land felt like, knew where I wanted to live.

According to the US Census, about 5 percent of American adults had a college degree in 1940; a little under 10 percent in 1960; about 15 percent by 1980; almost 25 percent in 2000, over 30 percent now.[83] This upward ratcheting of educational expectations means that there are vast numbers of students in college whose family members don't share a college experience. And because of that, there is a huge push to better understand the needs of first-generation college students, who are often not only less academically prepared than their fellows, but also share little of the cultural capital—the experience of literature and arts, the social networks, the confidence in institutional navigation—that their college-family peers have in the bank.

However, some of those first-generation students will be particularly successful at college, and decide that academia provides a suitable, desirable home. And for these folks, the strivers and climbers who offer ostensible proof of social class mobility, there is almost no understanding or support whatsoever. There is a huge literature on first-generation college students, and silence on what happens when that same group goes on to doctoral or faculty life.

I can tell you a little of what happens.[84] For your family, you become a

83. United States Census Bureau, "Educational Attainment in the United States: 2014–Detailed Tables," accessed April 28, 2015, http://www.census.gov/hhes/socdemo /education/data/cps/2014/tables.html.

84. The best and most touching accounting of this experience that I've seen is still Alfred Lubrano's brilliant book *Limbo* (Hoboken, NY: John Wiley and Sons, 2004), in which he describes his experience of being a class "straddler," and interviews dozens of others. He argues that straddlers in higher education experience the most uncomfortable limbo of them all. See also C. L. Barney Dews and Carolyn Leste Law, eds., *This Fine Place So Far*

class traitor. You are inexplicable: a source of pride, confusion, envy, and intimidation. You are still loved but no longer understood. You become the butt of jokes about not knowing how to do some task like replace a toilet gasket or make a good tortilla. Your siblings become self-conscious in your presence about their use of language. Your furniture is different from theirs; your car is different from theirs; your television habits are different from theirs; you buy books instead of fishing gear; you have soft hands. They will understand that you're a college teacher, but not why anyone would be motivated to study the folk music of late nineteenth-century French Canada. They are invested in instrumental knowledge; you have become converted to critical knowledge. You are a member of that class of people who once made them feel dumb and have the potential to do so again.

A friend about my age, now also in higher education, grew up with two younger sisters in a family headed by their mother, a waitress. When it became evident during high school that he was interested in reading and ideas and political engagement, his younger sisters began calling him "Grey Poupon," after the then-current mustard commercial featuring two chauffeured swells on picnic. It was the easiest language his sisters had access to for the fact that they felt he was aspiring above his station. More direct language is provided by Garrison Keillor, when he says that the Minnesota Lutheran parenting motto was: "Keep your voices down and don't think you're something special because you're not, believe me."

Among your colleagues, you overplay your hand. You study the habits, master the vocabulary, serve on yet another **committee**. You make sure that your **dissertation** is immaculate, beyond every expectation. Anything less will leave you exposed and endangered. You take nothing for granted; you always think your cover will be blown, your ruse revealed, your passport revoked.

When you teach, you hold in your heart the uncomfortable truth that you're leading your own students down that same path of cultural alienation, bringing them individual freedom while simultaneously interfering in their familial and community allegiances. You recognize more fully than most that college *can* change your life, in ways that cannot be predicted sufficiently to decide whether that's going to be a good idea. You love what college has done for you—*to* you—but you can never wholeheartedly cheerlead for higher ed, because you know what those gains have cost.

---

from Home: Voices of Academics from the Working Class (Philadelphia: Temple University Press, 1995).

Gg

Grades. Oh, how I hate grades. I hate them from a communicative stand-point, hate them from a statistical standpoint, hate them from a psycholog-ical standpoint, hate them from an economic standpoint, hate them hate them hate them.[85]

Let's go down the line of my objections. First, from a communication and content perspective, letter or number grades are a hyperreductive encap-sulation of four months' worth of work. Every semester for every student is a combination of ability and inability, of effort and slack, of insight and opacity. They might be brilliant at some aspect of the course and only de-cent at another. They might be the discussion catalyst who always brings an element of surprise and learning to the seminar, although they struggle with writing. Or, contrariwise, they might not be quite ready to engage a discussion of Hannah Arendt when they get out of bed, but more than ready to write brilliantly about her work at one in the morning. They might be merely great, or they might be the best student you've encountered in years. You're supposed to take the entirety of that experience, those dozens of hours of contact and dozens of pages of drafts and revisions and all those quizzes and exams, and reduce it not merely to a couple of paragraphs— which would already be painfully reductive—but rather to a single letter followed with a plus or minus?

Twitter has more nuance than a grade. At least you'd have 140 characters instead of two.

From a statistical perspective, grades are fatally flawed. The first great flaw is the lack of inter-rater reliability. Given a particular essay, can we be sure that two instructors would agree on its exact placement against a rubric? (Assuming such a rubric exists, which is already dubious.) A letter grade makes rhetorical claim to absoluteness: a student with an A-minus in Intro Bio was a "better student" in that course than the student who got a B. But that claim, in the absence of more than one reviewer, would not hold up in any other circumstance. Let's make a comparison: academic papers are **peer-reviewed** before publication, typically by the **editor** and by three

---

85. Don't even go there. A gentleman doesn't discuss his grades, but they were juuuuuuust fine, thanks.

reviewers in one's field. It's not at all uncommon to have one outlier in that review pool, who believes strongly in the merits of a paper that the others find lacking, or recommends immediate **rejection** of a paper that the other two are enthusiastic about.

When I taught Introduction to Academic Writing at Duke, I was one of about thirty instructors teaching about eighty sections of that course each semester. If we asked all thirty of those teachers to read and letter-grade all the work of all nine hundred or so students in a specific semester, do we really imagine that the final grades would align in more than the most impressionistic way? The fact is that different instructors have different emphases for their course, different values that they place on multiple aspects of performance. As they should.

Along with the inter-rater reliability issues for grades within a specific course, grades are also statistically misused to calculate GPAs. On the very first day of a basic statistics course, students are taught "level of measurement." *Nominal* data are descriptors of a category: race, gender, ethnicity, political party, right- or left-handedness, and so on. *Ordinal* measurement is for data that are hierarchical; naming someone as freshman through senior is ordinal data, for instance. The same is true for rankings from best to worst, or on a Likert scale from "strongly disagree" to "strongly agree." *Interval* measurement is for data that can be precisely quantified, and for which the units of measurement are a standard increment apart (that is, the difference between forty-five and fifty degrees Fahrenheit is the same as the difference between sixty and sixty-five degrees). And finally there's *ratio* measurement, which is interval measurement on a scale that has a firm presence of zero. (Zero allows you to calculate the proportion of something. You can't say that a fifty-degree day is half as hot as a one-hundred-degree day, or that an event that happened in 1996 is twice as contemporary as an event from the year 998, because you have to have a bottom of the scale to start from. You can, however, say that six doughnuts is half as many as twelve doughnuts, because zero doughnuts is a universally recognized tragedy, a true and utter absence.)

Anyway, not to get too far into that first session of Statistics 100A, but letter grades are ordinal data dressed up in ratio clothes, like a kindergartner wearing her mom's shoes. The distance between an A and a B cannot be accurately measured, much less be said to be the same distance as the gap between a B and a C. Just as we can't agree across instructors on whether a given student should receive a B-plus or a B for the course, we can't put that performance against a ruler and say that the A student was twice as good as the C student because four is twice as much as two. But as soon as we make the unwarranted translation from hierarchy to number, to say that B equals 3.00 and C-minus equals 1.67, enormous statistical mischief occurs. We wouldn't want to try to calculate an average between the words "fabulous" in one class and "not bad" in another, but once we pretend those words are numbers, we take that average between fabulous and not bad and calculate it out to two or three places beyond the decimal. Grade point average would never be accepted as a statistical method in social science, but we do far too much with it in higher education. We use it to give awards and scholarships, make class placements, and prohibit students from entering a major.

So those are two reasons why grades are terrible for education. A third is the emotional trauma they inflict on students and instructors alike. A high-achieving student may believe that he needs at least a 3.9 or so GPA to enter medical school, and so every grade becomes an opportunity to sustain or miss that mark. And there's not a lot of threshold there, since an A-minus is 3.67, and it brings your average down. It's like a baseball player who starts the season with six straight hits; every next at bat is likely to reduce his batting average from perfection. I've never had a student argue a grade at the end of the semester to get from a C to a C-plus; it's always the students who got a B-plus or an A-minus who want to get lawyerly and ask to see the exact calculation of grades or an explanation of precisely why their grade was lower than that of some classmate. The concepts of learning and growth and the deliberation of important ideas are all sacrificed to the false god of the letter grade and its evil henchman, the GPA.

The pressure on the instructor, who knows all of that, is likewise high — if a student is wavering between grades, how do we make a carefully reasoned decision? The final verdict must be singular and uninflected, even though we may be of multiple minds and highly conflicted. I always loved giving feedback on essays and drafts, and dreaded the end of the semester and the irretrievable submittal of grades.

Finally, we can think of grades as a form of payment: you do this work for me, I give you that grade in compensation. I like to think that, were I an employer, I would compensate my employees somewhere between fairly and generously. Having been an employee for most of my life, I know how much that means beyond the mere dollar amount: it means that my employer has gone out of her way to say that my work matters, and that my role in the company has value akin to her own. But even though grades are a currency (with accumulating balances that can be spent on crucial life capital such as graduate school or a better first job), I as the workplace supervisor don't have sole discretion in the amount of payment, any more than a Walmart manager can independently decide how much his stock clerks receive. Academic work is often thought of as a craft, a matter for the sole practitioner and her or his apprentices. But really, we left the atelier for the factory floor long ago, and we're now dealing with massive organizations that have informal but strong norms about payment and practices. The individual relationship I've created with a group of students and the ways in which I would like to reward their labors are interrupted and overridden by the larger structures and practices of a college or professional group.

So there are four reasons why higher education should abandon the practice of grading. Never gonna happen, though, so let me also say the following: First, if you're **teaching**, be clear with your students at the beginning of the semester about your expectations of performance, and do your best to hold firm to those expectations as the semester goes along. And take every opportunity to compare your grading and expectations to those of your colleagues, so that you can do your own calibration and understand your tribe's norms.

If you're a student, try somehow to get past the grade thing. If the work matters to you, do the best you can, and ask for detailed feedback, both positive and negative. Learn from that feedback, do some more work, and see if it gets better. You're trying to grow as a thinker, not be rewarded with a herring for balancing a ball on your nose.

However (there's always a however, isn't there?), for most undergraduate programs, a sustained GPA of 2.00 is sufficient academic progress; there are a lot of B-minus professionals in the world. Graduate school is different. Many doctoral programs require a cumulative GPA of 3.00 for good standing, and a grad faculty member might give a student a B as a form of wake-up call, a "shape-up or ship-out" message. If you're not steadily making A and A-minus in your first two doctoral semesters, I'd advise a frank conversation with your grad adviser about your prospects in the program. It's not time to panic; it's time to understand the expectations, and to be explicit about where your efforts should lie.

Graduate school, the. If your college offers degrees beyond the baccalaureate, it will have a separate division called the graduate school, with its own administration and hierarchy. The graduate school sets guidelines for master's and doctoral curricula; expectations for examinations and adequate progress; rules for **dissertation** committee membership, conduct of the **defense** and the awarding of the degree; and specific directions for preparation of your **thesis** or dissertation manuscript. The graduate school will almost always have a graduate student handbook, and that handbook will almost always be available online, usually even if you're not (yet) a student of the school. Download it, read it, master it.

Grant / grant proposal. People erroneously say that they're "writing a grant," but really the only person who can write a grant is the person with the checkbook. A grant is an economic contribution made by a person, organization, or government agency to support a project. Grants are usually competitively awarded, requiring proposals that outline the work to be done, the budget and timeline necessary, the qualifications of the allocated personnel, and the ways in which the proposed project advances the goals of the funder.

Many colleges will have an "office of external support" or "office of grants and external research" or "office of **sponsored research**" or some other entity designed to help you locate and apply for funding. Major universities may have more than one, located in particularly aggressive grant-seeking **departments** and research **centers**.

There are thousands and thousands of books and how-to's on grant proposal writing; I'll let you have at them, and talk about two other things instead. First, if there's any possibility at all, you should try to work with an experienced faculty member as she puts a grant proposal together for her own research. Do it as a member of her research team ... do it for free ... offer her a hundred bucks to *let* you help.[86] It's absolutely invaluable to walk through the process in a low-stakes way (low-stakes because it's not *your* project) before you have to do it competitively to fund yourself. Second, don't imagine that submitting a grant proposal is something you get to decide on in isolation. You'll need backup if nothing else: accounting data, your college's DUNS number, your **chair** or **dean**'s support for the **buyout** time you'll get because of the project. But you also want to make sure that you're not interfering with some larger plans or political background. Colleges are complex ecosystems, and your request to a donor for ten thousand dollars to do some small project may come three days before your **develop-**

---

86. Ira Glass, the producer of National Public Radio's *This American Life*, said that when he was attempting to learn how to write radio scripts, he'd put one together, take it to one of the public radio producers in New York, and pay them fifty dollars to read and critique it. It was much cheaper than tuition ... and, like Ira, you don't need a certification in proposal writing, you just need to get better at it, so paying by unit learning isn't a bad idea.

ment office was about to ask them for a five-hundred-thousand-dollar donation to the **endowment**. Anyone from an institution seeking funding is representing the institution as a whole, and the support needs to come from above. Start with your department chair, and if she seems too blithe about her OK, go to the dean's office. Better to check in than to blindside someone; at worst, it will just result in more people who know that you're serious and know a little about how to play the game.

Gray literature. When scholars conduct a **literature review**, they most often turn to the trusted sources: academic books and **journals**. But there's a vast body of other material out there that could be of use if only it were easier to get to. Gray literature, like the gray market in economics, refers to things for which recordkeeping isn't as thoroughly straightforward or tightly managed as in the mainstream. **Conference** proceedings, **professional society** bulletins and newsletters, official publications from all levels and agencies of government (and from international governments), reports from nonprofits and nongovernmental organizations—all of these can be vastly useful, and none of them show up regularly in standard academic database searches.

Google can be your friend here. You can use the same sorts of search terms as you would in ProQuest or ISI Web of Science, and a good web search will come up with a much broader set of starting points. Many of these sorts of documents have been digitized in recent years, especially now that they originate digitally in Microsoft Word or Excel anyway. With some thoughtful collaboration by your research **librarian**, you'll uncover a vast array of information that you would never have found by limiting yourself to journals and monographs.

There is another body of gray literature that's even harder to locate, or even to know about, because it's proprietary or classified. Every architecture firm that's designed dormitories, for instance, has provided each of its clients with a detailed needs assessment examining housing demand for the foreseeable future; a building program that specifies spaces, sizes, adjacencies, and general equipment and finishes; and a siting plan that relates housing to other campus functions, facilities, and systems. It would be of terrific research interest to understand the principles of college housing, and how those principles have changed in recent decades; but each of those informational and culturally rich documents is part of a confidential business relationship between the design firm and its client. Multiply that across engineering, technology, dotcom, security, finance, and so many other economic and governmental sectors, and you have a body of literature that likely exceeds the peer-reviewed academic pool as the earth exceeds the moon. You can often get access to some of it if you ask directly, but finding it and compiling it becomes a research project all on its own.

GRE. I'm assuming for the purposes of this book that you're considering entering an academic rather than a professional doctoral program, and thus I won't be discussing the other vast array of qualifying exams, such as the MCAT for med schools, the LSAT for law schools, or the GMAT for business schools. For most nonvocational graduate education, the test that counts is the graduate record exam, or GRE. The GRE is the postcollege equivalent of the SAT—the test that, along with your college grades, will unlock a door or leave it bolted.

I'll also assume that since you made it into and through college successfully enough so that you're now considering graduate school, your standardized test scores will probably fall within an acceptable range. You may find yourself struggling with one of the three focal areas of the test, though. I have a friend with a severe math phobia; she's actually better at math than she thinks she is, but she'll never be a candidate for a perfect quantitative reasoning score on the GRE because (a) she doesn't have the math background and (b) she struggles emotionally with math testing. The good news is that the three components—verbal reasoning, quantitative reasoning, and analytical writing—are scored independently, reported independently, and reviewed independently by graduate schools, which weight the most relevant components much more highly. So, since my friend is an American historian, her math score on the GRE didn't hurt her any (and was fine anyway, all fears aside).

As for any standardized test, you can find programs and study guides that will help you prepare, and practice tests that will give you a reasonably accurate sense of how you'll do. Your college may have a **graduate school** office with a collection of these research guides; your college's **library** and your public library probably do as well. But be cautious; the GRE was significantly revamped in 2011, and older test guides won't be accurate assistance.

Hh

Hard drive. The boxes of notebooks in the trunk of the car that's stolen. The film ruined in the leaky shipping container. The flash fire in the storage facility. Doctoral education is filled with horror stories of researchers losing field notes, photographs, and lab notes that can never be replicated.

In the era of the computer, the most common disasters are the lost or damaged laptop and the suddenly failed hard drive. One of my information technology friends says that there are two kinds of hard drives: the ones that have failed, and the ones that haven't failed *yet*.

Hard drives are cheap, and your sanity is costly. Build yourself a backup routine, and stick to it. Put it into your calendar program that every Sunday evening, you copy all of your critical work to a backup drive. Then take that backup drive to a different location, so that the burglary or the fire won't get both the computer and the backup. Send your files to a trusted friend by **e-mail** or a file-transfer service. Burn your photos onto CDs or flash drives, and take them away somewhere.

A cautionary word about cloud storage and e-mail-based backup, though. If you're doing work that requires **confidential** treatment of identities or actions, *do not* do your backups through online storage, no matter how well it's "password protected," or how many https reassurances you get. If you want to keep your credit card number and the photos of your trip to the Moonlite Bunny Ranch online, that's your business; but you do not have the right to endanger the privacy of your research participants to somebody else's so-called security protocols. Keep your research files on your own devices, and keep those devices in locations that can't be accessed by anyone else.

Honorific. I once worked in a running shoe store, and sold a pair of shoes to someone I'd not met before. The name printed on her check was Amanda P. Academic, PhD. That was fine ... but then she signed it Amanda P. Academic, PhD. I was like, "Oh, please. Did your mom name you that?"

The formulation "Dr. Lastname" is only used reflexively by physicians, dentists, preachers and K–12 principals and superintendents (none of whom typically have PhDs; they more often have an MD or DDS or DDiv or EdD.) If you don't want to be bothered at parties by people asking you about a sore on the inside of their lip, don't call yourself Dr. Lastname. (However, your pharmacy will return your calls, so that's a plus.)

You may choose to refer to yourself as Dr. Lastname in the classroom. How you refer to yourself and ask students to refer to you always felt like an issue of personal preference to me ... but then, I'm an older white male to whom students automatically defer. If you're younger, if you're female, if you're a person of color, if you're some combination of those three, you might ask your students to call you Professor Lastname or Dr. Lastname as a way of setting an expectation of authority and professional demeanor.[87] If you have a particularly difficult last name, "Dr. L" helps students have an endearing but comfortably formal handle for you. (I still fondly remember Mr. G—Andrew Grzeszkowiak—from seventh grade. I've probably misspelled it.)

I go by "Herb" in the classroom, even with freshmen, but that's also a conscious choice, an attempt to diminish the distance and formality that comes with my age. "Dr. Herb" wouldn't be so bad, but I'd run the risk of people thinking I was some hack talk-show psychologist.

The choices get messier when you need to address someone you don't know. If the Internet had no other uses, it would still be a wonderful place merely because I can look up someone's bio and know whether to write to them as Dr. Departmentchair or Ms. Departmentchair. For anyone with any kind of **doctorate** at all, start high and refer to them as Dr. Titleholder; they'll bemusedly dial you back if you overshoot. If someone really wants to be called Dr. Overachiever and you start with Carl, you've needlessly offended him.

There's an honorific on the back end, too, as my customer Amanda P. Academic, PhD, knew well. (More accurately, it's a title, but it falls in the same category.) "Carl P. Overachiever, PhD," is an appropriate thing to put on a business card or your **e-mail** signature. As a rule, only stick your doctorate back there. There's no good norm for a bachelor's or master's degree used as a suffix, unless it's a professional degree like an MDiv or MArch (and even that can feel like an overreach). If you've got a couple of them (like the increasingly common "Claudia P. Researchdoc, PhD, MD"), knock yourself out. However, don't double up and use "Dr. Preening P. Ostenta-

---

87. And, although I never thought about it actively when I was teaching, there are contexts in which even we old white guys ought to use "Professor Lastname," since going by our first names gives the signal that we're easygoing and cool, and that all those "others" are uptight and insecure. I know what I prefer personally, but if I'm part of a culture, I ought to act in ways that support that culture and all of its members.

tious, PhD"—go with the up-front "Dr." in person and the trailing "PhD" in print and call it good. We'll still respect you.

If you have an honorary degree from someplace, please for the love of god don't use it in either your prefatory or your trailing honorific. If you see someone else do it, run.

If you're in a professional rather than an academic setting, professional titles are okay. "Claude P. Architect, AIA" is fine (even though "AIA" technically denotes a membership in the American Institute of Architects and is *not* the only sign of professional licensure, it's the norm of the field), as is "Susanne P. Listener, LMFT." There has been a trend toward extended strings of postname abbreviations, which you should please avoid, thank you. For instance, Rebecca P. Jobsite, CE, AICP, RPLS, CRS might be a good person to hire when you're buying a piece of property, since she's a civil engineer, a member of the American Institute of City Planners, a registered professional land surveyor, and a certified residential specialist with the National Association of Realtors. She's also a little insecure, though, so make sure you write a nice complimentary note to her boss when the deal is completed.

Ii

IACUC. One of my favorite acronyms, "IACUC" sounds like a nineteenth-century folk remedy: "Give her a spoonful of IACUC and let's see how she does." Or like a waiter ogling a chef: "Eye a cook." Alas, an IACUC is an Institutional Animal Care and Use Committee, the on-campus group that supervises the appropriate treatment of scientific animals. There's also an entry in this book for the Institutional Review Board, or **IRB**, the related body that oversees the appropriate treatment of people in research. The IRB's oversight is often less stringent than that of the IACUC.

There are deep philosophical questions of animal rights and ethical behavior toward living creatures, questions far beyond the scope of this book.[88] If you're involved in laboratory science, you've already come to

88. There are religious traditions, for instance, that discourage the eating of root vegetables because one has to kill those plants in order to eat them, whereas fruit can be

some personal determination about how lab animals may and may not be ethically used, so at least let's be clear about exactly which living things are covered by your local IACUC. The fruit flies you gas by the hundreds to determine their bloodstream chemistry or their offspring's genetic change? You don't have to justify their housing and veterinary conditions. The plants you raise to review their rate of growth? No oversight needed. The aquarium in your **office**? Don't do any research on the fish or the snails, and you'll be fine.

But, as Tip O'Neill once almost remarked, all research ethics is local, and you need to learn the community norms. Your own campus IACUC might restrict its oversight to mammals. Or maybe to all warm-blooded animals. Or to all the vertebrates. Or to all the vertebrates plus all the cephalopods.[89] And it may make a difference whether those animals were harvested from shelters and pet stores or were bred and raised specifically for research.

Pity the poor fruit fly, with no one to advocate on its behalf.

Indirect costs rate / overhead. Let's say that you take your car in to the garage for service. You're in for a couple of hours, and you receive the bill for $560. You look at the breakdown, and see $400 in parts and $160 in labor. Really, $160 for two hours of labor? Some guy in that garage is making $80 an hour? That's more than $150,000 a year! Who needs a PhD when you can be a Honda technician?

Okay, so you've obviously spotted the logical fallacy in that little story, right? The $80 labor rate isn't the actual wage of the mechanic; it's the fully loaded cost of running a garage, including electricity and updated tools and facilities and training and bookkeepers and profits and—oh yes, the salary and benefits of the mechanic who replaced your brake calipers.[90]

When you write a small, individual **grant proposal** for summer funding, you'll probably only include what are called direct costs, or the money

---

harvested without lasting damage to the tree or shrub. Your own ethical stance with regard to other life is fundamentally yours, but your beliefs will intersect with the norms of a community in ways you need to understand and be comfortable with.

89. When I was a kid, I used to watch Richard Basehart in *Voyage to the Bottom of the Sea*. Those giant squid really were pretty smart, though ruthless. Duke University & Duke University Medical Center Animal Care and Use Program, "Policy, Species Covered Definition," accessed May 4, 2015, http://vetmed.duhs.duke.edu/PDF/Policies/IACUC %20Process/policy_on_definition_of_a_covered_species.pdf.

90. Moral of the story: *Stay in school*. You'll make more money, and you won't crush your fingers in a hydraulic press and end your career at thirty-eight.

that specifically supports the conduct of the work. This typically includes the prorated proportion of your salary, the materials or equipment you'll purchase, the **travel** expenses you'll incur, and the stipends for **research assistants** if you have students helping you. The accounting is easy when you write a targeted summer research proposal for twenty thousand dollars.

Once you enter the big leagues, though, your research starts to support the ongoing operation of the college, through the inclusion of indirect costs or overhead. Your salary is only a small part of what you cost the college: you also require health insurance and other benefits, a computer and network technology, a phone, stationery, an **office** (with furniture) to work in, a lab and some equipment if you're into that, a building to put your office and lab into, a campus to put your building on, and people to maintain all of that and clear the snow away in February. You require people in accounting to pay you and your research bills, people in human resources who manage your benefits and monitor labor laws, a **chair** and a **dean** and a **provost** and a **president** to supervise you, and a lobbyist to represent you to the state and federal governments. You're an expensive little beast, you are, and your grant funding is intended to lift some of the burden of your support away from your institution and onto an external funding agency.

If your institution has done any significant research funded by a major donor or by a governmental agency, the college probably has what's called an indirect costs rate,[91] which is a standard figure that the accounting magicians have developed about your actual, "fully-loaded" cost and not just your direct cost. That indirect cost rate is vetted through auditing procedures similar to the rest of your college's bookkeeping, a form of financial **peer review** so that there's some agreement that the number makes sense. Really research-intensive schools may have more than one indirect cost rate that they've negotiated with individual funding agencies or for different kinds of projects, but the short story is that you'll have to add another significant chunk of request to your proposal once you've named all of the direct costs of the project. For example, if you think your project will cost a million bucks in identifiable direct costs, and your university's indirect rate with the US Department of Health and Human Services is 58.5 per-

---

91. As always, there are oddball local terms. I've heard schools refer to this as their "F&A rate," standing for "facilities and administration." But if a school does any funded research, they'll recognize "overhead" or "indirect costs" as the umbrella terms, and then clue you in to the local argot.

cent, then your total request to HHS will be your million, plus an indirect of $585,000.[92]

As you can imagine, this is not work for beginners; and god help you if you're conducting research in conjunction with scholars from another institution with its own accounting procedures. I mean, you just wanted to be a chemist, right? And now you have to figure out how to be a bookkeeper too? The good news is that if your college does enough research to have an indirect rate, it has an office of **sponsored research** that will work with you to do the proposal submittal and the post-award financial management.

Major research universities will judge your contribution to the school in no small part by the amount of money you bring in as a researcher. I was told directly by one search committee chair that his university's **tenure** decisions were based foremost upon research funding; it was essentially a commissioned-sales position. But a major research university can make half of its entire income from research funding,[93] so if you're playing that game, you'd better know what the rules are.

Inside candidate/hire. When you're in a hiring pool, you know absolutely nothing about the other swimmers. And when you don't get the job, people try to say reassuring things, common among which is that "there was probably an inside candidate."

The notion of the inside candidate is that there's already someone known within the college whom the faculty would like for a new colleague, but they have to go through the motions of a formal search to give cover to their predetermined decision. For faculty positions, this is actually quite unlikely. Where would those inside hires come from? A young faculty member from another **department**? Departments are usually too rigidly defined for that,

---

92. This sounds like a tremendous bloat, yet another way in which "government inefficiency is bleeding this country dry." But private industry has an indirect costs rate, too, which is usually considerably higher; it's just hidden in the billing rate or markup for resale. Remember the Honda labor rate of eighty dollars an hour? That represents an indirect costs rate of well over 200 percent on your mechanic's labor cost. The rule of thumb for professional services is that your billing rate should be roughly three times your salary, to account for overhead, profit, and all those hours when you don't have enough clients. What looks like government inefficiency is actually just transparency; private industry is typically more expensive, in secrecy.

93. Massachusetts Institute of Technology, "MIT Facts 2014: Financial Data," accessed April 28, 2015, http://web.mit.edu/facts/financial.html.

and once someone's on the faculty, her **provost** and the relevant departments could just agree to reassign her without the need to go through a new hiring process anyway. **Adjuncts** who've proven their **teaching** abilities at that college? Please . . . they're invisible. The college pays them nothing, considers them expendable, and gives them no role in their department; the permanent faculty members scarcely know they exist, and consider them lesser beings if they do. Their own doctoral students, near graduation? The faculty will forever see them as students, not colleagues; and there's a general desire to recruit people trained at different schools, so as to broaden the thinking of the department.[94]

The inside candidate is a much more common phenomenon in administrative hiring. An experienced faculty member and department **chair** is chosen to become the **dean**; the associate provost becomes the provost, the longtime coordinator of the student learning center is selected as the **director** of the college writing program. Being an insider is no lock on an administrative position, but it does help, rather than being an active impediment the way it is in faculty searches.

Intellectual. In 2011, *The New Yorker* published a piece by Louis Menand called "Live and Learn: Why We Have College."[95] And although that subtitle promised to reveal why we have college, Menand did what all good professors of English must do: he complicated the problem. He put forth two major functions of college: social stratification through the sorting of talent, and basic training in the ways of thought and items of content that "people like us should know." Both of these functions—colonizing the natives, and sorting them into clusters of varied utility—are exercises of power, a word that curiously doesn't appear in his article. They are the things that college does *to* its participants.

Menand also hints at a third function, one seemingly brought by the students themselves: the function of credentialing, of knowing enough _____ to become a professional _____ and thus have a better income, more job security, and a higher material quality of life. When I teach first-semester master of architecture students, I often ask explicitly: If they could write

94. But not to make it *too* broad, mind you. You still have to be able to sing all the songs in the disciplinary hymnal, but your range might be a little different. They're just looking for an alto or a baritone to fill in those same comforting harmonies.
95. Louis Menand, "Live and Learn: Why We Have College," *New Yorker* (June 6, 2011), accessed April 29, 2015, http://www.newyorker.com/arts/critics/atlarge/2011/06/06 /110606crat_atlarge_menand.

one check for all the tuition money they'd spend in the next few years and just get their M. Arch today, would they take it? And sheepishly at first, but more vigorously once they see their fellows admitting it, more than half the students in the room say they would accept that bargain.[96] In their economic calculus, they've already been to an architecture school for their bachelor's degree, and thus know enough; many are already working in the profession. They just need to buy some very expensive letters to put after their name, so that they can stand on that platform to reach for licensure and a better professional life. If they could accomplish that in three fewer years, all the better. It's clear, then, that this third motive is also something students are compelled to rather than something they choose freely.

Because we are people who are selecting a doctoral education, or who are completing a doctoral education and hoping for a life in the academy, it is important that we all remember just what freaks we are. Most of our students do not share our intellectual enthusiasms; they are not willing to live for years on ramen and decorate the kitchen with towels from Dollar General in order to continue studying a phenomenological understanding of street patterns in the third wave of American suburbanization in the 1970s. They (and their parents, the college's board of trustees, the state's department of labor, and the US Department of Education) want to move on with their lives, to use their college education as an on-ramp to their chosen freeway. We, on the other hand, have become connoisseurs of the academy itself, have found a congenial home in a place that others consider transitional housing.

The seductions of discovery are great for those of us who are susceptible to its charms. Others may want to know enough to enter the marketplace and reliably sell their expertise; we stay in a place where we can never know enough, where the whole enterprise is founded on not knowing. If I could offer an attempted clarification of what the various degree levels are for, I'd say that the bachelor's degree is for acquiring a sense of judgment sufficient for the economic and civic engagement that Hannah Arendt called *the vita activa*, the life of social action; the **master's degree** is for developing the capability for ever-growing professional knowledge that takes advantage of the investigative techniques of one's field; and the **doctorate** is for never, ever knowing, for remaining perpetually on the edge of uncertainty and confusion. It's the X Games version of intellectual life, pushing ourselves to do intellectual stunts that nobody has ever even tried before.

96. This leads to a fascinating dialogue about what graduate school is for, after which I then have them read Menand so that we can keep arguing the following week.

These differing definitions of knowledge lead to a fundamental source of misunderstanding between teachers and students in higher ed. We mistake their **career** aspirations for intellectual apathy; they mistake our push for rigor and complication as picky, fussy overkill. We're enamored of ideas, and they want indoor jobs with low injury risk and no name tags.

Outside the walls, things are even worse. The model of expertise, of instrumental knowledge, is so strong in our culture that the possibility of the intellectual is nearly lost. Sartre divided the educated class into two fields: the *organic intellectuals*, who grow from and serve the needs of capital, and the microscopically smaller group of *critical intellectuals*, who get themselves involved over and over in issues that are none of their "business," but who feel driven to intercede in problems of power and subjugation.[97] The work of higher education is being pushed more and more toward the creation of organic intellectuals: the middle managers who sustain our institutions, the "creative class" who invent marketable novelties.

Knowledge is power— a power that is morally neutral and that can be used for many purposes. We have to remember that our work within higher education is an implicit argument about what intellectual life is, and is for; we have to engage that argument directly, rather than imagine that it isn't occurring.

Intellectual property. Back in the mid-Seventies, when I tried college for the first time, I was the president of the Michigan Technological University Bowling and Billiards Club. One of the perks of that exalted position was that the university hired me for one semester to teach a phys ed course in bowling. Mostly that meant taking roll, teaching scorekeeping, and answering random questions. Just as was true for me in Business Law or General Biology I, I doubt that anyone was taking PE0105 Beginning Bowling for the intellectual challenge.

In order to be hired for that $2.50-an-hour **adjunct** position, I had to sign a lengthy employment agreement that declared that the university would own all patents, copyrights, and licensing arrangements that derived from my Michigan Tech employment. I thought that was pretty funny, and that I wasn't very likely to develop much intellectual property in the bowling alley.

Now that I've been in higher ed for a while, it's not as funny.

97. Jean-Paul Sartre, "A Plea for Intellectuals," in *Between Existentialism and Marxism*, trans. John Matthews (New York: Pantheon, 1974), 228–85.

A college and its research **faculty** are engaged in a symbiotic relationship. The college provides space, equipment, salary, and sometimes **research assistants**; the faculty member provides the ideas, techniques, content knowledge, and labor. So when the Next Big Thing comes from a college researcher, who owns it? Who gets paid for it? Research-oriented colleges have specific agreements that each faculty member and research assistant enters into. For the most part, they're applied equally across the community; but if some rock-star engineer or biochemist gets hired, she might be able to negotiate a more advantageous arrangement as part of her recruitment package.

Here's some of the current Michigan Tech language, similar to what I signed thirty-eight years ago:[98]

If Proprietary Information or patents or copyrights relating thereto, are sold or licensed by the University, the University shall share income from such sale or license ("Income") as follows:

a. Initial Income up to $1,000 to me.
b. Income from $1,000 to $30,000 divided 15% to me and 85% to the University.
c. Income from $30,000 to $180,000 divided equally among the University, my department, and myself.
d. Income in excess of $180,000 divided 1/3 to me and 2/3 to the University.

So if you develop new genetic sequencing software that earns five million dollars, you'll get $1,645,450, and the university will get $3,354,550. That's why colleges hire more biochemists and fewer poets.[99]

But that's just the outcome of scientific and technological work, the miracle drug or killer app. What about the novel that gets published? What about the symphony or musical comedy or painting? Colleges have different rules about that, varying by how much they feel they've contributed

---

98. Michigan Technological University, "Patent, Research, and Proprietary Rights Agreement," accessed April 28, 2015, http://www.mtu.edu/hr/current/docs/patents.pdf.
99. Note also that the home department gets bubkes; just $50K maximum, the one-third of the strand between $30K and $180K. That's often a source of tension between the university that profits and the department that may feel itself to be underfunded and disrespected relative to its productivity. Chairs and deans will often attempt to negotiate some additional departmental funding from particularly successful research projects that emerge from their departments.

to the artistic creation. They may claim the copyright, or they may allow you the copyright but insist on the ability to use the material themselves without royalty. If your novella was supported by a **grant** from the National Endowment for the Arts or your state arts council, that group might have its own claims on ownership.

And it gets worse. In this age of **adjunct** labor, nobody knows who's going to be teaching a course in a couple of years. If you develop or improve a course, your college may or may not claim copyright in the syllabus, lesson plans, lecture slides (whether photographic or PowerPoint), lecture notes, or other course materials. If they allow you the copyright, they may insist on eternal free licensing. Either way, all the work you've invested in the course can be turned over to another instructor hired at the last minute to teach the course you developed.

And it gets worse than that. Every time you write an academic paper and submit it to a **journal**, the journal publishes it (with no payment to you) and owns the copyright. If you or someone else wants to create an anthology and include a paper you've published, the permission is granted by the journal **publisher**, and any payment for that reuse goes to the journal publisher. And if that academic paper might reveal a new material or technique, the college's intellectual property team might ask you to delay publication for a bit until they can tie down the legal rights to your discovery.

Scholarship is based on the free and open exchange of ideas, but ideas have economic value, and intellectual property law is a vast morass of negotiations. There is no correct or universal answer to who should own what; at any particular college, you should investigate how ownership rights work with regard to your scholarly and teaching materials. Or take up bowling.

Interdisciplinary. Nobody knows what this word means. Or, more accurately, you can't ever trust that someone using it means the same thing you do. Interdisciplinary is defined in at least the following ways:

- A project team or program comprising people from multiple **disciplines**, allowing specialized division of labor addressing different aspects of a problem.
- A person trained in two closely related fields, like biology and chemistry, or a field made up of such a dual-trained community, like biochemistry.
- A person from one field who borrows interesting concepts and theories from another field, such as the many cultural geographers

influenced by the sociological theories of Anthony Giddens, or historians who see cultural change through a feminist perspective.
- A person whose work is primarily based on a **method**, such as an ethnographer or a folklorist, and who sets that method to work upon seemingly unrelated phenomena over her career.
- A person who has taken liberal education to heart, and who feels the need to personally understand difficult problems or circumstances as complex, whole phenomena.[100]

This multiplicity obviously raises problems in conversations, in **job searches**, and in **tenure** and **publication** strategies. And the easiest way to avoid those problems is to never raise the issue at all, ever. That's because the enterprise of higher education, both for graduate students and for the body of **faculty**, is fundamentally clannish. You join a tribe, you claim fealty to that tribe, you endure the specific hazing and maturity rituals of that tribe, and you treat all other tribes with a mix of suspicion and condescension. It's kind of like fraternity or sorority rush; you have to believe deep in your heart that Zeta Tau Alpha is your one and only true sisterhood, and that membership in Alpha Chi Omega is unthinkable. Any hint that you might have mixed allegiances and you'll find yourself on the sidewalk with an empty beer cup.

Money follows disciplines. **Journals** are organized by disciplines. **Peer review** and **tenure** are linked to disciplines. Faculty hiring is allotted to disciplines. The whole structure of higher education is like the apocryphal story of auto wheelbases being the same width as railroad chassis, which were the same width as the ruts in the dirt from Roman chariots; it's just easier to reuse the existing structures and do it the way it's been done. No one asks hard questions about where you fit if your **doctorate** is in anthropology, but they sure will if you have a PhD in youth studies.

Interestingly, there is a *lot* of interdisciplinary work in higher education, bringing diverse ideas to bear on a particular phenomenon. Holocaust studies, for instance, is populated by folks from history, various social sciences, religion and theology programs, and several languages; urban studies by people from architecture and planning, from social sciences, from economics, and from systems biology. In many ways, this represents the best

---

100. The first, second, third, and fifth of these definitions are modified from Jeffrey Wasserstrom, "Expanding on the I-Word," *Chronicle of Higher Education* (January 20, 2006). The fourth definition, having to do with method over content, is my own.

that liberal education has to offer: a socially relevant way of thought that stretches your intellectual capacities in broad and sometimes uncomfortable ways, while retaining a clear object of attention.

If you receive a PhD from one of these interdisciplinary programs, though, heaven help you. You'll find very few similar programs in other schools, even fewer looking for new hires, and you will never be accepted in any of the parent disciplines. Interdisciplinary programs are almost always populated by senior faculty members who've been tenured within a traditional department; once they've found safe harbor, they're more securely able to venture into new waters. The major success stories, women's studies and American studies, are now secure enough to hire their own (and to act in that way, just like any of the other old patriarchies they mimic); but can you really wait forty years for your new PhD specialty to mature and ripen?

As a doctoral student, I was helped by one of my great **mentors**, Judith Kenny, to have an hour-long individual meeting with the geographer James Duncan, which was akin to having a personal audience with the pope. Duncan enthused about my **dissertation** proposal, asking more than once, "Are you *sure* this isn't a project in cultural geography?" (Although nominally in architecture, my work was deeply informed by geographic theory, literature, and methods.) At the end of our conversation, aglow with praise and encouragement, I asked whether it might be possible someday that I could find a faculty position in a geography department like his at Syracuse. "Without a degree in geography?" he asked, as though I'd inquired about getting a temp job as a neurosurgeon. "No."

Entering a doctoral program in any discipline is a long-term **career** choice as well as a more immediate intellectual enterprise. I cherish my time in environment-behavior studies; my faculty guides had their own degrees in psychology, architecture, art history, social ecology, cultural geography, and English, and I was able to do unique, high-quality work that integrated all of those intellectual origins. But I have found that the credential itself is bewildering to almost everyone, and offers absolutely no key to entry in any of the fields that I base my work on.[101]

Were I to do it again, I'd go through a program in cultural geography or sociology, focusing on exactly the same phenomenon of young people's

101. I do have long-term faith in the interdisciplinary project, and I believe that in another thirty years or so, it might be possible for a college to hire a new faculty member without disciplinary alliance in mind. The next thirty years, though, will be a lot like the last thirty, with bodies strewn across the beach as the next wave of the invasion comes in behind us.

uses of physical environments. I'd find quiet **mentors** from the other disciplines, but I'd keep my multiple citizenship a secret. You can be a pioneer, or you can get a job.

I will say, however, that having such a background has made me valuable and attractive as an **administrator**, who by definition needs to have allegiances that go beyond any one of the tribes. If you think you might someday want to be a **director** or a **dean**, an interdisciplinary education is terrific training. It's just unlikely that you'll ever get to be a faculty member, which is kind of a limiting factor.

IRB (institutional review board). If your research topic includes real live people, you've got to treat them right. This seems commonsensical, but let me tell you, it hasn't been. Stanley Milgram's obedience experiments, Philip Zimbardo's prisoner and guard simulations, invasions of privacy made public, disease treatments withheld—a grand menagerie of deception and pain has inhabited the preserve of human research.

This is not the place to get into a long discourse about research ethics. I write and teach about that in other parts of my life. In this context, what I want to let you know is that if your research includes living people, you will be asked to submit your research plans to a campus-based **committee** called the IRB, which is short for institutional review board, which in turn is short for institutional review board for the protection of human subjects in research.

The IRB (pronounced letter-by-letter) is charged with the oversight of research *before it occurs*; they think through the possible adverse outcomes that your work might cause to your participants. Typically, you submit a review application, and then you fall into a sort of flowchart of processes and procedures. For instance, let's say that your proposed research involves asking questions of volunteer adults about their preferences from among a set of photographs of buildings. There's probably someone in your **department** or division whom the IRB has sanctioned to give what's called an "expedited review" and a possible determination of minimal risk. In this case, it's unlikely that anyone will be physically harmed, beyond maybe a paper cut from the questionnaire sheet; unlikely that anyone will be psychologically scarred, unless the photographed buildings are really hideous; and unlikely that anyone will have their reputation tarred, unless they're in an architecture school and don't like the same stuff the other architects like.

But your research can get moved out of the minimal risk category pretty easily. First off, you might be working with a protected category of participants: minors, pregnant women, or prisoners. You might be making a physical intervention, like a blood draw or a drug administration. You might be asking the participants about sensitive topics like sexual behavior or criminal activity. You might be deceiving them, putting them into a simulated circumstance to learn their unguarded reactions. Or you might be paying them for their participation. Any one of those things can get your research the full IRB treatment.

If that's the case, you request a review and get put onto the IRB schedule. A month or so before your scheduled hearing, you provide a full accounting of your plans and the nature of the population you'll be working with, and the board members (**faculty** and administrators from your college, plus maybe the college attorney, and one "public" member who's not affiliated with the college at all) will read and think through your proposal.

You may or may not be invited to the IRB meeting at which your proposal is read; different campuses have different rules about this. For instance, at the University of Connecticut, the researcher *may not* attend the IRB meeting without specific invitation;[102] at the University of Alaska–Fairbanks, the researcher *can attend or not* as she chooses;[103] and at Butler Hospital in Providence, she *has* to go.[104]

The IRB, after hearing and deliberating, can come to one of three findings:

1. Go ahead as planned.
2. Submit specific revisions that respond to our specific concerns.
3. You're out of your mind.

Number 3 is, of course, rare. But so is number 1, except in cases of medical research in which the exact nature of the treatment, the population, and the protections can be precisely named in advance. Any kind of social research is likely to be much less clear-cut in its possible outcomes for participation. Under what conditions might participants' responses be embarrassing or

102. University of Connecticut Office of the Vice President for Research, "IRB Policies and Procedures," accessed May 4, 2015, http://research.uconn.edu/wp-content/uploads /sites/351/2014/09/IRB-Policies-and-Procedures.pdf.
103. University of Alaska–Fairbanks Center for Research Services, "Institutional Review Board Protocol Review," accessed April 28, 2015, http://www.uaf.edu/irb/faqs/protocol -review/.
104. Butler Hospital, "Instructions for Submitting Documents to the IRB Office," accessed April 28, 2015, http://www.butler.org/irb/instructions.cfm.

damaging? Under what conditions can you participate in a grade school without parental permission, and what happens if twenty-nine parents say it's okay to observe a classroom and the thirtieth says no? What do you do with an ethnographic field study, in which the protocol is invented on the fly to respond to changing circumstances and changed understandings? My own **dissertation** (particularly vexing, since it was an ethnographic study of high school students, who as minors were a protected group) involved three IRB meetings before final approval, and even then the board wasn't fully convinced, but at least trusted that I was thinking as carefully as they were about potential harms. And I had to file annual updates and inform them of any changes, so it's not as if I got a blanket permission to do as I pleased.

You may be imagining all of this review and potential interference in your work, and thinking, "Do I *really* have to do this?" Yes, you do. As always, there are noble reasons and punitive reasons to obey the regulations. The noble reasons are that it's always good to have intelligent and experienced people think along with you about the possible ramifications of your work, and that the board might find an improvement to your protocol that makes it simpler and safer. And many funders require evidence of IRB approval as part of their own approval and oversight processes.

The punitive reasons, though, are massive. If you don't get IRB approval of your study prior to conduct, and someone discovers that (or, worse, complains about how they're being treated), you could be barred from using any of the data you've collected; you could be prohibited from publishing in many **journals**; you could be disqualified for future consideration by funding agencies; the college might not defend you if there's a lawsuit; and you could be dismissed from grad school or from employment for **research misconduct**.

The details of how the IRB process works on your campus are, of course, outside the scope of this book. But you need to know them, and a simple search of your college website for "IRB" will get you started.

Jj

Job posting / position announcement. A genre of literature more deeply studied than Joyce, and with as many nuances and subtexts. Let's start with an example, from the *Chronicle of Higher Education*:[105]

> Massachusetts Institute of Technology
> Program in Science, Technology, and Society
> Faculty Search: Assistant Professor
>
> MIT's Program in Science, Technology, and Society invites applications for a tenure-track faculty position at the level of **assistant professor**. The area of study is the history of science and/or medicine with a focus on the modern period. Graduate and undergraduate teaching and advising are expected. Interest in establishing scholarly connections at MIT beyond the STS Program is desirable.
>
> Candidates must hold a Ph.D by the start of employment. The offer is contingent upon completion of the degree by the start date of employment. Candidates must be able to demonstrate excellence in research and teaching. The appointment is anticipated to begin in academic year 2014–2015.
>
> MIT is an Equal Opportunity and Affirmative Action employer and strongly encourages the applications of women and members of minority groups.
>
> Applications consisting of a cover letter, current curriculum vita, statement describing current and future research plans, a statement of teaching philosophy, and three letters of recommendation should be submitted via the Academic Jobs Online website at https://academicjobsonline.org /ajo/jobs/2942. Please, no hard copy submissions. Applications will be

105. Chronicle of Higher Education, "Assistant Professor, Massachusetts Institute of Technology, Program in Science, Technology, and Society," accessed May 4, 2015, http:// chronicle.com/jobs/0000790595–01. Note that this ad is for a job that would start more than a year after its posting. If you want a job at a research university, you should be reading ads in the summer of the year before. Less selective schools advertise later.

reviewed beginning October 15, 2013. The process will continue until the position is filled.

I'm not even looking for a job, and I can feel myself start to sweat. What is this telling me? What do I need to think about? Let's do a line reading.

First, I'm interested in the fact that STS is described as a "program" rather than a "department." So I go to their website and see that STS is indeed organized not as a department, but as a **research center**. Undergrads can minor in STS, but they can only major in it as a double major with something else. STS does have a doctoral program, though, so there'll be expectations of serving on doctoral committees. It will be worth looking at the **curriculum** of the doctoral program, to see the core courses you might be expected to teach.

Almost all of the **faculty** actually either have appointments in other departments or hold specifically endowed faculty positions, so it appears that MIT hasn't yet committed to a full departmental status.[106] There are a couple of other junior faculty members whose appointment is only with STS, but until a few of them get **tenure**, it's looking like a rough ride for new faculty. They're *listing* the position as tenure-track, though, so they're offering the carrot of permanence. Tenure at MIT is notably difficult in the best of circumstances,[107] and given STS's status as a program rather than a department, this one seems particularly tough. But it looks like a great gig while it lasts, and people do go on to good careers at other schools after being rejected for tenure at elite research universities, so let's keep going.

They want someone with a background in "history of science and/or medicine with a focus on the modern period." They didn't capitalize "modern," so they may mean the Modernist period of the 1890s to the 1950s, or they may just mean contemporary. Given STS's mission of "understanding major events of our time and ... addressing these and other major public issues," I'm betting that "contemporary" is the preferred synonym for "modern" in this instance. (That's only a good guess, though; not a certainty. I'd want to find out what other researchers in this unit are working on.)

Let's continue. We already know that STS has some academic interest

106. The program was started in 1976, so be patient.
107. Maybe fewer than half who start as assistant professors make it through the tenure review. Jessica Lin, "Unraveling Tenure at MIT," *The Tech* (online edition) 130, no. 28 (June 11, 2010), accessed April 28, 2015, http://tech.mit.edu/V130/N28/tenure.html.

in undergrads but offers its own stand-alone PhD, so it's no surprise to see "graduate and undergraduate teaching and advising" as part of the expectations, and in that order.[108] But it's also interesting that "interest in establishing scholarly connections at MIT beyond the STS Program is desirable." Certainly it's good to not just sit protected within your department (which isn't really a department), but what exactly does "establishing connections" mean? Do they want you to try to get a joint appointment, so that STS only has to pay half your salary and you have greater institutional safety (or twice as many people who are willing to deny you tenure)? Do they want you to be on doctoral committees in one of their more established **disciplines**, as well as within STS? It would be great to already know someone at MIT in history or in one of the scientific fields related to your **dissertation**, so that you can talk about your partnerships-at-the-ready. Better see who's in those departments.

"Candidates must hold a PhD by the start of employment. The **offer** is contingent upon completion of the degree by the start date of employment." Trust me, they're serious about this. You can *apply* before you defend your dissertation, but you had better be sure that you'll complete it within the next six months before they get into final candidate reviews. Some schools will hire a faculty member **ABD**, but that number is decreasing as the stock of idle PhDs grows, and a major research school will only want mature fish, not hatchlings. Note also, though, that since the appointment is "at the level of assistant professor," they want someone whose dissertation was completed relatively recently. Essentially, you have about a two-year **career** window during which you can apply for this job: the dissertation must be done, but if it was done very far back, you're obviously damaged goods and not fit for MIT.

"Candidates must be able to demonstrate excellence in research and teaching." Not capability, but excellence. You need to be able to point to peer-reviewed, published scholarship *now*, preferably in important **journals**. You need to assemble your course evaluations and letters from your teaching supervisors. Getting hired as an assistant professor at MIT is going

---

108. This being an elite research university, it will be advisable (once you're hired) to get onto a few doctoral committees as fast as you can, so that by the time that your tenure clock rings, you can demonstrate that you've led PhD students to successful completion. Don't *chair* anybody's committee, though; you want a more senior scholar to bear the bigger risks, and you don't want your students penalized because your colleagues decide to haze you.

to require a level of scholarship that might already get you tenure at a small liberal arts college, because the level of scholarship required to cross the MIT tenure threshold will be extraordinary.[109]

"MIT is an Equal Opportunity and Affirmative Action employer and strongly encourages the applications of women and members of minority groups." I'd take this at face value and not imagine that "equal opportunity" or "affirmative action" means that you don't stand a chance if you're white or male. (See the entry on **minority preference** for some data on this.) Institutions are under a lot of pressure to make sure that they're effectively reaching out to diverse pools of applicants, and they need to keep careful records to demonstrate the percentage of both student and faculty applications that come from women and persons of color. You'll probably be asked at most schools to fill out a card later in the process for the human resources office, on which you indicate your appropriate ethnic, gender, veteran, and disability status.

Now, let's look at the next paragraph: all the stuff you have to assemble for your application (which will be completed using an online submittal process, by the way, so presume that all of these things have to be in a PDF format for uploading):

1. A **cover letter**. Think of this as a proposal, which carries with it all of the elements of any other proposal: this is what I want to do; this is why I'm the right person to do it; this is why you will benefit from partnering with me.
2. A current **CV**. Reread the section of this book on curriculum vitae.
3. A statement describing current and future research plans. This is where they want to see your so-called **research agenda**. As a doctoral student, you may be staggering from exhaustion as you carry your **dissertation** across the line, but MIT wants to know what your next ten years of research might entail. What area of knowl-

---

109. It's not uncommon for senior faculty, when reviewing a mass of highly qualified, highly talented applicants for a new faculty position, to remark on the far greater scholarly productivity this generation has achieved as doctoral students than they themselves were required to demonstrate when they went up for tenure thirty years ago. "I could *never* get a job now ... hahahahahaha." And there's something vaguely creepy and certainly condescending about that, like bragging about the million-dollar house that you bought as a new assistant professor in 1982 for thirty thousand dollars. Demographics can be just as much a source of undue privilege as aristocracy.

edge do you propose to advance, and what are the stages of scholarship that will allow you to become a leader in that advancement?

4. A statement of **teaching** philosophy. Remember that this position expects both undergraduate and graduate teaching, so don't just wax enthusiastic about bright-eyed freshmen being introduced to the world of ideas. As a grad-student **teaching assistant**, you may never have led other grad students, so at least talk about your upper-division undergrads and the ways that you're preparing them for grad school.

5–7. Three letters of **recommendation**: one from your **dissertation chair,** and the other two from senior scholars in your field from another college (preferably of stature similar to that of MIT). Investigate MIT's submittal system; do they really want *you* to submit your recommendation letters, or is there a link that you can forward to your colleagues so that they can upload their own letters and preserve their confidentiality? A good automated system will let you log in and upload documents repeatedly, so that you can advance your application as far as possible while still waiting for that one last letter of recommendation to come through.

As with any area of criticism, you'll do at least as much work understanding the text as its authors did in creating it. And even then, you'll need to read all of the program faculty **biographies**, so that you know their areas of interest. How can your work dovetail with theirs, so that their own agendas can be furthered? Find their most recent doctoral graduates, and get the **abstracts** of their dissertations so that you can see the kind of work that faculty members encourage through their student proxies.

Finally, as you submit your application, find out how you can verify that all of your materials have been appropriately received and noted. Too many schools still don't send out an acknowledgement letter when your file is complete; you need to know who you can call if you haven't heard anything within a couple of weeks.

Reading a job posting is every bit the literary event that reading philosophy is, including analysis of all of the paratexts and epitexts that accompany the core. It would make a fun drinking game to get half a dozen friends together, have each one choose an ad they're considering responding to, and do this kind of close read of each one (with multiple web browsers open). You'd all benefit from it, and you'd not feel so damned alone as you went through this miserably arcane process.

Job search. This whole book is your job search. Your job search doesn't start when you've completed your PhD; it doesn't even start when you're **ABD**. It starts from your choice of which doctoral program to attend, and which faculty member to work with. It starts from your first paper in your first doctoral seminar, your first time attending your national conference. It starts with your choice of **dissertation** topic, and of whom you reach out to for guidance.

The nominal job search, the year or two or three you spend at the end of your doctoral studies, has to be set up with a string of **publications**, a **network** of connections, an increasing reputation as a young star in your field. You have to be known, and you have to know that being known is a currency you can spend.

Your faculty must stand ready to help you with your search, also from the very beginnings of your doctoral journey. They have to steer you toward the right journals for early publications; they have to guide your dissertation research in marketable ways without channeling it so tightly that your enthusiasms are dried out of it. They have to talk you up among their colleagues, and tip you off to an upcoming opening in their friend's **department**. It's absolutely fair to ask your potential dissertation adviser where her students are currently working, and what she did to promote their early **careers**. In fact, it's essential.

We live within a paradox. We sensibly plan for our futures; no one wants to wind up sick and penniless, burdened by student loans they have no prospect of repaying. And yet we also live for the enjoyment of the day and of our friends and families. If we spend all of our time planning, we can miss the true joys of the moment; if we live wholly in the moment, we run the risk of a diminished future.

Doctoral education is a singular embodiment of that paradox. Done the way I did it, it's like a powerful travel experience, in which every moment reveals some new thing about the world, or some new aspect of your own self. I love to travel without an agenda, to encounter what's around the corner and spend five minutes or five hours as the circumstance warrants. My doctoral education, like my trips to Venice and Victoria, has been of immeasurable worth. Neither has been capital I could convert to faculty life.

Done another way, doctoral education is a constant slog along the Monopoly board, making strategic rather than emotional decisions. In the end, you can find yourself cornering the market on cardboard properties of dubious value, exquisitely prepared to take on a career that you no longer care about.

Your challenge will be to sustain a workable and enjoyable balance on the rope between those two necessary poles. Much of the news I bring in this book is hard, I know, but that's only because I assume that you, like me twenty-five years ago, are about to enter or complete graduate school in romantic enthrallment to the glories of knowledge and to the seduction that you, too, could be an initiate into this clan. You're skewed toward the daily joy, and don't know enough yet about the long game. I, on the other hand, have just left higher education, having had great success in ways that I no longer cared for. Through this book, I hope that I'll be useful to you as the far pole that tightens the rope upon which you're about to step.

Journal. At present, there are approximately 2.38×10^{23} academic journals in active publication. Well, actually that's the estimated number of stars in the universe; but according to Arif Jinha at the University of Ottawa, there are roughly twenty-five thousand refereed scholarly journals currently published worldwide, accounting for something like a million and a half articles per year.[110] These journals differ by **discipline** and subject matter, obviously, but they also differ in other ways that are crucial to your **publication** plans.

Foremost among these differences is reputation. We'll talk in a minute about some empirical ways to assess whether a journal is "important," but those are still secondary in most fields to the journal's perceived importance. Every discipline has one or two journals that are considered the authoritative source, the highest bar. The *Annals of the Association of American Geographers*, the *Journal of Organic Chemistry*, the *New England Journal of Medicine*, and the *Lancet* are academic equivalents of the *New York Times* in both quality and prestige of publication. If you have a publication in one of those flagship journals, your **CV** comes to the top of the pile; you should surround that citation record with blinking lights and stars. Ask your faculty members and colleagues what journals they think are the most important and prestigious in your field, and you'll quickly center in on just a few answers.

Aside from reputation, though, journals now calculate what's called an impact factor, which is simply the average number of times that its articles are cited. (See the entry on **citational power** for more detail.) The impact factor can be calculated annually or over a specified range, and each of those methods has its own strengths and shortcomings. For instance, the short-range calculation is most important in the natural science fields, where the

110. Arif E. Jinha, "Article 50 Million: An Estimate of the Number of Scholarly Articles in Existence," *Learned Publishing* 23, no. 3 (2010): 258–63, http://hdl.handle.net/10393/19577.

channels of research are straighter and flow more quickly; journal articles published in 2014 are often cited in articles published in 2015, and a rapid factor is sensible. In the social sciences and humanities, the nature of published work is very different; the creation of a publishable manuscript may take years, the relevant research is published in a far broader array of journals, and a strong paper may make meaningful citation of works that themselves were published decades earlier.[111]

As I've noted earlier, impact factor and reputation are not necessarily linked. In my field, the two highest prestige journals are probably *Environment and Behavior* and the *Journal of Environmental Psychology.* But *JEP*'s impact factor is 2.55, whereas *E&B*'s impact factor is only half that, at 1.28. The *Annals of the Association of American Geographers* has an impact factor of 2.11, whereas the more focused *Urban Geography* is at 1.70. If you want your work to be noticed, consider whether the journal's articles are actually read and cited, and are not just trophies on a particularly gilded shelf.

Another factor to consider is the average time to publication. Some journals are notorious for sitting on their submittals for a long time, in some cases more than a year. That's most often a result of the **editor** and **publisher** not having a sufficient pool of **peer reviewers**, so that each individual reviewer is swamped with requests that she just can't fit into her larger work life. The major journal publishers can often tell you what the pace of review has been for a journal you're interested in; Elsevier's website, for instance, has a five-year running record of time to first decision and time to final decision for each of its journals. You want to have a judgment and an opportunity to revise in short order, so that you can resubmit to another journal if need be.

Finally, the world of academic journal publishing, like all publishing, is experimenting with different economic models. Historically, a journal was made available by its publisher at one price to individual scholars, and at a second very high price to university **libraries**; that higher subscription cost—sometimes in the tens of thousands of dollars per year—was justified by the potentially larger number of users, and because college libraries were the goose that could always squawk up another golden egg. But several forces have come together at once to change that model.

111. Among the many flaws of the impact factor method is that citation is in part a function of access; the more researchers who have access to a journal, the more who will cite its papers. So the publisher's salesmanship matters a lot, getting the journal into as many libraries as possible; so does its decision to make articles broadly available online.

- Journal publishing is increasingly consolidated in fewer corporate hands; Reed Elsevier, Wiley Blackwell, Taylor & Francis Informa, and Candover & Cinven each publish more than a thousand academic journals.[112] And, as in all fields, oligopoly puts upward pressure on price. Publishers often bundle journal subscriptions like cable TV packages. Libraries spend a lot more per journal to pick and choose than to buy a package, but the package is more expensive than the smaller number of journals a library might have selected on its own.
- The increasing number of journals and published papers means more subscription costs for major research libraries that attempt to have strong academic breadth. The members of the Association of Research Libraries spend, on average, more than four times as much on journals now as they did twenty years ago.[113]
- If a library chooses a journal's online access, it probably has to pay the annual subscription fee forever, or else that school's community will no longer have access to the older content it has already paid for. Back access isn't a problem when a library quits subscribing to a paper journal, since the paper copies are the library's property and are stored in perpetuity.
- Some publishers charge **authors** a fee to make their materials broadly available in electronic format. Publishing in the journal is still free, but adding **open access** rights, which increases the reach of your work, will cost you.
- Still other publishers are shifting the cost of publication from subscriber to producer. Historically, if a publisher asked you to pay for publication, it was a clear indicator of a "vanity publisher," a house that charged exorbitant fees so that the unwitting and overreaching could say that they were published.[114] But now, with the increased

---

112. University of California Berkeley Library Collections. "Hot Topic: Publisher Mergers," accessed April 28, 2015, http://www.lib.berkeley.edu/scholarlycommunication/publisher _mergers.html.

113. University of California Berkeley Library Collections, "Monograph and Serial Expenditures in ARL Libraries, 1986–2005," accessed April 28, 2015, http://www.lib .berkeley.edu/Collections/pdfs/monser05.pdf.

114. Those still exist, too, as do vanity conferences. I supervised an adjunct faculty member who unfailingly asked me every year for five thousand dollars to go to "an Oxford conference" in England. Of course, it was really a flattering come-on for a summer continuing-education week put on by a business affiliate of Oxford University and cash-

number of print and **online journals**, subscription models may not always be effective, and author surcharges ("page fees" or "acceptance fees") have sometimes made up the difference.

Academic publishing was always an odd business model anyway, in which the journal publisher received the labor and **intellectual property** of hundreds of scholars for free, and then sold it for quite a pile (occasionally charging a copyright fee to the authors themselves if they wanted to use their own articles in later anthologies). All of the **authors**, **peer reviewers**, and **editors** participated because there were no other options for disseminating and getting credit for their work. Now, however, other options exist, mainly online—but as with any frontier community, there aren't yet good rules in place.

The basic upshot is that you should ask your more senior colleagues for advice about any venue you're thinking of publishing in. They can help you get the most **career** credit for your work, and can also help you avoid an expensive mistake.

Ll

Learning management system / course management system. There's software for everything. There's software that interfaces with a chip in your shoes to tell you how far you've walked. There's a smartphone app that tells you the speed of your pool break shot. There's software that tells you how many lottery tickets you need to buy, and what numbers to play to guarantee a return. So it's no surprise that there's software to organize your teaching life.

Your college will almost certainly have one or another of the learning

---

ing in on its name. In general, if you're contacted by a publisher or conference promoter to submit your work, and that contact isn't accompanied by a detailed personal note indicating how this person came to hear of you and your research, it's a fake. Beware, and check journals and conference organizers against *Beall's List of Predatory Publishers*. Jeffrey Beall, "Beall's List: Potential, Possible or Probably Predatory Scholarly Open-Access Publishers," accessed May 4, 2015, http://scholarlyoa.com/publishers/.

management / course management systems (LMS or CMS) that allow you to support your courses electronically. Although the systems differ, all will let you post syllabi and readings, receive homework, moderate discussion boards, calculate and record **grades**, set course-visible calendars for due dates, divide large classes into smaller groups, and allow the group members to single-click for team **e-mail**. Most of them do a lot more than that, but you'll never use the extended features.

Like Kleenex and Xerox and Jell-O, there's a trademark that has become a generic term for LMS: Blackboard. Blackboard's LMS owns about half of the higher education market, and Blackboard has regularly bought out other businesses with competing and complementary functions. The biggest current competitor is actually the open-source software Moodle; there are others that you might encounter as well. Blackboard is attempting to sell the smart-university model, in which their software organizes courses, monitors swipe card access to buildings and parking lots, houses student debit cards, manages emergency notifications, facilitates on-campus **committees** and working teams, and enables **assessment** analytics for students, courses, faculty members, **departments**, and the college as a whole.

Privacy? That's so twentieth-century, dude.

Actually, an LMS has a form of privacy control at its core, which is **intellectual property** protection. You have to be a registered member of a course to see its contents, which means that copyright permissions for syllabi, assignments, and articles only extend to the enrolled students. (Course access also expires once the course is complete, so if you're a student, make sure you've downloaded all the documents you want to keep before the semester ends.) You typically can't invite others to join the course if they're off campus, which means that you can only make limited use of guest speakers and critics. The upside, of course, is that once content exists in the LMS, you and the students have access to it at any moment from any log-in location, including laptops and smartphones.

Once the LMS exists on a campus, it's only as good as the instructional technology staff a college hires to make it work. When I came to Duke University in 2002, Blackboard was like the fluorescent light in my office or the water in the bathroom; it just worked. I received no formal training in it, but I was using it effectively in my first week and creatively within a month. Other schools—usually those with big aspirations, no money, and lots of adjuncts who need training—run into constant technical glitches. Your officemates will likely have better, faster solutions to your problems than the instructional technology staff, because your colleagues have already had the same problems you have, and they've figured out workarounds.

Library/librarian. One of the great joys of academic life is that you have both permission to read and access to a treasure house of ideas. If, like me, you went into academic life because reading was as natural to you as holding a spoon, you will be treated to a banquet the likes of which you have never imagined.

Books, yes, of course—books by the hundreds of thousands, books by the millions. Ten million, when I was a student at Berkeley. Books old and new, books to be discovered and rediscovered and treasured. My God, I love books.

Magazines, too. Or more precisely, periodicals: popular magazines, academic **journals**, newspapers, trade magazines, organizational newsletters. Periodicals for casual intercourse, to take pleasure with on a cold afternoon between classes. Periodicals that become lifelong partners, reliably taking you ever deeper into the mysteries of thought.

Other stuff as well. Maps, music, movies, microfiche of dead publications photographed for preservation. Images and government records. Architectural drawings, writers' notebooks, scientists' letters, composers' drafts. Your own college's archives.

The contemporary library also has electronic resources, databases both general and specific: JSTOR, Web of Science, ERIC, WorldCat, BioOne, Scopus, hundreds and hundreds of them. The digitizing of scholarship has become the norm on an ongoing basis, and is picking up speed backward into the archives as well. Every field has its own electronic repositories that bring far-flung intellectual ingredients into the already rich local cuisine.

There's stuff you can get at freely, and stuff that's protected; material you can photocopy and scan, and material you can only take notes about; material you can touch, and material that only trained and gloved professionals can handle.

Just thinking about a top-tier academic library is like remembering a favorite trip—the joys of discovery, the planned excursions, and the constant surprises. I remember doing an architectural history paper about the Bhagwan Shree Rajneesh and his followers' takeover of a rural village in Oregon in the early 1980s, and discovering to my astonishment that Berkeley's Moffitt Library had microfiche of the entire history of the Rajneeshpuram community newspaper, which I spent more than a month reading. I remember finding the 1948 Norwegian anthropology journal that gave the account of discovering the first Trelleborg Viking camp.

Oh, sorry. It's like talking about your vacation slides . . . .

So what do you need to know about libraries as a young scholar? You need to know that the quality of the library where you go to grad school or where you take a job is a vital element of your decision, and will have enormous bearing on your satisfaction and your capability. You need to know that "the library" is probably a shorthand for a number of general and specialized collections that may exist in multiple locations around campus. You need to know how to use a library in both focused and serendipitous ways. You need to practice your keyword searches and database selections, and to use the reference librarians as coaches in your training. You wouldn't try to be an Olympic athlete without coaching, and you shouldn't try to do **literature reviews** on your own either.

You need to be able to lay your hands on that paper from 2003 that was only published as part of a **conference** proceedings. But you also need to know that because of the miracle of categorization, every book you find from your sharpshooter's search will be surrounded on the shelves by five feet of related books in all directions. Find your book or article, draw an imaginary zone around it, and scan all the titles; you'll almost certainly find something else that's just as interesting as what you came for.

For every useful item you find, read its bibliography and take advantage of all of those resources as well. I didn't understand this for the longest time. When I first started my doctoral program, we were reading about 250 to 300 pages per week for the main introductory proseminar. This was prior to the age of the PDF, so the articles were left on reserve for us, and we photocopied them all at ten cents per page. I, being clever, wasn't copying the bibliographies, and thus was saving a couple of dollars per week. After all, we weren't going to be discussing the bibliographies in seminar, right? It took another, wiser student to suggest kindly that I might find the bibliographies useful because they contained resources for my own further investigations. Even after being a star undergraduate, I had many things to learn about scholarly life.

And finally, remember that a library is its librarians as much as or more than it is the materials. A talented reference librarian (thank you, Greta) is an invaluable partner and advocate for your scholarship, for the development of your **teaching** materials, for the training of your own students in librarianship, and for colleagueship of surprising and innumerable forms.

As a graduate student or an early career **faculty** or an **adjunct**, you will face innumerable indignities and slights. Whenever you feel you can't bear another minute of the incredibly small-minded amateur politics around you, go to the library and remind yourself why you got started with all this. Ideas still matter; the library has more of them than any other place.

Literature review. Literature reviews have several purposes. The most fundamental are the researcher's own preparation and confidence. We use literature reviews to discover what is already known about some phenomenon, and to learn where the edges of knowledge are ragged. This allows us to build upon the achievements of the field while not replicating work already accomplished.

But if our own preparation were *all* that lit reviews were for, we wouldn't include them in our **publications**. Literature reviews also act as communicative devices, as language elements in our conversations with the field. We use them to convince colleagues and **editors** that we have the background for the work, and to leave the trails of our efforts behind us so that others can see the work we've relied upon. A good literature review is an essay in itself, one that might form the basis for the readings and intellectual framework for an upper-division college course.

Let's also be clear that not all literature reviews are created equal.

Life is good when you're a lab biochemist. Let's say that Dr. Francine Pipette is one of about ten people in the universe studying the effects of folic acid and glycine supplementation on embryo development and folate metabolism during early pregnancy in pigs.[115] She doesn't have to explain any basic nutritional chemistry or digestive biology to her readers. She probably knows all the other nine people in her field—hell, probably a third of them are working in her lab. There are only four or five **journals** that this kind of research could ever be published in, and she's only interested in what's been published in the very recent past. So Dr. Pipette's lit review in advance of a new piece of research will take most of a day to complete.

On the other end of the scale, let's imagine Dr. Melody Thirdwave, a researcher in women's studies, thinking about a study of gender experience of musicians in major American orchestras and the ways in which those ultimate roles are rooted in gender patterns of childhood music education

---

115. You think I'm kidding, don't you? F. Guay, J. J. Matte, C. L. Girard, M. F. Palin, A. Giguère, and J. P. Laforest, "Effect of Folic Acid and Glycine Supplementation on Embryo Development and Folate Metabolism during Early Pregnancy in Pigs," *Journal of Animal Science* 80, no. 2 (2002): 2134–43. I was only kidding about Dr. Pipette's name.

(boys given trombones, girls assigned flutes). Professor Thirdwave, probably working alone, will have to conduct a lit review encompassing at least music education, orchestral history, larger social history, and gender and childhood theory. For a qualitative study like this, even the **methods** section alone will need a literature review. The relevant literature (and only the researcher herself will understand her own criteria for relevance, and those criteria will change constantly as her insights evolve) might be spread across hundreds of journals and thousands of books published across the span of decades. Her literature review will take two consecutive summers away from teaching and advising, and she will never be confident that it is complete enough that she can begin working on the project itself. The broader your research topic's relevance, the more others will already have been thinking about it, and the more that will have been written on matters that you'll touch on. And the relevant material will be dozens or hundreds of pages each, not a handful of six-page reports in the *Journal of Organic Chemistry*. An exhaustive literature review is as impossible as hand-washing every blade of grass in the yard, and the relevant literature is continually being added to while you're making sense of the parts you already know about.

Allow me to make up a rule of thumb about the scope of a lit review in interpretive scholarly fields, which I'll call "the second-level rule." First, you have to cite and discuss the ten or so studies that are conceptually closest to your own. These are the siblings who must be named. But a lit review is not just an inventory; it's an analysis. So you intuit the major intellectual categories within your sibling literature, topics that your own work will likely address, and conduct a lit review on each of those topics, with another ten or a dozen articles apiece.

That second-generation analysis will have you up to 80 to 120 citations, which is a pretty good starting point for a **dissertation**-length study. My own dissertation had 111 citations, and it was fundamentally ethnographic; a literary analysis might have double that number.

You need to make friends with a good research librarian. And I don't mean meeting her once or twice and going through your own ideas. I mean taking her out for a coffee or three and really getting acquainted both socially and professionally. Most research librarians I've ever met are truly talented research thinkers who've decided to specialize in the work of resource management rather than the actual conduct of the research. If you can work with a librarian as a collaborator in your work, if you can help her understand the intrigue and the power of your research plan, you can expect to get **e-mails** at random moments with some amazing resource that you'd never have thought of on your own. And you'll have another intelligent friend to share ideas with, and to commiserate with over the inevitable periods of feeling stuck or inadequate. I've never seen a librarian listed as a **coauthor** on a paper, but I can certainly imagine the circumstances where that would be fully warranted.

Mm

Master's degree. What is a master's degree, anyway? In some professions, the master's is the threshold to professional life and certification: architecture has the M.Arch, fine arts has the MFA, finance and management have the MBA, religion has the M.Div, and so on.

But the undifferentiated mass degrees, the master of arts and the master of science? They don't lead to a creation of knowledge or advancement of the field; they often don't require much in the way of independent thinking at all, being mostly just a further array of coursework. The master's gives you a chance to pursue a different "major" than you did the first time, and marks you as an even more diligent student than your BA or BS colleagues (having reached the 10-percent threshold of national educational attainment, rather than the 30 percent or so of the US adult population who hold bachelor's degrees). The master's degree may be a necessary step on the path to a PhD; many doctoral programs only allow entry to master's grads. In my case, I went right from undergrad to my doctoral program; I just had to take extra coursework compared to my master's-holding friends. I could have organized my credits in a way that got me a master's degree along the way, but chose not to.[116]

The US Bureau of Labor Statistics shows that in 2012, having a master's degree is correlated with higher income and lower unemployment than

116. Many programs encourage the en route master's degree so that you "won't leave empty-handed" if you wash out of the doctoral program. It's kind of like having a reflective blanket and some drinking water in the trunk of your car in case you get lost.

that of persons having only a bachelor's degree.[117] You need to consider your own professional context and investigate whether a master's degree will likely improve your pay or placement; engineering, for instance, seems to financially reward the master's.[118] A master's degree usually gets you an automatic pay raise in K–12 teaching, and might qualify you to teach in a community college. But given the debt burden you're likely to incur, I'd avoid most MA or MS programs without a high likelihood of financial payoff. They're a middle ground: beyond a college degree, but not really part of academic life.

Mentor. Think of your remarkable intellectual talent and your body of knowledge as a highly refined fuel. It's densely loaded with potential energy, but when handled wrong, it's just an inert bucket of liquid. In order to ignite your fuel, you need to mix it appropriately with the surrounding atmosphere, and you need some kind of an ignition source.

You're responsible for refining the fuel. This book is my attempt at providing the atmosphere. And your spark has to come from a mentor.

We use the word "mentor" sloppily. Teachers can be mentors, but often aren't. Supervisors and employers also can be mentors, but often aren't. Parents and older relatives can be mentors, but often aren't.

A mentor offers useful and reliable guidance to the norms and practices of a culture. She's the person who tells you which fork to use, how to get your work in front of an agent, why you don't applaud between movements of a symphony and how to tell when it's *really* over. In short, a mentor is someone who helps you gain welcome entry to a community that matters to you.

Here's a different metaphor. A mentor is the tugboat captain who helps the ship's pilot navigate the unfamiliar waters of a new port. A little nudge starboard to stay in the shipping channel; the knowledge that pier 12 isn't wholly stable and doesn't want to be approached sideways; all the little as-

---

117. As has been true for a long time, getting the PhD is good but not great for your employment and income prospects; the professional degree is where it's at. United States Department of Labor, Bureau of Labor Statistics, "Earnings and Unemployment Rates by Educational Attainment," accessed May 5, 2015, http://www.bls.gov/emp/ep_chart _001.htm.

118. For instance, starting salaries in the American Chemical Association's 2011 survey. Susan R. Morrissey, "Starting Salaries," accessed May 4, 2015, http://cen.acs.org/articles /90/i23/Starting-Salaries.html.

sists that allow the high-powered, heavily laden ship to come in easily to a place it's never been before. Without that tug and its captain's knowledge, the big ship is just as powerful and just as full of treasures; but it's going to get hung up on a bar or swept into a bridge abutment because of simple ignorance of local conditions. A mentor provides that local knowledge.

Mentors explain unseen pitfalls and find hidden opportunities. Mentors make connections between their students and their own professional **networks**. And it's not enough to say, "You should send your work to my friend at USC." No, a real mentor sends an **e-mail** both to her student and to her friend at USC, introducing them to one another and explaining why they'll enjoy one another's thinking. She takes them both out for a drink at a **conference**, and fosters their conversation. Students' success is part of a doctoral adviser's job, and good mentors take it as seriously as they do the classroom and the **dissertation** draft.

If you find someone nearby who you think is capable of being a mentor to you, share an entry of this book with them and ask for local examples of the broad definitions I'm offering. If they're a real mentor, they'll laugh about it, take you by the shoulder, and start telling you about all the secret handshakes in use and the loose stair treads to avoid.[119] If they don't have time, if they think you should just focus on your work, they're not going to be mentors in the most necessary way. Move on, and don't try to get blood out of a stone; there'll be others. Your **dissertation chair** doesn't have to be your mentor— nor does your dean, nor does your research supervisor. Mentorship often comes from surprising corners: an **administrative assistant** who's seen it all, a **librarian** who deals with enough grant-based **lit reviews** to know how your college wants proposals written. Listen, be humble, soak it all in. There is no unnecessary knowledge in any culture, and academia's knowledge is held in many offices.

Meritocracy. Ha. That's funny. Tell me another one.

Malcolm Gladwell's book *Outliers* is a necessary corrective to our com-

---

119. I got married a few years ago to a Jewish woman, which came as no small surprise to my Midwestern Protestant family. In so doing, I've picked up bits and pieces of Yiddish expression, which brings no small amusement to my wife. One of the most apt words I've learned, one that doesn't quite have a simple translation, is *mensch*. A *mensch* is a person who's kind, who has integrity, who's easygoing—a good guy. Just saying the word brings a sense of fondness and warmth toward the person to whom you're referring. That's the core trait of a mentor, I think: just being a *mensch*.

mon conception of meritocracy.[120] The general cultural story is that there's a nearly mathematical formula for success, which has two components: talent and hard work. If you do something for which you have a lot of talent, and if you work harder than those around you, you're assured to be successful. Gladwell's great service is to say that there's a missing variable: that success equals talent plus hard work *plus opportunity*. And he fills that book with stories of hockey players born in February, computer magnates born in 1955, and why a sixth of the richest people who have ever lived on earth were born in the 1830s.

I don't want you to waste your talent and your hard work because you didn't have the opportunity to learn some things about the landscape of higher education that would allow your talent and effort to find purchase. Your PhD, no matter how good it is, is a form of lottery ticket that allows you to be entered in the drawing for a **tenure-track** faculty position. But in the lottery, the more players entering the game, the bigger the prize pool. In the academic job market, the number of qualified players is continually rising, and the prize pool of tenurable jobs is at the same time continually shrinking. Most of those new **doctorates** are smart and hardworking, just like you. And only a small percentage will find tenure-track positions.

Let's check this. There are about fifty thousand PhD degrees granted by American universities each year, up 20 percent in ten years,[121] and about twenty thousand hires for tenure-track faculty positions.[122] So assuming that you're in a field of average competitiveness, you'd think that your odds of finding a job are about 40 percent. But of course no, because you're also competing against the hundreds of thousands of PhDs who didn't get hired last year or the year before that or the year before that—or against those who took positions with low-ranked schools while intending to go back on the market for more suitable positions, or those who took positions with high-ranked schools and have been denied **tenure** there. Your odds are, frankly, poor.

Talent is a given, and hard work is a given. I'm assuming that of you. They're not universals, but they're hardly uncommon. So if you have two of

120. Malcolm Gladwell, *Outliers: The Story of Success* (New York: Little, Brown, and Company, 2008).
121. National Science Foundation, "Science and Engineering Doctorates: 2011," accessed April 29, 2015, http://www.nsf.gov/statistics/sed/2011/data_table.cfm.
122. American Federation of Teachers (Higher Education), "American Academic: The State of the Higher Education Workforce 1997–2007," accessed April 29, 2015, http://www.aftface.org/storage/face/documents/ameracad_report_97–07for_web.pdf.

the three traits, how do you manufacture the third: opportunity? You have to become known in your field. You have to be productive, and have senior friends who can guide you through the weeds to the good fishing spots. You have to have advocates who are excited about your work and your potential.

As the old saw goes, it's not what you know, it's who you know. Or, more accurately, it's *who knows you*. If someone is eager to receive your application, you'll have a potential different from that of someone whose PDF comes through the Human Resources e-mail portal. "Oh, yeah, I met her at a **conference** last fall. She did a great **presentation**." Now you're a potential asset, unlike the dozens of anonymous arrivals who are seen as obstacles to ever getting the search completed.

But although I can advise you how to play your best, like teaching you to count cards in a casino, I can't stress this highly enough: you may do everything right and not win. There is no mix of actions you can take that will absolutely assure your success. There are lots of things that can assure failure, sure, and let's avoid those. But the notion that you can guarantee a great outcome? Nonsense.

And can I be blunt once again, and self-incriminating at the same moment? Yes I can. Let me borrow liberally from the philosopher Joe Jackson:

Pretty women out walking with gorillas down my street.
From my window I'm staring while my coffee grows cold.
Look over there! (Where?)
There goes a lady that I used to know.
She's married now or engaged or something so I'm told

Is she really going out with him?
Is she really gonna take him home tonight?
Is she really going out with him?
'Cause if my eyes don't deceive me,
There's something going wrong around here.[123]

It's not a trait I'm proud of, but I think of some nontrivial number of people I know in tenure-track positions, and I think to myself: "Really? *Him? Her?* Really?!" And I think of the roughly two-thirds of all instructional personnel at US colleges who are neither tenured nor tenure-tracked, and about

123. Joe Jackson, "Is She Really Going Out With Him?" on his debut album *Look Sharp!* (A&M/Polygram Records, 1978).

some of my brilliant colleagues who deserve to work at Stanford or Penn but have somehow stalled as long-term contingent instructors at small professional colleges. I know from direct observation that academic meritocracy is a hoax.

According to the National Center for Education Statistics, in fall 2010 there were about 415,000 persons with academic rank (**professor, associate professor**, or **assistant professor**) employed in American colleges and universities.[124] The rest of us with PhDs (about 1.5 percent of the adult population, or roughly three million people) are retired, working in higher ed **administration**, working in other kinds of employment, or hoping hoping hoping for one of the 415,000 to die or quit from the right field at the right moment so that we can invest in yet another ticket to the academic Powerball.

If you are among the 415,000, please reflect for a moment on your good fortune, and use this book to think of specific strategies you can employ to help your students to join your ranks. If you are among the larger number on the outside looking in, please know that you are not a diminished person, not a lesser thinker, not a failure. You are the uppermost tier of the higher education world. Anyone who can successfully complete a **dissertation** from a solid university is playing at the top of the field; there just aren't enough spots on the team, and your capabilities haven't matched one of the existing gaps in service that you happened to know about. This is not your fault. Try not to second-guess yourself. Try not to fall prey to helplessness and despair.

This is not about your **career**. It's about your life. You can have a good life without the career you'd imagined when you were eight, or eighteen, or twenty-eight. Be ready to be fluid, don't make it an all-or-nothing game in which you stay on the market for a decade of bitter self-doubt.

If your work is good, take pride in your work. Recognition is often outside your control, but the character of your **research**, **teaching**, and writing is not.

Method/methodology. Our language is afflicted with post-fit words having to do with compulsive behavior, and we have been subjected to the terms

---

124. United States Department of Education, National Center for Education Statistics, Institute of Education Sciences, *Employees in Postsecondary Institutions, Fall 2010, and Salaries of Full-Time Instructional Staff, 2010–11*, accessed April 29, 2015, http://nces.ed .gov/pubs2012/2012276.pdf.

workaholic and *chocoholic* and *textaholic*. And I'm discouraged every time I encounter one of these words, because it's such a shoddy construction. The suffix *-ic* makes an adjective out of a noun: *anorexic* means struggling with anorexia, *spastic* means suffering from spasms, *nostalgic* means colored by nostalgia, and *academic* means reflective of academia. So an *alcoholic* is someone afflicted by alcohol. Simple enough, right? But I don't have an addiction related to my love of chocohol, and that kid with the overdeveloped thumbs doesn't have an addiction to textahol, and your boss doesn't expect you to dedicate yourself to workahol. If you base your whole life's worth on how hard you work, you'd more accurately be "workic," which looks and sounds terrible.

I think that our fancy with the word *methodology* is much the same. It just sounds important, and feels nice to say. But of course, the suffix *-ology* means "a body of knowledge," as in biology and pharmacology and philology and musicology and theology. So *methodology* should rightly be a body of methods, an understanding of the array and theory of methods that one might use in one's field. It's a *system* of methods, a collective to be understood. Individual people and projects employ their *methods*; to question someone's *methodology* is not to question what they did, but rather to question their understanding of appropriate research methods in general.

This is akin to someone saying that they're working on a **grant** rather than a *grant proposal*: you'll hear it all the time, but that doesn't make it right. Please, help stop the madness; don't talk about your methodology.

Now, since we're talking about research methods, you may think as a stellar undergraduate that you're ready to jump right into your **dissertation**, that it's just a longer and more thorough job of the papers you wrote as a junior and senior. Trust me, young novice; you know nothing of the methods of your field. If you're in the laboratory sciences, you need to understand lab books and instrumentation and sample purity and materials acquisition and measurement techniques and lab safety. If you're in the quantitative sciences, you need to understand a broad array of statistical techniques and, more importantly, understand how to select the right statistical tool for the interpretation you're attempting to employ; just understanding the math, already hard enough, is far from sufficient. If you're in the qualitative social sciences, you need to understand techniques for interviewing, observation, participatory research, record keeping, and double-entry field notes. If you're in the historic or literary fields, you need to understand the different ways of reading a text, its author, its time, its precedents, the mode and circumstances of its creation, and its sponsorship or patronage.

And it's not enough to have read through these things and studied them well enough to pass an exam. You have to practice them so thoroughly that they come to hand instantly when needed. Even though I'd read a lot of interview guides, I was unbelievably bad at interviews for at least two years. There's a musicality to research methods, the technique put into service of the art, that can't be learned through anything but repetition. "She looked like she learned to dance from a series of still pictures," said Elvis Costello;[125] and so will you until you get some soul in your methods.

Crazy as I am, I took three methods courses in architecture, one in anthropology, and one in history. And I use them all. If you have electives to spend in your doctoral program, you cannot go wrong spending them on methods courses in adjacent fields. You'll build your repertoire, and you'll learn how those other folks think.

Minority preference. The anthropologist John L. Jackson, Jr. argues in his book *Racial Paranoia* that in contemporary life, where overt racial barriers are illegal and overt expressions of racial prejudices are discouraged, racism holds its continued power largely through operating inside our own heads; we create readings of situations that stem from our own presumptions about what the other person or group intends.[126] We act not merely on the objective facts we see, but on all the hidden interpretations we instantly bring to those observations. Jackson argues that the only way for us to get beyond those paranoid readings—on any front—is to be honest about what we perceive to be happening and what we're feeling about it.

The facts of personnel selection are always secret, as they should be to protect the privacy of those involved. But in higher education, whether in grad school admissions or **faculty** hiring, the stakes are high and the criteria are intentionally vague. Programs are looking for a "good fit," and the makeup of that fit is only partially about one's intellectual prowess. Put another way, you have to have the goods in order to be considered; but there will be a pool of folks who are judged to have the goods, and after that point, the decision is based on the preferences of the hiring community—preferences that may be invisible even to them, and which may only emerge through their deliberations.

Decades of those tacit preferences about "good fit" resulted in an

125. Elvis Costello, "Satellite," *Spike* (Warner Brothers, 1989), audio CD.
126. John L. Jackson Jr., *Racial Paranoia: The Unintended Consequences of Political Correctness* (New York: Basic Civitas: 2008).

American faculty that was largely white and male, and who started their faculty careers in their late twenties and early thirties. Individual **departments** would never admit—or even recognize—that those preferences were part of their deliberations, but the overarching demography of higher education seems to indicate that they were in play.

Many white and male candidates believe that the advantage has since swung in the opposite direction, and that a woman or a person of color will always have the hiring advantage in a small pool of qualified candidates. The University of California system has done interesting research about this from its own five years of hiring from 2006–7 through 2010–11, comparing the percentage of tenure-track hires by gender to the national creation of new PhDs by gender.[127] The findings seem to suggest that gender bias in favor of male candidates, at least, is still operational in hiring:

- In life sciences, 48 percent of all PhDs were awarded to women, but UC hires were only 33 percent female.
- In math, computer Science, and engineering, women received 18 percent of PhDs and got 4 percent of the jobs.
- In the physical sciences, women received 25 percent of the PhDs and got 29 percent of the jobs.
- In the humanities and social sciences, the new docs were 53 percent female, but women got only 41 percent of the new hires.
- In education, women earned 64 percent of all new PhDs and got 67 percent of the new jobs.
- In the professions, women received 45 percent of the PhDs and got 29 percent of the positions.

So in education and physical sciences, women got a very slightly disproportionately higher number of the new jobs relative to their numbers in the marketplace, but the discrepancy was not so glaring that we can imagine some vast feminist hiring conspiracy. In the other four realms, the historic male bias persisted in pretty substantial proportions. Taken as a whole, the supply of relatively fresh PhDs in the United States was about 42 percent women, but the UC System hires were two-thirds of that amount, at 29

127. University of California Office of the President, "UC Tenured Faculty, New Appointments 2006–07 to 2010–11 & Academic Availabilities (1990 to 2004 National Doctoral Degree Recipients) Universitywide," accessed April 29, 2015, http://www.ucop.edu/academic-personnel/_files/newhire_tenuredgender.pdf.

percent. It seems that women continue to face greater odds in tenure-track hiring, and that the "*of course* they hired the woman" gambit isn't based in the empirical world.

How about ethnicity? Looking at the same system's hires over the same time, and using the same methods, here's what they found.[128]

- In life sciences, 19 percent of all PhDs were awarded to minorities, UC hires were 16 percent minority.
- In math, computer science and engineering, minorities received 26 percent of PhDs and got 26 percent of the jobs.
- In the physical sciences, minorities received 18 percent of the PhDs and got 9 percent of the jobs.
- In the humanities and social sciences, the new docs were 15 percent minority, but they got 25 percent of the new hires.
- In education, minorities earned 19 percent of all new PhDs and got 16 percent of the new jobs.
- In the professions, minorities received 18 percent of the PhDs and got 23 percent of the positions.

So it seems that hiring biases related to ethnicity are somewhat relieved, especially when compared against biases regarding women; overall, the national pool of recent PhDs was 18 percent minority, and UC tenure-track hiring was 22 percent minority—a pretty decent match.[129]

Admittedly, this data is only from one academic system, albeit a very large, very important one that is politically committed to equity in hiring; if we were going to see "reverse discrimination," we'd expect to see it at UC. Part of the dilemma we face is that good numbers aren't easy to come by. But really, the lack of data on gender, ethnicity, sexual identity, social class, and other candidate characteristics is just a small part of the larger fact that from the outside we have no idea about what goes on within the

128. University of California Office of the President, "UC Tenured Faculty, New Appointments 2006–07 to 2010–11 & Academic Availabilities (1990 to 2004 National Doctoral Degree Recipients) Universitywide," accessed April 29, 2015, http://www.ucop.edu /academic-personnel/_files/newhire_tenuredethnicity.pdf. Note that these numbers only include US citizens and permanent residents, not international PhD recipients or hires.

129. When the category of "minority" is reduced further to "underrepresented minorities"—Native American, African American, and Chicana/Latina—the UC system-wide hiring is 9.5 percent, compared to a national pool of 8.6 percent; essentially a wash.

sealed gearbox of grad school selection and faculty hiring. We don't know
how many applicants there are for a given spot, and we don't know what
their qualifications are, so we can't assess for ourselves whether our not
getting a job has been due to the general talent in the pool, a typo in our
cover letter, the spilled salad dressing on our tie in the interview dinner
with the search committee, or the fact that we're white, black, female, male,
old, young, straight, LGBT, tattooed, not a veteran, or what have you.

As people with PhDs, we're trained to be analytical—to gather as much
data as we possibly can, and to interrogate it for pattern. We want to know
why some phenomenon or another has happened. But when it comes to our
own hiring, we're left with no information whatsoever except for the raw
binary outcome of getting or not getting a job **offer**. We put our intellectual
horsepower to work on interpretation anyway, because it's our strength, and
we can spin out some mighty interesting stories in the absence of empirical
data.

Here's some data. The job you want has 80 candidates, or 180, or 800. So
let's imagine an opaque jar with 180 marbles: 179 blue and one gold. You
want the gold marble, and you're now allowed to enter the drawing (already
a remarkable achievement, by the way; congratulations on that), so you
stick your hand in there and grab one. If you pull out a blue marble, you
can't reasonably intuit that you're an incapable marble picker, nor can you
presume that the game is rigged against you in particular. If you go to four
county fairs and draw a blue marble from four tubs, that's still a 98-percent
likelihood, but it doesn't *feel* like randomness, and you might start to believe
something about the game or about yourself that's unsupported by the data.
A false supposition is more comforting than no supposition at all, which is
what the current system offers us.

Nn

National search. When a college needs a new employee, they go about finding one in different ways. When they need a service or clerical employee, they advertise in the local paper, just like any car dealership or restaurant; nobody's going to move halfway across the country to work in some university's food-service operation. But when that college needs a **faculty** member or an **administrator**, it has a couple of choices: it can promote from within its ranks, or advertise broadly and see who emerges from what comes in through the mail. The goal of the national search is to make a position visible to thousands or tens of thousands of potential scholars, and through brute arithmetic to find the single best candidate in America for that work.

National searches imply the use of national media, most often the *Chronicle of Higher Education* but also *Inside HigherEd* and disciplinary **journals** (architecture schools seem to avoid the *Chron* in favor of the *American Collegiate Schools of Architecture [ACSA] News* and the *Journal of Architectural Education*, for instance).

There is a temporal correlation between the posting of a position and its prestige. Major research universities and renowned **departments** will start advertising in summer and early fall for positions set to begin in the subsequent August. By September through November, the state schools and liberal arts colleges start to advertise; by April, there's nothing left but community colleges and emergency limited-term replacements, feeding on the desperation of the starving herd.

These massive searches have several stages of winnowing. Let's say that Nobel MacArthur University is searching for an assistant professor of twentieth-century Japanese literature to join its faculty of award-winning novelists, poets, and literary theorists. They receive 489 applications. (These numbers are not hyperbole, by the way; there are **disciplines** in the humanities that routinely have more than 500 applicants for attractive positions. It's not unlike a hiring day at Walmart in some shattered industrial town, except there's no visible line around the block.) A **committee** has been established to read and review these applications—probably five or six faculty members; let's say six. Each reviewer will thus have about eighty applications to review; at ten minutes apiece, that's almost fourteen hours. So most of them get not ten minutes, but more like a minute each, during which badly formatted documents, **cover letters** with awkward sentence structure, applicants who have clearly misunderstood the nature of the position, and those with degrees from "nonrelated disciplines" are placed onto the very large pile of disinterest. The good ones get two minutes, and are placed onto a smaller pile to be reread.

So let's say that of our eighty applicants, we've put fifteen into that second pile. The other sixty-five people have wasted fifteen hours apiece in creating and submitting their application materials, a thousand hours of desperation and futility compressed into a stack of paper about half a foot tall. Five other reviewers have created similar piles.

Lesson number one, then: If you're not serious about a job, if it doesn't really speak to you, if you can't make the case for why it interests you and why you're the right person to do it, don't bother. Your life will merely flash before someone else's eyes before dying in the heap of neglect.

Lesson number two: if you *are* serious, your materials had better be formatted to perfection. They should be easy to read, and calmly and professionally attractive, using a coherent layout across documents. Don't give the reader any easy reason to neglect your good ideas.

Now, the fifteen applications that remain get their ten minutes each, in which the cover letters are read closely, and the **CVs** perused for quality of prior **publications** and **presentations**. (Teaching record? At Nobel MacArthur University? Please.) Those fifteen now become perhaps three or four about whom the reviewer can be an enthusiastic advocate. Of course, there are five other reviewers, each of whom also has three or four candidates, so we're still at about twenty live ones.

When the review committee meets after that round, the twenty will be discussed and winnowed down to ten or twelve that none of the reviewers is adamantly opposed to. And you will never know the basis upon which that reduction was grounded. This is the meeting at which the job description as written is amended into the job description that the search committee really wants, through an inductive and unspecified process of qualitative analysis regarding the applicants and their materials. Someone on the committee might be opposed to your interest in Japanese literature written since 1995; someone might feel as though your **coauthored** papers are a sign of intellectual dependency; someone might be excited by your secondary interest in Japanese industrial design. The passions and biases of the review committee, impossible to name in the posting (or even to predict), come out in full force at this moment of reduction.

Ten candidates remain, more or less. The dead will typically not be informed of their demise until after the hire has been made, and perhaps not even then. And if they are, the letter they receive will offer no hints of why their application was not advanced. In publishing, good proposals are often rejected by way of a brief personal note, saying that the **editor** didn't think it was right for the **publisher's** marketing plan, or that she didn't have a good audience for that genre. In academia, good applications that are rejected receive no feedback of any kind whatsoever. Number 11 gets the same content-free letter as number 489.

The ten left standing will each receive an **e-mail** or brief telephone call from the search committee chair, congratulating them and inviting them to participate in a **telephone interview** or **conference interview**. E-mail is increasingly common, since it saves the awkwardness of having to leave a phone message. (Do I tell your voice mail that you've made the cut, or do I just ask you to call me back?)

The phone or conference interview is a miniature version of the first read; of the ten conversations, four will become obvious, flaming wreckage within minutes of starting. The twenty or thirty minutes allotted will still be respected; it's not like an audition where you can get called off the stage within four bars of starting your song: "Thank you. Next." But the final eighteen minutes will be agonizing for all concerned. If you're on the phone, be grateful you can't see your interlocutors reading e-mail or doing Sudoku on their iPads.

But six of the candidates will be pretty good, and each will have her or his advocates among the committee. Six is probably too many for the university to afford to bring to campus, so the search committee will meet again to reduce the number of finalists to three or perhaps four. That meeting is difficult for all concerned, since each of the six might prove to be a valuable colleague, and could take the department or program in an exciting new direction. This is the meeting at which surprising alliances will be formed among the search committee members, teams of two or three reviewers who form agreements about particular candidates' unique strengths. Those candidates with a single advocate will be left aside.

Nobel MacArthur University will now pay the expenses for three or four finalists to fly to campus, stay in a moderately attractive hotel, and go through one to three days of **on-campus interviews**. Each of those meetings can kill you. If the **dean** isn't impressed with your research and **grant writing** agenda, you're dead. If the **department** faculty as a whole aren't impressed with your ideas and collegiality, you're dead. If your sample class wasn't interesting and well structured, you're dead. If you prove to be either boorish or shy at meals, you're dead. If your **presentation** drones on or your PowerPoint isn't loaded properly, you're dead.

One of the finalists will die extravagantly, almost certainly—will commit some blunder (or step onto a hidden local mine) that leaves him sprawled in his own entrails on the muddy ground. But it's quite likely that there will be two or three astonishingly good candidates in the end, each offering a different path for the department to take. At that point, the decision is about the future of the program as much as it's about the individual candidates.

If you make it to that point, congratulations. You're clearly at the top of your scholarly game. You may not have a job; runner-up is at least a 50-percent probability. And if you don't get the **offer**, you will never, ever know why your rival did. Try not to damage yourself or your surroundings when you read the glowing press release about your rival's hiring, the first time you will ever know his identity. Mourn for a while, go through all five steps of grief: denial, anger, bargaining, depression, and acceptance.[130] It won't help you to hear me say it until you get to acceptance, but if you had a campus interview, you really are that good. Get back in there and do it again.

Networking. I once heard a conference speaker, Gabrielle Foreman of the University of Delaware, explain my history of difficulty in professional life in two sentences. She said: "For **first generation** students and students of color, asking for help feels like begging. For more privileged students, asking feels like networking."

I have rarely heard anything as true as that. If you're a working-class kid, you're taught from the tricycle onward to figure it out yourself, to keep working, to suck it up and do it again and take care of your own problems. Nobody's gonna help you but yourself, and people in power are not your friends. And so you work, and you keep your eyes and ears open and pick up the information you need. There's no Uncle Richard who's going to get you the internship at the bank, no grandmother who pledged the same sorority at the same college as you, no dad who's the **provost** and has the e-mail roster of fifteen thousand names.

Friends, let me tell you this: The game is rigged, and the people who know people win. Always. So if you're going to play the game, you need to

---

130. This reference to grief is not merely a metaphor. You will grieve about not being hired. And it will take time, and a lot of support from friends and possibly professionals, to go through it and reemerge.

manufacture the same tools as your strongest competitors lucked into by birth. You need to know people, and those people need to know you. You need to be able to send an e-mail or pick up the phone and have the right person happy to reply.

Think of networking from the other end of your life span. If you were in your fifties or sixties and had a successful **career**, and one of your students asked you for career advice, would you turn her down? Of course you wouldn't. So it's okay to be the one who's asking. When you discover a particularly wonderful teacher, take advantage of her office hours once in a while—not just about your homework, but about your larger plans. Ask her to meet you for a coffee. Ask her which **journals** she reads, who her influences are, what her next big project is. Make it clear that if the project has space for a junior worker, you're available and interested.

When you hear someone say something smart at a **conference**, introduce yourself afterward and thank him. If there's not a mob around him, ask him a direct question of advice, framed around his own experience. "How did you start . . . ?" or "How do you choose between . . . ?" It ought to be a question you want the answer to, but it also ought to give the person the chance to talk about himself. He doesn't know your circumstances well enough to answer "How should I . . . ?" questions, but he'll be both flattered and capable of talking about himself and his choices.

If you're working in a support position putting on a meeting, if you're managing an organization's membership and mailing list, or if you're part of a research team with a senior practitioner, you have entry to a larger, more experienced, and professionally rooted community. Those people are in the place you want to get to. Find the ones you want to learn from, and ask them a specific question about their individual work or their career. You'll be embarrassed, sure, because you'll think you're the only person who doesn't know this stuff. But the generous people, the ones you want in your network, will be happy to reply. The nonresponsive ones will never be helpful anyway, so let their silence act as a warning.

Asking for help needs to be specific rather than general. It needs to be occasional (for any individual respondent) rather than constant. It needs to be confident and curious rather than panicked or narcissistic. And you need to learn how to do it. Start with the people you trust most, and be honest about the fact that it's hard for you to do. They'll coach you through it, and if they're really interested in you and your work, they'll make the next steps easier. They'll send you and your networking target a joint e-mail by way of introduction, they'll bring you to the right session at the conference, they'll invite you for a drink at the right time and the right place.

Hard work on its own is good for moral superiority, but for hard work to be effective, you need fertile soil: a community of potential colleagues who know about you and are eager to work with you. Networking is not begging; it's a vital way to learn the knowledge and the community that will matter to you. And that's why you're in graduate school, isn't it?

Oo

Offer.[131] I hate the concept of haggling, of asking if I might have a slight discount from the windshield price of that 2007 Civic. It feels Dickensian: "Please, sir, may I have just a bit of meat pie?" "Bugger off, urchin." And after your long journey as a student supplicant, you've been trained to be humble, to be grateful for whatever scraps of time and attention you receive from your betters, to bow and scrape and say "Yes sir" and "Yes ma'am" and to prostrate yourself.

But now you have a job offer. Get up off the floor, and don't automatically grasp at whatever crumbs are on display. The offer may be the only time in the next six years that this college will overtly express a desire for your presence; you're not going to get this kind of pure compliment once you're in the building as an **assistant professor**. Thus, the offer and its subsequent negotiation are the most advantageous moments you'll ever have to set the expectations for your support.

We think of a job offer as mostly having to do with salary, and salary *is* important, but an academic job offer entails a bewildering array of components, many negotiable. (Make sure, by the way, that you keep a personal copy of every single thing you sign.) Any college worth the name has a **faculty handbook**, a statement of the mutual requirements of institution and individual. The moment you get an offer, download or request an

131. First off, if you're reading this entry because you *have* a job offer . . . holy crap! Dude, you completely rock! Congratulations times four million! *Woohoo!!* OK, back to work.

electronic copy of the faculty handbook, and study it as if your comps are tomorrow.

Your offer letter and the faculty handbook together will include some or all of the following:

- *Salary*. You've heard of Google, right? Google "new **assistant professor** salary" and your prospective institution. The offer they've made didn't come from nowhere, they're not trying to cheat you, but have a look and see what's happening in other **departments** in your division. You might get them to come up as much as 10 percent; since your starting salary is the baseline for all subsequent annual increments, it's worth the request. If they can't do it, they can't; let it go.

- *Contract length*. You can see the entry for **contracts** for more details, but you should know whether your prospective school is offering you research summers or the expectation of full-year engagement. Likewise, you should know the timetable and sequence of steps leading toward **tenure**, which may be negotiable if you have prior tenure-track academic service at another institution.

- *Benefits*. These are less likely to be negotiable; they come as a package, managed by human resources and not influenced by a **chair** or **dean**. Common benefits include health insurance, retirement contributions, access to gyms or health centers, and life insurance. Make sure you know what the benefit package entails and when it kicks in; your employer's retirement contributions might not begin until the second year, for instance.

- *Office*. Probably also not negotiable, since it's managed by a **facilities department**. But you can at least know whether you'll have a solo **office** or a shared office, and it's possible that you might get to choose between those two conditions.

- *Start-up costs*, such as computing and software, or experimental or fabrication equipment. Your department made you a job offer explicitly because of your research excellence; they know what you do, and they know more or less what it costs to do it. If they expect high research productivity, they're prepared to equip you for your success. You should be thinking about research costs even before the offer comes, so that you have a well-reasoned request in hand. That request will probably take the form of a dollar amount with a few key items specified, rather than a detailed shopping list of parts and pieces; but you have to have that detailed shopping list to make the overall request. If you've received an offer from a **teaching**-oriented school, though, they're not going to be interested in or able to afford costly experimental equipment, and they won't expect your **publication** record to be the same as that of someone from a research-intensive school; the start-up available to you will be vastly lower. (See the separate entry on **start-up costs** for a little more detail.)

- *Intellectual property agreements.* If you invent or publish something with economic value, your prospective employer will claim some proportion of that value. If you create a course, your prospective employer will claim some degree of use or ownership rights to its content. For the most part, this is a nonnegotiable, unless you're a real star in your field. If you're going to be worth hundreds of millions of dollars in pharmaceutical licensing fees, you can probably negotiate your share upward; the university might be happy to take a slightly smaller proportion from a massive pot. For the rest of us mortals, just shut up and sign it. (Again, there's a separate entry on **intellectual property** in this book that might be helpful.)
- *Moving allowance.* Since this is a one-time cost, you may have a little bit of room to negotiate over this one. If you have an extensive or complicated household, or if you have a piano or a pool table, or if you're moving a huge distance, you might be able to get the baseline threshold raised. The moving allowance will almost certainly take the form of a postmove reimbursement, so save every single receipt related to your move, and be prepared to submit an extensive expense report once you're in. If you're comfortable enough to have a Ferrari collection that needs relocation, you probably ought to contribute to your own move; but if you live more or less like most people, your new school should get you to the new job. It's important to note that the allowance is a one-time offer, so think carefully about finding your first place to live after you accept the job. If you move into some plywood palace expecting that you'll move again after your first year, your college won't assist you with that next relocation, even if there is money left below the allowance's ceiling from the first move.
- *Housing assistance.* That caveat aside, some colleges own a small amount of near-campus housing—usually small detached homes or rowhouses, less often apartment buildings—that they make

available to incoming faculty, visiting scholars, and so on. It's nice enough ... and it's usually below market rate, walkable to school, with quiet neighbors. Like the freshman dorms, faculty housing might make a usable landing spot while everything else in your life is in flux. Aside from physical building stock, some schools are equipped to support you with low-interest home loans if you decide to buy a home, and that offer will not expire after your first move.

- *Immigration assistance.* If you're a citizen of another nation, you already know far better than I do how complex US immigration laws can be. The human resources office at your prospective college will have experience supporting international scholars, and will usually provide the legal support to get you and your **partner** and kids into appropriate immigration status. If they can't provide this assistance, they had no business offering you the job.

- *Partner and family assistance.* If your partner is on the civilian job market, wearing one of the standard collars of pink, blue, or white, he'll be on his own with regards to employment in your new community. But if he's a fellow academic, and if your prospective employer wants you badly enough, it's just possible that they might find appropriate work for your **trailing spouse** as well. (You ideally should have raised this possibility during one of your **on-campus** meetings with a **chair** or **dean**.) This negotiation is going to take some time, because it's going to involve everyone up to the **provost** to make it possible; new faculty lines don't appear all that easily. Along with work for your partner, the college may offer free or reduced tuition for your kids; there may be faculty child care; and if your college has an education program, it may run or partner with a "lab school" that your younger kids might have access to.

- *Memberships and travel costs.* Most departments have a set allowance for membership in **professional societies** and for **travel** to their meetings. But it's like start-up costs: if they knew when they made you the job offer that you're part of the team working on the Large Hadron Collider, they'll understand that you have to get over to Switzerland every few weeks. If your professional life necessitates extensive travel, and your offer's been made on the basis of continued scholarly excellence, they'll get you where you need to be.

Just because all of these things are negotiable, though, it doesn't give you license to be a Donald Trump pain in the ass. They like you right now, and this is not a time to make enemies. Here are some thoughts to keep in mind, a sort of decision-making flowchart.

First, is the offer on the table acceptable? Could you have a good life for a few years with what they're making available? If so, that's great; everything you might request from here is just a gloss on a good start. Push for 10 percent on a couple of things, but don't be a jerk, and take the job already.

Second, if there's one thing that's insufficient in the offer but which you believe to be nonnegotiable, name that and accept everything else right away. If you absolutely have to have some particularly outfitted lab to do your research, starting without it means that your entire assistant professorship will be hindered. If you absolutely have to have immigration assistance for your husband, starting without it means more or less surrendering your marriage. So if there's one thing that's absolutely not going to work, make that clear, and tell your prospective employer that everything else is just fine, so that you can both focus on the sticking spot. But don't be tempted to give up something that's not connected; it's not a board game. If your prospective employer says, "OK, we'll handle the immigration, but we'll reduce your salary by ten thousand dollars a year," say no thanks. Otherwise, it's the start of a relationship that will always be marked by unnecessary drama.

Finally, there's the big question, the dirty little secret of academic life, the question you're never, ever supposed to ask: Do you really *want* this job, in this place, with these students and these colleagues? You're supposed to be so grateful at having been brought into the mansion that all other considerations of life happiness are off the table. And you know the odds; having cheated the hangman once, do you want to go back out there again? But friends, I've taken a couple of jobs while consciously ignoring all of the blaring alarms and warning lights, and they've been miserable experiences. A tenure-track job offer is a proposal of marriage, at least a six-year commitment that all parties hope extends to thirty years or more. If it's good, there's nothing better. If it's bad, it's all-consumingly bad, in ways that other kinds of work relationships rarely entail. I've had a colleague say, in regards to his college's underperforming students, "Oh, all our new faculty want to kill themselves their first year here." The unspoken next sentence is that after that first year, they lower their expectations, drink more, and become cogs in the mediocrity generator.

The job offer is not merely about your job. It sets the conditions for your life in crucial ways. Don't automatically say yes without careful reading and real deliberation of your (and your family's) desires.

Office. Graduate students occasionally get a shared office with one or two other colleagues; in less affluent **departments**, they get a gang office where twenty-five or thirty will sit in a warren of desks, sharing one phone, one printer, and three or four networked computers (you have a laptop, right?).

Offices are often linked to a role rather than a person. If you become a **teaching assistant**, you might get office privileges, because you'll be holding office hours with your undergrad students. If you become a **research assistant**, you may get a desk in the research program's office. But as an undifferentiated member of the proletariat, you'll be remanded to the bullpen.

The bullpen can actually be a lot of fun. There'll always be people in there ready to commiserate or to laugh with you over the crazy reading you just finished. There'll be more senior students to coach and offer warnings, and less experienced students looking for your advice. At its best, the group grad office is a familial, funny place.

Don't expect to get any work done there, though. You need to stake out someplace quiet where you can read and write without distraction or interruption. The library may have carrels or study rooms you can reserve; there may be a chair and a desk back in the closed stacks to which you can get access. And of course you might be able to set up your home office to give you that quiet concentration, if you can convince the rest of your family to leave you alone when you need focal time (which will be both frequent and extensive).

More senior faculty often don't consider this, just as K–12 teachers don't, but not everybody's home is conducive to study. If you're one of six kids in a small apartment and the TV's always on and mom has a succession of not-very-stable boyfriends, the concept of "homework" fails on multiple levels. So too for graduate students, who often live on meager incomes (or loans) and somehow just can't dedicate that third guest bedroom to an office. Your home office may be your laptop, your backpack, and a wing chair at Panera Bread.

Once you become a junior faculty member, your office takes on another role—not merely focused garret or grad-student group home, but a place from which you can exercise hospitality. We hear all the time about some successful person or another who "just wants to give back"; as a faculty member, one of the ways of doing that is the welcoming chair, a cup of tea, and a casual place where your students and colleagues can come to test ideas or admit that they're overwhelmed. Being a good host is an underrated capacity in higher education, and one that is just as crucial here as it is in any community. We are engaged in social, emotional work, not merely forebrain intellectual exercises; fostering connections and emotional well-being will set you apart from your colleagues, and will make your workplace healthier and more engaging.

Office hours. Civilians really don't understand the concept of office hours, because civilians go to the office at eight-thirty and stay there until five o'clock. During those hours, they're paid to be in their office. That's office hours; pretty simple. But, as with so many things, that's not how we roll in higher ed.

In academia, **faculty** members are expected to hold office hours for somewhere between two and four hours per week; let's say Tuesdays and Thursdays between one-thirty and three p.m. During office hours, students can expect to just drop by and find their professor available for conversations. So (your uncle might ask you), "You're in class for nine hours a week, you're in your office for three more, that's only twelve hours a week, and for that they pay you sixty thousand dollars and insurance? Where the hell are you the *rest* of the time?"

Well, if you're wise, you're in your lab running an experiment, or in the archives finding research material, or away from campus altogether and writing another academic paper. Thinking does not survive interruption, and if you're in your office you will be interrupted, guaranteed. The world of **scholarly activity** requires a selfish attitude toward time, only bits of which can be grudgingly frittered away on student contact outside of the classroom. It's bad enough when the **department** chair asks you to be on another **committee**; you sure don't want to give away more time voluntarily.

You'll see more on this idea under the entry on **teaching load**, but the notion that students can just drop in on their instructors and chat is a nostalgia rarely applicable in the contemporary academic landscape. There are at least two reasons for this. First, both students and faculty are more mobile and have more allegiances. The student working a full-time job and squeezing classes around work won't be on campus to ask questions, and the **adjunct** instructor who's busy driving from one school to another to patch together a living won't be on campus to answer those questions. Second, even faculty at "teaching-focused schools" are under increasing pressure to be academically productive, so the hours they might have spent in their offices they now spend away, doing their own research and building their **CV**. A student who stopped by to hesitantly discuss a possible shared interest won't bolster the faculty member's credentials, though that possibility of changing lives is ostensibly the reason why we're all working in academia instead of in some research think tank somewhere.

And office hours can change lives. I was an undergrad at Berkeley, working on an architectural history paper on the Trelleborg Viking camps of tenth- and eleventh-century Denmark. I stopped by my student mailbox and found a note reading something like, "I'd like to talk about your research paper. Paul." I didn't know who Paul was—he was not my instructor, or my **TA**, or any of the other students I knew—so I decided for some now unknown reason that the note must have been left by Paul Groth, a cultural geographer teaching in the landscape architecture department who was interested in things like barns and roads and thus, presumably, the military encampments of the Middle Ages. I stopped by Paul's office one afternoon, and though he hadn't left the note, he was curious about the *Danevirke* and the Jutland peninsula, and we talked about the movie *Babette's Feast*, which had been set in that region. After an hour I thought both that Paul was a pretty good guy and that this scholarly life stuff was even more pleasurable and wide-ranging than I'd imagined. That mistaken reading of a scrap of paper, and the office hours that came from it, were the first germination of my intellectual desires.

So please, if you can bear it, extend your office hours beyond the three or four per week mandated in the faculty handbook. Much of it will be spent answering more e-mail, but you never know who might unexpectedly appear before you, waiting for his life to be opened anew.

On-campus interview. You've done a great job so far. You've survived several sets of winnowing, from two hundred applicants to fifty considered, to fifteen interviewed by phone, to four invited to the school. Quick statistics question: What are your odds now? Yes, that's right, they're still only one in four.

"On-campus interview" is shorthand for multiday event, just as "decathlon" is shorthand for having to be really good at ten dissimilar athletic events conducted over the course of two days. Here are the events that may be part of your on-campus interview.

First, there are all of the logistical arrangements you'll make with **administrative assistants**: booking your flights, reserving your lodging, transporting yourself to and from the airport. If you come off as a prima donna or as completely indecisive, news of your demeanor will travel through formal or informal channels to the committee.

You will have an opening dinner the night before your formal events, usually with the members of the hiring committee. Ostensibly, this is an opportunity for you to settle in and get comfortable before your grueling interrogations. Don't believe that for a second; this is in fact the first of those interrogations, and one that sets the tone for your entire visit. There'll be far more chit-chat than there will tomorrow, more about your flight and the weather and all, but most of the conversation will still be about your intentions and attitudes toward the job. Eat lightly (and neatly; linguine with red sauce creates about a 95-percent chance of looking sloppy at some point over dinner), drink only if your hosts begin, and then only a single glass of wine. No beer, which is gauche even if it *is* an Otter Creek Black IPA; no girly cocktails; none of that regionally microdistilled gin you always wanted to try; just wine. If your hosts suggest buying a bottle of wine, accept their choice, even if reds give you a headache. No dessert unless every single person at the table decides to indulge; if so, a small dessert or coffee, not both. This moment of dessert or coffee is the most relaxed you'll see your colleagues for the coming days, and you might be able to probe a little more about the position and the **department** in ways that might be really useful tomorrow.

Next morning, set two alarms: yours plus the hotel wake-up call. Be clean, be ironed, be ready twenty minutes before the car comes for you. You will now have some combination of the following: interview with the full **department** faculty, interview specifically with the department **chair**, interview specifically with the **dean** of your division, interview with faculty senate leaders, interview with **director** of **sponsored research**, interview with undergraduate students, interview with graduate students, public scholarly **presentation**, sample class. Most of those venues will be polite and engaged, and will give you a chance to interact genuinely; occasionally, you'll run into an interviewer who takes this as his opportunity to be hostile or confrontational. Defuse that with nonviolence. Refuse to defend yourself or your research choices, and instead ask him about what kind of scholarly work he finds most valuable. All he really wants is a chance to feel important, so let it be about him instead of being about you. He'll waste a few minutes of the hour, but so what; you'll come off as a star by not mud wrestling with the local pig. (If the hostile party is the dean or the ongoing department chair, beware of taking the job. If it's another member of your prospective department, you'll just know who not to hang out with if you get the **offer**.)

Let's take a moment to examine two of the events more closely. The scholarly presentation is your chance to really shine, both intellectually and socially. You have the floor, you have an uninterrupted thirty minutes, you have the props and the prompts ready. You're going to do four things here. You're going to impress upon your audience the freshness and importance of your research topic; you're going to convince them of the rigor of your approach to the topic; you're going to make it apparent that you can extend this line of inquiry well into the future; and you're going to demonstrate that you fit the culture, whether stuffy or folksy, earnest or ironic. They don't really want to know about your research; they want to know about *you*, and you're using your research talk as a way to portray yourself.

The other unique event is the sample class. Most often, one of the search committee members will be the regular instructor, and you'll be assigned to teach the class session on the day you're in town. The students may have been told of your pending arrival, or may not. They may have been assigned something of yours to read, or may not. (If so, they may have read it, but likely not.) The class may be a small seminar of twelve students, a standard efficiency pack of twenty-five, or a lecture of a hundred or more. You should ask about the circumstances, ask what the students have been most interested in recently, and get a copy of the syllabus. When you arrive, regardless of the group's size, you might consider treating the session like a seminar. Your best **teaching** will come through helping students learn something themselves, enabling them to consider and reconsider a problem, so come in with a set of good framing questions and do your strongest facilitation.[132] You want the students to shine, and to leave excited; the observing members of the faculty will notice. It also clearly displays a second skill; if you lecture again, that's just a repetition of the abilities you already showed at your scholarly presentation.

If there are enough events, you'll be scheduled for another dinner with a different group but the same rules, with you once again as the grilled main course, and with some combination of trials held for the second day. Bring a full change of clothes, including shoes and jewelry; you should be wearing nothing on day two that you wore on day one except your watch and your wedding ring (if applicable). In your briefcase for both days, only the following: extra copies of your **CV**, **research agenda**, or other application materials; your business cards, and the ones you collect from others, in two identifiably different containers; reliable pens; a fresh legal pad or Moleskine journal; a small canister of Altoids or TicTacs; a small canis-

132. My favorite seminar-methods book is still Michael Strong, *The Habit of Thought: From Socratic Seminars to Socratic Practice* (Chapel Hill, NC: New View Publications, 1997).

ter of your preferred pain reliever; and a package of hand wipes or a well-sealed zip-close bag with a damp washcloth. If you have a laptop or tablet computer, you probably won't have the opportunity to use it during your series of events; consider leaving it behind at the hotel. Your phone should be silenced but on; you may get a call or text from someone on campus, and you don't want to miss a connection or schedule update. Check it discreetly between sessions, and don't spend any time on personal calls, texts, or **e-mails**.

You may get a few minutes between one of these events and the next, or you may not. I was once interviewed in an extraordinarily humane way: two days of sixty-minute conversations separated by twenty-minute breaks, where the interviewing teams came in succession to one conference room and I was given a small temporary office in the same suite. I have also been interviewed in an unbroken sequence of sixty-minute conversations, each in a different building, with no gap time between interviews, so that my campus host was always escorting me into the next group five or ten minutes late—a whole sequence of bad first impressions. Be opportunistic about your use of the bathroom, and drink a little less water than you normally would, just in case.

At the close of the events, reiterate to your hosts how exciting and intellectually invigorating your time on campus was, and that you're looking forward to the possibility of working with them. Chat brightly in the car with your escort on the way to the airport; get through security in plenty of time to get on the plane, regardless of local reassurances that "our airport is really small and casual." Only in the gate concourse can you loosen your tie and have a beer or something messy to eat.[133]

Once you're home, wait a day or so, and then send a follow-up e-mail of gratitude, individually, to each of the people on campus with whom you spoke at any length. The messages may share much of their text in common, but each should have some tailoring to its individual recipient: a line or two on something that person said or some aspect of her research that you found interesting.

If you do all of those things correctly, if you hit every mark in the decathlon, your odds will have increased from one in four to one in three or even one in two, because it's almost a certainty that one or two folks won't have done these things. But even if you've done a great job, you're now utterly at

---

133. Even there, you might run into a member of the search committee on her way to a conference, so maybe wait until you're home.

the mercy of people who are talking about you behind your back. Their goals and their needs are going to intersect with your personality and your abilities (and those of the other finalists) in ways that are entirely out of your control. As Martha Graham once said, "What people in the world think of you is really none of your business." You've done your part and done it well. Good luck.

Online journal. I had a friend, now deceased, who made her living by creating and selling crochet patterns. It wasn't an extravagant living, but it kept her in food and gasoline and bought her a small house. Toward the end of her life a few years ago, though, that income dried up, because the market for crochet patterns had evaporated. Why spend five dollars on a pattern at the fabric store when you could almost certainly download it—or at least one like it—for free?

The same logic holds true for **intellectual property** of all sorts. We increasingly believe that writing and music and video just ought to be available. And one would think that for academic publishing, free access should be especially easy, since academic publishing has always worked on the same model as Twitter and blogs and the *Huffington Post*—unpaid writers giving their ideas away. Academics, it was presumed, were paid by their home institutions to teach and to do research, and that research was intended to be freely available to the broader scholarly community. The **journals** themselves were once published by the scholarly societies as a service, and subscription rates were relatively low. But, as always, capital seeks new markets, and thousands of journals were bought up by a few commercial **publishers** who have successfully monetized the process. The academic publishing houses organize **peer reviewers** and **editors**, compile and print the selected works, and distribute the bound objects to libraries for an annual subscription fee ranging from high to outrageous; from there, the research can be consumed by other scholars. The **authors** remain unpaid, occasionally even paying "page fees" for the privilege of publication, even as the publishers record vast profits.

In recent years, there have been several attempts at **"open-access"** scholarship, in the mode of Wikipedia, in which anybody could publish online without the mediation of a publishing house, and the cream would just rise to the top. These have not been successes, at least in part because **tenure** committees still reward publication in the big name peer-reviewed journals. Publishing academic work online is generally seen as being merely one step above a blog, worthy of little if any recognition.

It may be that in a few more years, there will be online means of academic publication that are held in high regard. If you value your **career**, you won't be on the forefront of making that happen, publishing your work out on the bleeding edge of academic acceptability. And this represents another way in which academia supports stasis. It ought to be the established scholars, the ones who have tenure and thus academic safety, who push back against the power of the journal publishers and work to create new public-access scholarly venues; but those are exactly the **faculty** who've made their bones in those old venues, and who are now set to become the editors of exactly those journals. They've got nothing to gain, except for freeing their institutions from hundreds of thousands of dollars of journal subscription fees and supporting the next generation of scholars. Where's the payoff in that?

Here's a model. The American Association of Colleges and Universities[134] could establish an **endowment** that would allow it to either launch new journals or buy back long-standing publications. It could end up with a stable of tens of thousands of online journals across the full range of academia, and charge lower subscription rates because it wouldn't have the paper distribution costs or the high profit motive that currently interferes with intellectual transmission. Authors who publish in the AAC&U journals wouldn't get paid, just as they don't get paid now; however, their *libraries* would receive a proportional subscription discount for every article published by one of the school's faculty members; let's say one hundred dollars per published paper. This would allow all colleges to benefit by eliminating the substantial profit margin in the publishing system. In addition, the major research universities (who already subscribe to far more journals and pay millions of dollars for subscriptions) would get significant contributor's discounts on their library periodical budgets, while smaller, teaching-centered schools would get smaller discounts. This would bring economic benefits to the colleges that support the most productive researchers, a direct and measurable return on investment that schools could recognize and publicize.

Until such time, though, you're part of a culture that adheres to the existing model. Violate it at your peril.

Open access. The easier it is to access a full paper online, the quicker it'll get used and the more often it'll be cited. You can make that happen by

---

134. For instance. Or, frankly, the US Department of Education, though that would be (gasp) socialism.

publishing in an open-access **journal**. As opposed to the subscription model in which the reader-subscriber pays for the journal, open access makes journals free to readers and charges the **author** a publication fee. (*You*, the hapless author, have already given it away for free in either case; now you can pay the journal a thousand bucks or more to help them give it away too. As they say in some neighborhoods, "Nice little research ya got there ... be a shame if anything happened to it.") Institutions that do lots of **sponsored research** often contribute to their scholars' publication fees, and you can budget for it in the direct costs of your **grant** if your research is externally supported.[135]

There are hybrid forms, of course. There are journals that are closed-access for a certain "embargo period," so that subscribers get first use, after which the electronic files are made public. There are journals that allow authors to personally distribute their work to colleagues, but not in the same formatting; it can't "look like" the journal's page layout. And there are journals that have significantly reduced peer-review standards, or none at all. As always, you should investigate the impact factor and selectivity of any journal in any format that you're considering.

Your best ally in figuring all of this out might actually be your **librarian**. Libraries are at the center of the global debate about journal costs and who bears them, since it's college and university libraries that pay the greatest proportion of academic journal subscriptions. Librarians are typically big fans of open-access publishing, since they want to be able to steer their patrons quickly and efficiently toward the best information, whether it's a part of their own holdings or not. So it's likely that they'll be up to date on the latest developments in open-access publishing, and that they can guide you through the "gold option" (author payment for publication) or the "green option" (standard subscription models that also allow you to archive or distribute your own work), and help you navigate the legalese of publisher websites.

135. Open access, though it sounds lovely, is yet another way to rig the game against adjuncts and independent or nonaffiliated scholars. Nobody's going to help those folks pay to play. Most adjuncts get library access as part of their contract, so they've typically been able to take advantage of college resources in locating scholarly literature. Shifting the economic burden onto authors, rather than onto subscribers, will eliminate some of the utility of that small consumer benefit while adding an impossible hurdle to adjuncts' participation as producers.

Pp

Partner. I'm an old guy now, with a lifetime of language use behind me. So even though I'm an advocate for gay marriage (and, as a justice of the peace in Vermont, have officiated at one), it still sounds funny to me when one of my colleagues talks about her wife, or when my friend talks about his husband. And of course, there are familial relationships of all sorts, from friends with benefits to long-term unmarrieds to polyamorous tribes. So let's just use the word "partner" to cover all of the relationship permutations.

Being the partner of a doctoral student or new hire has numerous and poorly considered implications.[136] There are microspatial implications, with the home office and vast file of photocopied articles being necessities in ways that the dining room or guest bedroom are not. There are mezzospatial implications, such as choosing each year's vacation by merely extending one's trip to the national **conference** by a couple of days: "Look, honey, after this year's trip to Irvine, next year we'll be in Kansas City!" And of course there are macrospatial implications, such as when the academic partner gets an **offer** from the University of Alaska–Fairbanks. I once interviewed an aspiring musician who had moved from rural northern California to the San Francisco Bay area. She was preparing to move again. "In this business, there are only three cities that matter: Los Angeles, New York, and Nashville." You go where the work is.

There are emotional implications, the calming of fears and the insistence that it's time to get off the computer for a while. There is the soothing after a failed interview, the reassurance of capability and desirability in the face of recent evidence otherwise. There is the political planning of departmental strategy, the testing of ideas with an intelligent layperson.

If you get a faculty position, your partner becomes the faculty wife, regardless of gender. If your partner is a white-collar professional, she will be welcome at the cocktail parties and potlucks; if you host one at your own home, she'll be expected to be the good hostess, regardless of her **career**

---

136. This entry is focused on relationships in which one partner is an academic and the other is not. For relationships in which both partners are academics, see the entry on the **two-body / two-career / trailing spouse problem**.

status, while you do the subtle political work that marks any "casual gathering" of like professionals.

If your partner's collar is pink or blue, he'll never be taken seriously as a member of your social group. He will always have to decide whether to come to the gathering and be supportive while being ignored or patronized, or to stay home and have you be the guy whose partner never participates.

Your partner will always be the one presumed to have time to take kids to gymnastics or to the doctor. Any mention of your own responsibility for your kids' well-being marks you as less than a serious scholar.

Being the partner of an academic is not unlike being the partner of a professional baseball player. She's uprooted for a new city at a moment's notice; her partner is always in danger of not getting promoted to the major leagues, or not staying once he gets there. The bad days at work are very public and require a lot of reassurance; the good days at work fill him with adrenaline that takes hours to come down from, with stories that must be retold. There aren't many days off from the training regime; and when camp opens every season, she's not going to see him for awhile.

Peer review/reviewer. A fundamental rule of research in higher education is that faculty judge the work of other faculty, and that it takes a scholar to recognize the scholarly quality of someone else's work. So peer review is the uppermost standard of scholarly recognition; it implies that established members of your **discipline** have found that your work has been competently conducted and makes a meaningful contribution to the field.[137]

Ideally, peer review is conducted "blind," or with the identities of **authors** and reviewers not known to one another. The goal is that the work is judged only on its content, not on its author's prestige. But in small fields, it's apparent from content or style who's written something. In my own field, there's one **department** with four faculty members who have done variants of the same study a dozen times or more in new locations. I may not be able to tell who the lead author is on a particular version, but I know that it's come from that program and I know that I'm tired of reading it

137. It can also lead to an ossification of disciplinary norms, wherein senior researchers struggle to understand the importance or relevance of new modes of theory and interpretation, and thus reject novel approaches to scholarship. As Thomas Kuhn has pointed out, intellectual paradigms change slowly, and they require the generational change of a community's membership to fully take hold.

again.[138] And the **editor** certainly knows from whom a piece of work has come, and that may influence her decision on whether to review it at all. Your name can get you published with minimal review, or it can keep you off the review docket altogether.

All academic endeavors rely on volunteer reviewers. Faculty members are asked to serve on doctoral committees for students from other departments or schools, conference organizers review dozens of submittals for **presentations,** the department's faculty review applications from prospective graduate students and prospective new colleagues, and established scholars act as reviewers for academic journal papers and funding agencies. In just the past three years, I've reviewed about forty manuscripts for journals and another three hundred **abstracts** for conference participation, forty or fifty graduate school applications, a couple of hundred student **portfolios** for progress to their next curricular segment, and another two hundred student abstracts for a national **undergraduate research** event.

I don't have time for any of that, but I try to make time, because it's how the enterprise works. That workload, however, limits the degree of subtlety I can bring to any individual review. If there's any lapse of clarity in one's argument, if the **methods** aren't presented methodically, or if the researcher can't convince me that the work is important, I'm going to be cranky—and you *do not* want a cranky person making a decision about whether or not you'll get published. If the work seems important and well argued, then I'm more than willing to put a few hours into close reading, offering diagnosis of smaller problems and suggestions for improvement.

For a book or journal article submittal, a reviewer will offer a written commentary directly to the author, as well as a second set of comments to be seen only by the editor. Usually, there's also a scalar judgment, ranging from "Accept as is" to "Accept with modifications or significant changes required" to "Unlikely to be acceptable even with revision." The editor bundles these comments and sends them along to the authors, along with her own decision. If the decision on your submission is to ask for revisions, you should celebrate (briefly), because your manuscript is not dead on the floor somewhere. But then study the comments, and revise carefully. You may be asked to submit, along with your revised manuscript, a comment sheet that responds point by point to each of the reviewers and discusses what you've

138. There are a lot of one-trick ponies out there. It reminds me of the old line, "I love his book, and I read it every time he writes it."

done to address their concerns (or why you believe that a particular concern is mistaken, or that the point they've raised is covered somewhere else).

Ultimately, academics live and die on their reputations among their colleagues. Even entire colleges go through **accreditation** reviews that are conducted by "a jury of their peers." This means that if you intend to do innovative work, you have to conduct yourself in a nonthreatening, respectful way. You have to demonstrate how your work follows in the tracks of the prior generation, even if it doesn't; you have to have precedent to draw upon, and that precedent has to be respected by the people reading your work.

Placement. I'm working on a novel in which one of the characters is about to go to a doctoral program. I looked at various **rankings** of grad programs in the relevant **discipline**, and visited the programs' websites so that I could write about my character's pending experience with some background. One of the **departments**, a nationally elite program housed in an **R1** university, showed the placements of its 2014 graduating **cohort**, a very successful and high-horsepower group of six new PhDs. Those six students all got positions immediately, as one might expect from such a great program. But wait: only one got a **tenure track** faculty line, and the other five got ... **post-docs**? The year before that, five grads—one TT line, three postdocs, one visiting scholar. Postdocs are fine and all, but they're neither **faculty** jobs nor guarantees of jobs; they're temporary shelter (and another line on your **CV**) while you stay out on the market. The program's glowing 100-percent placement rate suddenly looked pretty tenuous.[139]

One of the key pieces of data that you absolutely must know before selecting a doctoral program is its detailed and complete record of placement for graduates in the past five years or so. It should be easily available, either from the department's website or from the department **chair** directly. If the department doesn't have that data, it's not following through with the obligations of its program, simple as that. (Placement data is a lot harder to collect for undergrads; there are lots and lots of them, they scatter to the winds the day after commencement and don't reply to e-mail from the alumni office, and they haven't developed an intimate and ongoing relationship with specific advisers. In a doctoral program that graduates half a dozen students a year, collecting and maintaining this data is easy, and

---

139. My fictional character, by the way, doesn't know this yet. Won't *she* be surprised to find out!

ought to be a reflex.) If the department has the data but won't give it to you, I would suspect the worst.

Before this book went to press, it went through **peer review** by two anonymous colleagues in higher ed. They made several suggestions that improved what you're reading, but one of the things that simultaneously gratified and depressed me was their utter, wholehearted agreement with the numerous times in this book that I've recommended against an **interdisciplinary** doctoral path. And their exhortations to avoid intellectually appealing but **career**-endangering programs put me in mind of a legal doctrine known as *attractive nuisance*. The idea is that if you own a piece of property that is both enticing and dangerous (the most commonly used example is an unfenced swimming pool), you should be held liable if some child is injured or killed in it, even if the kid was trespassing and had no permission to be there. One of the core principles is that kids don't realize the risk involved, and that innocence places an extra burden on the property owner to take strong measures to keep them out.

Well, kids, I'm here to tell you that some doctoral programs may well be attractive nuisances. They're enticing, whether because of their purported convenience or because they study some urgent, real problem through a gloriously intelligent intersection of **methods** that will never take root in any of the intellectual monocultures that we call **disciplines**. And I've done my best in this guide to help you recognize their dangers. But someday, somewhere, an enterprising legal mind will take up the principle of attractive nuisance, and the game will be on.

Plenary.[140] The Latin vocabulary arises once again, from *plenus*: full, complete, greatly crowded.[141] A plenary session at a **conference** is one that has no competing sessions scheduled at the same time, so that theoretically everybody at the conference can attend. A conference can have more than one plenary, but typically only one *keynote*, which opens the conference and ideally sets the intellectual agenda for the rest of the event.

140. This does *not* rhyme with "canary." Accent on the first syllable: *PLEH-nuh-ree.* Faculty often complain that students can't spell, but that's because young people have grown up in auditory environments—TV and music and live teachers—and they don't have an immersion in seeing words on pages. On the other hand, I have read millions of words, but because I spend all my time reading, I don't have any friends, and thus don't know how those words are pronounced.
141. My friend Dennis Munk offers an alternative etymology, in which *plenary* is Latin for *time to check your e-mail.*

A plenary speaker is only sometimes hired for the quality of her speaking; more often, she's "important" in some way that benefits the conference host. She may be a public official or corporate leader who has supported the organization in the past, or whose future support is desired. She may be asked to give a talk as part of being honored with a career or service award. She may be a "big name" whose primary function is to sway the undecided to register for the conference. In any of those cases, the talk itself might be completely fabulous, but that's not why she has been asked to speak.

My suggestion for attending plenary talks is to sit at the aisle near the rear, hope for the best, and prepare for the worst. The talk will be well amplified and will usually have one or two large projection screens for the PowerPoint, so even at the back of a huge auditorium or banquet hall, you'll have good access to the material. And if it's a terrible droning bore, as far too many academic speakers are, you can cut out after ten minutes and go for a walk. They're not taking attendance.

Popular press / trade press. When I think of the major **intellectual** forces of public life in my lifetime, I imagine people like Jane Jacobs, Jean-Paul Sartre, Simone de Beauvoir, Rachel Carson, Joan Didion, Susan Faludi, Betty Friedan, Martin Luther King, Paul Goodman, Vaclav Havel, and James Baldwin. They wrote largely for the general public, rather than for a disciplinary audience, and they were not academic professionals.

If you're in academia, you have to remember that your **career** prospects are determined solely by what other academics think of you; the "peers" of peer-review are others engaged in university life within your **discipline**. So a paper published in a middling **journal**, read by a hundred other scholars and cited by six of them, will be worth far, far more toward your career advancement than a newspaper or magazine story read by tens or hundreds of thousands. Rachel Carson's culture-shifting books *Silent Spring* and *The Sea Around Us* have been cited broadly in academia, but they themselves were never published within the frameworks of academic publishing; the same is true of *Slouching toward Bethlehem* and *Backlash* and *Against Interpretation* and *The Second Sex* and *The Death and Life of Great American Cities* and *Growing Up Absurd* and *The Fire Next Time*. All of these books are far more daring, wide-ranging, beautifully written, and publicly influential than the stuff that lives in the journal bubble.

As an early-career scholar, though, your **CV** entry for popular-press **publications** mustn't be too large (maybe not even more than one item). Too much public writing indicates to academic reviewers that you're not serious about your work, since you're wasting time and energy rather than developing more peer-reviewed papers.

My first **mentor** toward graduate school, the cultural geographer Paul Groth, once wrote a moving essay called "Tithing for Environmental Education."[142] In it, he proposed that persons with some knowledge about how the world works actually have a responsibility to share that knowledge with a broad public.

> Each of us with the ability to see the local environment has a duty to teach that ability to some part of the public. Setting aside some time every other week—tithing—could get the project started.... We must teach a way of seeing the built environment as an ever-changing quilt woven by our group experience of social, political and historical forces all within the realities of the bioregion.

If the work we do matters in the world, we shouldn't sequester it behind the locked portcullis of the academy. But public scholarship is perilous for junior members, and Paul's call for a tithing of our time for public awareness has gone largely unheeded in the face of academic reality. That's one of the reasons why I've left academia; I wanted my time for projects like this book, in which I could talk to the genuinely curious, rather than the captive audience of a handful of colleagues.

Portfolio. In other sections of this book, I have implied that your applications for grad school or **faculty** positions will have two components: the **cover letter** and the **CV**. However, if you're in the studio or performing arts, you'll also likely be asked to submit a portfolio of your work, and the portfolio is as weighty a concern as the other two.

A portfolio is not merely a visual collection of your best completed work; that's just a catalog. Instead, you're using the portfolio as you use everything else in your application: to portray yourself as a thinker in your field. What kinds of problems interest you, and how do you attempt to engage them? You're narrating your thinking visually, showing not merely the finished object but also its development or its underlying concerns.

As a student applying to grad school, you include more process work, since you're applying for a position in which the sketch, the diagram, and

142. Paul Groth, "Tithing for Environmental Education: A Modest Proposal." *Places* 7, no. 1 (1990): 38–41.

the study model are what you'll talk about most often. This leads toward organizing projects chronologically, starting with your older work and coming to the newer. Within each individual project, chronology also reigns, from a description of the given problem through early analytical steps toward understanding context and constraints, the gradual development of a concept, and the emergence of that concept into final form.

As a professional applying for a faculty position, you'll offer a little less of that background work; your readers assume that you're competent at getting from blank page to completed object, and would like to see more of the range of ideas you're capable of engaging. So your projects might be organized thematically. A public-art sculptor, for instance, might show a few projects that address community history, accompanied by an overarching statement about how local history informs her work. Then she might show a few projects that were driven primarily by a response to the site, and discuss the ways in which she conceives of physical and social context. You know the categories your work fits into; make sure that you're using the language of your **discipline** to describe them, and take charge of the way we read you.

And you really do have to take charge of how you're read, with all of your documents, because they'll be read on the first pass in almost no time whatsoever. For instance, in major architectural competitions, there might be just as many entrants as there would be for a faculty position, and each entrant is judged only on how it's portrayed on a set number of a set size of posters (or, in the trade, "boards"). Thus they're "read" at a blinding pace; the concept of "reading" work is almost a meaningless term at this speed, and should really be replaced with "evoking the viewer's prejudices." Here's the landscape architect Martha Schwartz discussing her experience of a first reading of design competition entrants:

> At first we went through every one in about ten seconds. That's awfully fast. But by the time we started getting into it, we realized that we could see whether or not there was any merit in a project in even less time. We actually got it down to about five seconds.[143]

Each of those entries was at minimum two boards, twenty by thirty inches each, comprising a dozen or more drawings and explanatory text

143. Quoted in Jack Nasar, *Design by Competition* (Cambridge: Cambridge University Press, 1999).

and hundreds of hours of construction. Consuming them in five seconds apiece—or even a more leisurely and considered ten seconds—is merely an exercise in visual preference, not unlike a focus group for a new Doritos logo. "Nope ... nope ... that one's interesting ... nope ... nope ...."

This offers an important lesson for the designer and artist. When you ask your peers for their considered feedback, you often encourage them to take their time, to discuss it, to sit with it and see what questions or ideas emerge. But it's equally important to find reviewers unfamiliar with your work, give them your portfolio and two minutes to flip through it, and ask for their immediate impression. That's how they'll be read by competition juries and faculty hiring committees.

Postdoc. The sociologist Hugh Klein once wrote an enlightening paper on how we have historically created more and more "stages of life," based on the exigencies of the economic system around us.[144] Where in agricultural and hunting communities there were essentially babies and workers, there is now an accumulation of stages based on the knowledge needed for independent craft or farm life (childhood), successful factory employment (adolescence), and the "information economy" (young adulthood and the ubiquity of college). Our economy is such that it's just not viable to be married and independent at age nineteen any more, so college is a norm at least in part to defer adulthood until one's late twenties, when the new couple can have a couple of jobs and some economic security. Besides, all those young people in college and grad school aren't counted in the unemployment statistics, which makes the numbers tolerable.

The postdoctoral position plays a similar role in higher education. The current system of lean operation means that there just aren't enough open positions for permanent **faculty** to absorb the number of doctoral graduates, thus creating Marx's "reserve army of the unemployed." Like any army, this one is dangerous and must be mollified. So we tell all those **adjunct** teachers that their service is appreciated and will one day pay dividends, and we also develop adjunct researchers, highly educated laboratory assistants who do the labor of managing major work while the credit goes to their **tenured** faculty sponsors. In the laboratory sciences, it's not unusual to string together one postdoctoral position after another, "postdoc" now

144. Hugh Klein, "Adolescence, Youth, and Young Adulthood: Rethinking Current Conceptualizations of Life Stage," *Youth and Society* 21, no. 4 (1990): 446–71.

being an expected stage of life after baccalaureate and **doctorate** (and ideally before **assistant professor**).

The Office of Research Integrity at the US Department of Health and Human Services has developed nine categories of what they call the "responsible conduct of research" or RCR—one of those categories is the **mentorship** of trainees and postdocs.[145] But as in any relationship, the exact degree of effort and reward is always negotiable and always open to question. And being a bad mentor is not going to disqualify a scientist from future funding the way that plagiarism and fake data would, so the RCR is just a toothless nudge to the lab directors to play nice.

We have this notion that if you're smart, work hard, and wait your turn, you'll get your due. But the world is not so linear, and the economics of higher education are such that temporary employees offer enormous benefits to the institution. So let's be clear. The research postdoc gives you experience. It gives you **publications**. It gives you recognition. It gives you hope. It may not give you an academic **career**.

There are also **teaching** postdocs, such as the one I held at Duke University's Writing Program for four years. The basic logic, funded by a major foundation, was that we would come in and teach first-year writing courses under a particular (and well conceived) pedagogical model, and then move on to take this newfound commitment to academic writing with us into our early faculty careers, spreading the practice of revision like Johnny Appleseed. That postdoc gave me teaching experience and confidence, a lot of good colleagues, an income that was marginal but included health insurance, four years on the **CV** that didn't fall under the category of "nonrelated experience," and the opportunity to participate in a couple of major **assessment** initiatives that led directly to my **administrative** life. It opened no doors to the faculty—at least in part because I was forty-eight years old when I completed it, rather than thirty-two.

If you're considering a postdoc of any kind, you owe it to yourself to investigate its publication, **authorship**, and **intellectual property** practices, and what the previous holders have gone on to do. Is it a launch pad for industry or faculty careers, or a scrap yard that gets a little more service out of those destined for rust?

---

145. United States Department of Health and Human Services, Office of Research Integrity, "Responsible Conduct of Research, General Resources," accessed May 4, 2015, http://ori.dhhs.gov/general-resources-0.

Poster / poster session. During my first year of grad school, we were told that the **department** would cover a (very small) portion of our travel to the national **conference**: $100 if we were just attending, and $150 if we were presenting. Even in 1992 that didn't go far, but it was a nice gesture for their students. I was asked by an alumna of the program to be part of a session having to do with history and the built environment; she didn't get much more specific about it, but since I'd just come from an undergrad focused on architectural history and cultural landscape study, I figured I could wing it until more information arrived. She said something about a poster, which of course I assumed was the flyer on the wall outside our event room. So when the associate **dean** came by to find out how many of us were presenting, I told him that I was on the poster. I guess I was thinking, you know, like the movie star whose name comes above the title. He looked at me somewhat quizzically, but he allotted me $150 rather than pressing the issue.

As it turns out, of course, I was entirely mistaken about the concept behind this session. At major conferences, there are several different kinds of **presentations**, including the individual paper, the discussion panel, the workshop, and the poster session. The first three all involve people sitting around, talking and listening as some body of ideas is presented. The poster session is just a big room—sometimes a dedicated gallery space, sometimes the hall where the refreshments are served during breaks—where researchers display large-format posters of their research projects and findings. The poster session is typically reserved for the display of single experimental or quasi-experimental projects, or for session proposals that didn't quite make the cut to be assigned to an attended room. So a poster session didn't mean my work was important; in fact, at this particular conference, it meant exactly the opposite.[146]

The tradition of the poster session comes from the physical sciences, in which the poster acts as an abridged version of a paper, getting data and findings out quickly. There's a big title, an **abstract**, a brief setting of the problem, **methods**, data (including tables, graphs, or diagrams), conclusions, and a bibliography. It turns out that this works terrifically well for

146. I've since served on conference organizing committees that offered the opportunity to present posters to conference proposals that either missed the mark of the conferences or seemed otherwise not quite right. For lots of organizations, conference registration represents a huge proportion of their income, and those who present are more likely to register (and have their expenses paid by their home institutions) than are those who are merely attending.

the physical sciences, since the full-scale paper might only be two to four pages long, and the paper-to-poster compression ratio might be less than two to one. But imagine having a single poster, four feet by three in size, to portray a meaningful summary of your analysis of the nonfiction of David Foster Wallace as read through Heidegger's concept of *gelassenheit*. First off, your paper's probably sixteen to twenty-four pages long, so the compression ratio is going to be well over ten to one. Secondly, your work is meant to be considered, pondered, savored slowly; the poster is just a billboard to be observed as you go by on the freeway.

Outside the laboratory sciences, poster sessions tend to be kind of sad affairs, like a junior-high dance where everyone stands stiffly in their nicest clothes and hopes that someone comes over to talk to them. Each presenter is stationed next to his attractive graphic board on its easel, a stack of full papers ready to hand out to the eager throngs of excited scholars … and then watches forlornly as the important people walk by on their way to get drinks and canapés.

Presentation. I often hear the common belief that lectures are "less effective" learning environments than seminars, labs, or other "engaged-learning" modes. And that may be true, given how poor most people are at lecturing. But I had the sublime experience of taking architectural history at Berkeley with the late Spiro Kostof. Spiro came to the United States originally intending to study drama and theater, and that background served him well in academia. Twice a week, four hundred of us crammed into Dwinelle Hall to watch a seventy-five-minute lecture of stunning clarity, daring connections, and great humor.[147] Students brought their friends or visiting family members to class, and he was rewarded with a great ovation at the end of the semester.

There's a reason that the recorded TED lectures have gotten more than a billion views in six years. Large presentations have a theatricality about them that must be acknowledged. You're in the front of the room, standing; the others are seated and facing toward you. You speak; they are silent. You can move; they sit still. You control the slides, the lights, the props, the topic, the pace. It is, for a brief time, your room.

147. You can watch Kostof's lectures, too. University of California, Moffitt Library, Media Resource Center, "Spiro Kostof Lectures: Architecture 170B, Spring 1991," accessed May 4, 2015, http://www.lib.berkeley.edu/MRC/kostof.html. They're a treat.

If you buy a comedy record or CD, you'll notice that even though it's usually a recording of a live performance, an unbroken hour or more of stand-up comedy, the recording will be divided into tracks just like a music CD, and each of those tracks—a few minutes long—has its own title. As a stand-up scholar, you must also divide your allotted time into specific "bits," sequenced thematic elements that allow you to energize the room, or to slow it down, or to return to an earlier idea. You don't just push "start" at 10:00 a.m. and push "stop" at 11:15; you divide those seventy-five minutes into six or eight big elements, each of which is its own scene. Listen to comedians or famous speeches, and you'll hear specific approaches to subdivision, pacing, and repetition. And you'll hear a lot more silence than you're expecting. You don't need to fill every single second with your voice. You know the phrase "hanging on her every word?" You get that by leaving them time to hang, to anticipate.

I often hear colleagues on their way to conferences talking about writing their PowerPoint on the plane. Please don't. If you're going to speak at a **conference**, you absolutely must know how much time you have allotted to your presentation, how the technology works, and whether your slide template and your font are stable across brands and generations of software. I was at a conference years ago with ninety-minute sessions, each of which had three presenters. You might think, based on simple arithmetic, that each presenter would plan on something like twenty-five minutes of talk followed by five minutes of questions. The first presenter had numbered her slides 1 of 47, 2 of 47, and so on; at thirty-five minutes she was on slide 3, and the moderator firmly called her to a halt.[148] Don't do that, either. Practice your talk, know how long it takes, print your script or notes in 18-point type and 1.5-line spacing so that you can find your place quickly after making eye contact with the room, and staple the pages together so that you don't drop them and have an impromptu reordering.

Please remember that reading on a page is not the same as listening to words. You might change some of the sentence structures from the text

148. I was once at the presentation of a dissertation proposal in which the student had no idea how to frame her remarks. She had gone on for an hour and ten minutes, unsuccessfully attempting to herd her ideas into some sort of cogent enclosure. Her dissertation chair finally interrupted her, saying, "We only have two hours, and several of us probably have some questions for you." Another committee member added, "And you haven't talked about your methods yet." At which point she turned gray, and vomited into a nearby trash can. Meeting adjourned.

version to the spoken version, making the syntax sound something more like the conventions of daily speech. The room will be filled with people who have come to see and hear you, not to read your words. Give them an experience worthy of their time and appropriate to the context.

President. The contemporary college president has four fundamental roles. She sets the intellectual or social mission that the school will pursue. She coordinates the senior leadership and makes major fiscal and strategic decisions in consultation with the board of trustees. She acts as the college's hood ornament, attending public functions and ceremonies, making nice with dignitaries. And she raises money. Although all of those are crucial functions, no one person is equally good at all four.

Major corporate boards hire CEOs to accomplish what the board sees as the next big strategic phase of development. The cost-cutting, belt-tightening CEO cleans house and brings the institution back from the brink. Then he's replaced by the growth CEO, who knows how to add relevant business functions through merger and acquisition. After a few years, he's replaced by the innovation CEO, who sees different market opportunities and helps to update the company brand.

College presidents are likewise not uniformly skilled at every possible aspect of the business of higher education, and good boards of trustees set the mission of the incoming president carefully. The growth president is probably not the same person as the intellectual mission president, and neither of them are the same as the strategic partnership president. The trustees have to take a hard-eyed look at what they believe the college needs next, and must find the president who can accomplish that; this may not be the president they currently have. As a result, the average length of service of college presidents is shorter than ever, at seven years, and more are coming from backgrounds outside higher education.[149]

As a doctoral student or early-career **faculty** member, you'll likely not have significant dealings with the president, and may not even be able to recognize him from across the street. If this is true, you probably have a decent president, because he's attending to problems at the correct scale, and you don't reach that scale. But presidents can fall prey to Louis XIV syndrome—*L'université, c'est moi*—and start to personalize and micromanage

---

149. American Council on Education. "Leading Demographic Portrait of College Presidents Reveals Ongoing Challenges in Diversity, Aging," accessed April 29, 2015, http://www.acenet.edu/news-room/Pages/ACPS-Release-2012.aspx.

everything they come into contact with. Every *Dilbert* cartoon featuring the pointy-haired boss represents the worst of what college presidents can be: petty, narcissistic, bullying, and oblivious to the actual nature of the work conducted around them. A good president, on the other hand, finds opportunities for the people around her to succeed, locates resources, rewards talent, accepts occasional mistakes (especially mistakes of exuberance), and gets out of people's way. I've known both kinds.

Presidents are constantly flattered, beset by hucksters telling them how smart they are and how they'll be even smarter if they partner with organization X or start program Y. There's a "shiny-object" problem that requires a powerful discipline to ignore. And ignore it the president must, for at least two reasons. One is that there has to be an intellectual mission that sets one college apart from its peers; a college that is nothing but an attic full of once-attractive knickknacks has only dust at its heart, and can never thrive. But the other reason why presidents have to have discipline is that they have power, and every public suggestion that a new program or a new initiative or a new partnership might be in the works will set dozens or hundreds of people into motion, whether planning for the new project's success or planning to thwart its implementation.

For the most part, you'll be deep in the academic ocean, well below the turbulent surface. But new presidential initiatives can have impacts even at your depth. If a new president's agenda is (or the old president suddenly decides) to define the mission in terms of public engagement, or to convert the reputation of your teaching-oriented school to an institution of higher scholarly attainment, the blast wave can travel through several layers of **administration**. The **provost** begins to implement the new mandate, giving each of her **deans** their orders; those deans then call together their department **chairs** and impart the new initiatives, and the chairs then return to their offices and let the faculty know the new rules of engagement. Typically at that level, someone will suggest calling a **committee** to explore ways of increasing public engagement in the department's **curriculum**, and peace will be restored; committees act as an institution's shock absorbers, preventing the sudden and shifting infatuations of the executive wing from having any noticeable impact in campus life.

Principal investigator / PI. On television and in the movies, the PI gets to drive cool cars, get into gunfights, and have pretty clients and molls mooning over him. Remember *Magnum, P.I.*? Jim Rockford? Sam Spade?

Well, in higher ed, the reality of the PI is somewhat different. The principal investigator is the lead researcher on a project, the person who takes the supervisory role and bears final responsibility for its outcomes. The **grant proposal** is submitted under the auspices of the PI, the PI gets primary credit for its **publications** or other **intellectual property**, and the PI is likely to be the one who gets some amount of stipend support from the grant's funding.

You'll occasionally hear something like, "Who's the PI on this one?" Remember that the PI isn't necessarily the project manager or the person doing most of the work. In bigger research **departments**, the PI can be the lab leader or **director** of a research group who coordinates across projects, touching any one of them only rarely. For small projects, the PI, project manager, and research grunt are all the same person.

Most funding proposals have their **authors** and teams clearly identified as part of the proposal content. This is appropriate, since one of the characteristics of a high-quality proposal is a high-quality team. But it also means that the PI has name-recognition value as well as capability value; a proposal from a PI with lots of federal funding can have a better likelihood of acceptance than a proposal from a lesser-known scholar, even if the big-time PI isn't going to have much role in the conduct of the research. So let the PI get the credit, so that you can actually get the work.

Priority/prioritization. The architectural historian (and my dissertation chair) Tom Hubka spent many years examining New England farm buildings as both an expression and a facilitator of farm life.[150] As part of his research method, he looked at household diaries of farm families to understand how they spent their time. What he found was that over the course of a year, both men and women spent about fourteen to sixteen hours a day at work—but within that consistency, there was enormous seasonal variation in the types of work conducted. Maple sugaring occupied eight or ten hours a day in March and April, dwindling down to three or four hours of cleaning and storing in May before disappearing for the rest of the year. Fence building happened when crop work didn't; woodlot management for men and canning for women took place in the winter after harvest. Both the men and women of Maine's farms were balancing ten or a dozen major

---

150. Most prominently in Thomas C. Hubka, *Big House, Little House, Back House, Barn: The Connected Farm Buildings of New England*, (Hanover, NH: University Press of New England, 1984).

functions over the course of the year, constantly shifting across tasks as the seasons made resources available.

Once you decide what your array of highest priority projects ought to be, you can set them into a seasonal array that allows them to come to the fore at the best time. That's one of the functions that the nine-month **contract** has always held; it was expected that you'd be away during the summer, conducting the reading and research that you'd spend the rest of the year analyzing and reporting on. Once classes begin, you're doing nothing but **teaching** and advising and **committee** service, so you'd better take advantage of those three months.

And of course, things will come up that aren't part of the big plan. Dwight Eisenhower famously differentiated between things that were *urgent* and things that were *important*. Higher education is filled with things that are urgent, and **e-mail** winds that urgency up to a high pitch. If you can shut off the e-mail server for a few hours a day, you'll surprise yourself at how many things you didn't really need to do after all.

You will never do everything you'd like to do. You will never do everything other people would like you to do. You will never do anything quite as well as you might like to do. So you're already off the hook, to some extent; you're going to be just like everybody else in terms of not getting all of your work done and your ideas expressed. For smart, attentive people, enthusiasms will always exceed capacity. My wife and I joke about the Post-It wall of pending projects. She or I will come up with some great idea—doing a *New Yorker* cartoon about Moses bringing commandments down to the cats, for instance, or developing a voter guide to the public offices and functions of our town of eight hundred people. Worthy projects, but not worthy enough to get to the top. So we create an imaginary Post-It with three or four words, call it Post-It project #947, and let it go.

Learning how to let go of potentially good work, how to say no to interesting opportunities, is the work of a life. Donald Hall, in his book *The Academic Self*, advocates for writing a statement of professional purpose every year or so, and using it to help focus your attention on the big goals.[151] And while I admire and believe in that approach, I think it's more rational than maybe our lives ought to be. So along with the statement of purpose, keep your Post-It list and look at it periodically. If one of those ideas seems

---

151. Donald E. Hall, *The Academic Self: An Owner's Manual* (Columbus: Ohio State University Press, 2002).

to keep calling you, maybe it's a project and not a momentary enthusiasm. It might not fit the frame of your overt purpose, but it may be important in a way that your conscious intellectual mind doesn't yet have language for.

Professional expenses. A study by the National College Players Association and the Sport Management Program at Drexel University estimates that the average scholarship athlete receives a package that runs $3,000 per year short of his or her actual expenses of attending college, and that 85 percent of scholarship athletes are below the federal poverty line even after including their tuition and room and board stipends.[152] And they can lose their scholarships and eligibility altogether by accepting a little weekend money or some clothes from a friendly booster.

You may have never considered yourself in the same category as an elite college athlete, but the similarity of the unbudgeted expense is real. As a doctoral student, you already pay tuition, buy books, and photocopy articles. But you will also have other professional expenses, none of which you'll be warned about.

A good laptop is $1,000, plus another $1,000 for essential software. Your college bookstore might be a good source, since they can take advantage of all of the educational discounting that hardware and software makers offer. If your field uses a specialized software package, like Adobe's Creative Suite ($500 to $1,700, depending on features), IBM's SPSS ($2,600 at minimum), or QRS's NVivo (license $700 per year), you might be able to get an institutional discount for that as well; ask whether it's available to you as a student or **faculty** member before you go out and spend that much money. You'll replace the hardware and the software every three years or so.

Don't forget the periperhals. Your physical contact with ideas comes through the mouse, trackpad, and keyboard; spend a little more and get the ones that really fit your hands.

I cannot adequately express my recommendation that you get a second monitor. Having your Word document open in one big window and your spreadsheet or your browser open in the other, so that you can move ideas back and forth without having to minimize windows, is a huge boost to your productivity and sanity. Monitors are comparatively cheap; you can

152. Ramogi Huma and Ellen J. Staurowsky, *The Price of Poverty in Big Time College Sport* (Norco, CA: National College Players Association, 2012), accessed May 4, 2015, http:// www.ncpanow.org/research/body/The-Price-of-Poverty-in-Big-Time-College-Sport .pdf.

get a twenty-three-inch hi-def widescreen for under $200, a fraction of the cost of the laptop.

Cables, flash drives (both travel-sized and 500GB to 1TB backup drives), speakers, or headphones: another $300. Oh, and another $50 a month for internet access.

You'll be able to get used office furniture for your desk and filing cabinets, so figure another $300 for that if you don't already have it. Don't scrimp on the chair, though. Or consider setting everything up at a greater height and standing to work. Bad sitting will kill you.

You'll need a good professional briefcase. A nylon briefcase or laptop case will probably serve for around campus, but I'd get a second really nice one and keep it in the closet for **conferences**. You don't want to be hauling the one with the broken zipper tab and faint acid shadow of cleaned-up cat vomit into an interview. Figure $150 for the pair. As with men's shoes, there are only two colors, black and brown; use a colorful bit of string on the zipper tab to tell yours apart from the dozens of other identical cases around you.

Speaking of shoes, we gotta get you some clothes: again, some daily wear and some show clothes. You might be able to wear jeans every so often, if they're in perfect condition, but you have to make up for it with all of the other accessories; the shirt, jacket, and jewelry all have to be pretty stylish. You'll need enough daily clothes so that you can look nice at work and not have people talk about how you wear that same shirt every Thursday; you need ties and grown-up shoes and scarves and stuff to accessorize properly. Let's call every one of those things an average of $40 to $60, which should be a perpetual part of your budget, since they do wear out eventually. Get an iron and an ironing board to go with it; another $40. Pick up a flat ceramic tile or kitchen trivet for a dollar to put the iron on, too, so you don't go burning the apartment down while you practice. Watch a YouTube video or something if you don't know how to iron.

You need at least two suits or conference dresses for interview-level professional dress. Yes, you need two; you'll go to faculty interviews that extend across two days, and you can't wear the same clothes on the second day. (If there's a third day, you can wear the day 1 suit again, but with a radically different shirt and tie combination so that people won't remember it.) Figure that you'll spend the same on two suits and their shoes that you spent on your laptop. Don't put your suit in the washing machine, either. Welcome to the world of dry cleaning.

So we've allocated about $3,000 to $4,000 for computing, and another

$2,000 to $3,000 for your clothes. Now let's add the cost of membership in one or more **professional societies**, about which the next entry will give you more ideas. You'll probably go to at least one of those conferences each year as well, and that's $2,000 easy; see what your **department** offers in the way of offsetting your travel expenses.

With all of this, a realistic doctoral student budget would be $4,000 or $5,000 in first investment costs, a $1,500 annual replacement and renewal budget for clothes and computing, and $2,000 a year for your memberships, conference, and travel. Like Ohio State football players, you may get a "full scholarship" and still be hurting for money. For one thing, graduate **teaching or research assistantships** are often just tuition offsets, and so they don't cover the cost of your apartment, your heat, your canned soup, or your beer. Add these other expenses, and you'll see that even the most generous graduate departments often leave their students well short of solvency.

Professional society. Everybody's got to get out of the house once in a while; take a road trip. What better way to do that than to convince your boss that it's work and that she should pay for it?

The roster of professional societies grows constantly.[153] Every established **discipline** has one or more. Geography, for instance, has a couple of them: the American Geographical Society and the Association of American Geographers. Then there are long-standing **interdisciplinary** groups, such as the Environmental Design Research Association, with members across the design fields and the social sciences, or the National Women's Studies Association, with members representing almost the entirety of academia.

But even within those, there are moments when small groups of scholars decide that their own interests aren't sufficiently represented in the larger organizations, and thus start their own specialized groups. Thus we have the Rural Women's Studies Association, and the National Society of Hispanic MBAs. And the major national groups can have local offshoots, such as the nine regional branches of the American Political Science Association. Most of these will have their own **conferences**, their own **publications**, their own staff or volunteer management.

Think we're done? Hardly. Just as **faculty** and **administrators** operate in parallel universes on their campuses, there is a parallel body of organiza-

---

153. And of course, I'm restricting this whole conversation to the American context. Other nations and consortia of nations have similar assortments and numbers of professional societies.

tions and conferences that are about the practices and operation of higher education rather than its disciplinary contents. Again, there are the overarching (the American Association of Colleges and Universities), the thematic (the National Association of Schools of Art and Design), the consortial (the National Association of Independent Colleges and Universities), the hierarchical (the Council of Graduate Schools), the regional (the New England Association of Schools and Colleges), and the pedagogical (the Council on Undergraduate Research).

You can also choose an organization by role: the American Association of University Professors, the National Postdoctoral Association, the Association of Research Libraries, the Association of Deans and Directors of University College and Undergraduate Studies, the Association of Governing Boards of Universities and Colleges, the National Association of Graduate-Professional Students, and the New Faculty Majority (a national **adjunct** faculty group).

At their best, these organizations convene the like-minded, allowing us to broaden our exposure to interesting ideas and innovative practices we never would have encountered on our own campuses. Those same organizations, though, can act as make-work service projects that pad the **CV** and eat your time. They can also be shadow governments, equivalent to country clubs and Ivy League alumni groups, where agendas are set and informal recruitment occurs.

As a doctoral student or early-career faculty member, you aren't going to get a lot of financial support for your membership in academic groups or attendance at their meetings. Your **department** might fund one such group per faculty member, or perhaps only provide a stipend much smaller than the cost of a single conference attendance. And yet academic societies and conferences are where your name is made, where you become visible and (one hopes) desirable. So, supported or not, you have to go.

If you're a grad student, join the organization that puts on the most important conference your **dissertation chair** goes to. After all, she's the one who's going to introduce you around, talk you up, get you known; to do that, she has to be seen as a reliable witness, a long-time leader. Keep a list of the other organizations you might be interested in, and hang onto those for later life. You might be able to take out an individual membership in a few of them for seventy-five to a hundred dollars each per year, which will at least get you their **journal**, and access to their list-serv.

Once you make it into faculty life, retain your membership in your earlier group—you'll be setting up leadership credibility later on—but casually poll around your new colleagues and see which groups they belong to. If there's a central tendency among the group, your department **chair** will know about it, and will be more inclined to fund your membership and participation as well. (Some organizations offer institutional memberships to departments or colleges, so you might get some automatic privileges if you can find out about them. Your chair and **dean** will know.)

My own experience of working for a dozen years with the Council on Undergraduate Research has been enormously powerful for my own intellectual growth and **career** path. It's also periodically overloaded me with work that sat on top of my already sixty-hour weeks; as the saying goes, "If you want something done, ask a busy person." So I've been part of the governing council for the full time (I came in at the earliest stages of the social sciences division, and they needed the help), chaired my division for four years (and thus also sat on the executive board because of that role), participated in organizing three consecutive national conferences, worked on a merger team with leaders of a related organization, helped to facilitate a dozen professional development weekends, reviewed hundreds of conference proposals and student research summaries, and led a working group to refocus the nature of our flagship publication. In the process, I've gotten to be more broadly knowledgeable about practices at other colleges, discovered how my colleagues have moved through their careers, and learned new ways of fostering the growth of my students.

A good professional society membership is hard work, and is worth every minute of it.

Professor. When you were an undergraduate student, you may have politely called all your teachers "Professor Lastname." In fact, most of them probably weren't professors at all, though (to quote Hemingway) "isn't it pretty to think so?"

Here's your abbreviated field guide to the birds of academia. The most basic division is between **tenure-track** (TT)[154] and non-tenure-track (NTT). Within the TT genus, there are species of increasing rank: **assistant professor** for the newcomers, **associate professor** for the ones who've passed their **tenure** reviews, and professor (informally "full professor"; or even "full P," if you're down with the hip kids) for those who are fifteen or twenty

154. This is the most common term, but occasionally you'll hear variants. The University of California system officially refers to "ladder rank" rather than tenure track, for instance.

years in and acknowledged as being lifelong leaders in their fields. There are *endowed professorships* (almost always associate or full professor), such as the *Russell Cleveland Professor in Guitar Studies* at the University of Texas in Dallas—a position named for its patron, a Dallas investment manager and guitar collector. There are *distinguished professors*, typically full professors late in their **careers** whose work has been deemed to have brought particular notability to the university. There's also the *professor emeritus*, a rank equivalent to an honorable discharge after one's tour of duty has ended. *Emeriti* (what *is* it with this Latin fetish?) often get to keep their offices, phones, e-mail, library privileges, and so on, and many continue to be active scholars even after their faculty careers have officially ended.

The lesser genus, NTT, also includes several species: **adjunct** professor, instructor, lecturer, visiting faculty, and so on. The identifying marks in the field guide will be dominated by their contingent status; all of the NTT are employed under contracts that have expiration dates: usually semester by semester, sometimes year to year. Rather than being "let go," their contracts are simply not renewed. (There is an NTT with a longer contractual period, often called a *professor of the practice*; this is usually someone with experience in a related profession who is brought into a **department** for an extended period, three to five years being common.)

In birding, there is a common expression for the innumerable sparrow-like creatures that are hard to identify at first glance: they're LBBs, or "little brown birds." NTTs are the LBBs of the faculty aviary. They outnumber their flashier TT cousins two to one or more, and do more to nurture the ecosystem of undergraduate learning while consuming far fewer resources themselves. Members of the two genera rarely interact; NTTs often approach TTs with friendly gestures, believing themselves to be related species; the TTs typically flee in horrified nonrecognition, building elaborate safeguards to keep themselves in and NTTs out.

Birds of a feather . . . .

Program rankings/ratings. I saw a cartoon many years ago that attempted to explain dating and sexual attraction. We all, the cartoonist posited, have a number stamped on our foreheads that relates to our sexual attractiveness—10.0 for the rarified air of professional athletes whose parents were both models, 5.0 for average people, and downward from there. The author further posited that, although these numbers are invisible and none of us actually knows our own number, we will invariably find ourselves dating persons whose number is ± 0.2 from our own. If we shoot above that, we'll find ourselves humiliated and frustrated; if we go below that ... well, why would we? Beauty is power, after all.

The world of college and program ratings works something like that when it comes time to apply for your teaching position. It is very hard to gain a teaching post at a college more prestigious than your own doctoral program; you can only date level or downward.

- Is your **doctorate** from MIT or Stanford? You're a ten, and have no upper limit. The lower limit is that if you apply for a job at a three, like Formerly Secretarial College, they'll assume that you just want a one-night stand on your way to a more suitable relationship.
- Is your doctorate from a major state research university like Michigan or Wisconsin or Missouri? You're an eight, and may never see the finalists' list for jobs at the tens. However, there are lots of high-powered public universities and excellent liberal arts colleges who will love to court you. The threes and fours will still be suspicious, but might be able to be flattered if you're a smooth talker.
- Is your doctorate from UMass Boston or UC–Merced? You're a five, prepared to continue a life within the state-comprehensive systems, community colleges, or less selective private colleges.
- Is your doctorate from any of the online for-profit schools that are likely to sue me for defamation if I mention them by name? Congratulations; you're a one.

It's important to note that this is not an ethical question, but rather a strategic question; you can live a satisfying, productive, and socially beneficial life as a three or four. But if you aspire to date James Franco or Kate Upton (or whoever this year's version of media perfection might be), then you need to do everything in your power to strive for nine-ness and beyond. You also need to know that you'll never get there if you're genetically or educationally a five. So think carefully about your desired teaching and research life, and about what kind of college offers that life to its **faculty**. Then make sure that the graduate schools you want to enroll in are *at least* at that level, and preferably a step or two above.

Colleges as a whole have rankings or reputations. Your school's program in its specific **discipline** will as well. So, for instance, there are some schools almost universally regarded as tens: Stanford, Princeton, Yale, MIT, and so on. But if we look at economics **departments**, U. Chicago and Northwestern come higher on the list than their general rankings; for physics, Cal Tech and Cornell rise high; in civil engineering, U. Illinois–Champaign-Urbana tops the list. You *must* know these standings, and get yourself into a school that's ranked appropriately for your dating preferences. Look at the current faculty of schools you'd like to teach in, find out where they got their PhD's, and you'll have your answer.

And to be blunt, your adviser or potential adviser has a ranking as well, which is also taken into account in hiring possibilities. If your doctoral chair is well-liked and well-published, you'll have more open doors as you move through the hiring process. If one of those two things is missing, you'll have reviewers taking sides before the details of your work are ever examined. If both are missing, if your doctoral chair is both a jerk and a deadwood (or an unknown), you're really walking into a team sport as a solo player, dragging the weight of your decision along with you.

Provost. Vice president for academic affairs, academic vice president, chief academic officer, provost. All of those titles describe the same role: that of being the college **president**'s senior leader in charge of the school's intellectual mission. The provost is a member of the president's leadership team, working in concert (one hopes) with other vice-presidential leaders in charge of finance, operations, athletics, fundraising, community relations, and other core business functions.

To return again to our simple hierarchy pyramid, the **faculty** of a **department** are organized by a **chair**; all the chairs of an academic division report to a **dean**; and the deans of all the divisions are supervised by the provost. Thus, the provost at a big school is three steps removed from daily faculty life, four steps removed from grad students. And you may never even know who she is; at a smaller school the role may be similar, but the lived experience may entail closer contact.

I know a few provosts, and I think it's probably the hardest job in academic life, akin to being secretary of state during international conflict. The provost has to convince the public and the troops that the president's strategy is not only sound but brilliant to the level of inevitability; and simultaneously he has to tell the president in private that he's out of his freakin' mind. The provost has to listen to the concerns of deans and chairs, of grad students and **postdocs**, and try to help improve their lives in the twenty minutes left before he has to go off to a dinner with an alumnus considering a major donation. He is seen from below as being immensely powerful and often ominous, and yet he is beholden to be the president's proxy in all academic dealings. It's an enormously diplomatic job, one that academia itself isn't preparation for. Faculty life is ideally based upon unfettered research, **academic freedom** that allows one to be an inconvenient voice of truth. Moving from being an intellectual soloist to being a voice in the unified executive choir is a long journey, and a trip in a direction opposite to that for which we were trained.

Publication. You've heard of "publish or perish." This centrally binding rule of higher education simply indicates that you're expected to be a productive scholar in your **discipline**, contributing to the body of knowledge that your field relies upon. This is most often shown by publishing papers in relevant academic **journals**. How many publications, and which journals, is a matter of professional judgment by your colleagues, and that uncertainty will give you many sleepless nights.

The "publications" area of your **CV** will have subdivisions. In the humanities and social sciences, a book (along with several papers) is a common threshold of **tenure** at research-intensive universities, so if you've published a monograph, or if the book based on your **dissertation** is under contract with an academic **publisher**, list that first. Laboratory scientists, on the other hand, almost never write books, so their papers in elite disciplinary journals are most prestigious and would be listed first. Publications of lesser but still useful weight include **book reviews** or topical synopses, and progress notes or preliminary findings in the natural sciences.

If you're in a research university, don't bother much with publishing in any forums other than academic journals or university presses. If you work at a smaller liberal arts or comprehensive state school with a public-service mandate, however, you may get **career** benefits from publishing in the local and regional **popular press**, especially if it's about your own field and the benefits your research, your students, and your college bring to the surrounding community. Professional publications in practitioner magazines may be of use in professional departments, but less helpful in other disciplines.

There's a commonly used classification of **scholarly activity** that runs as follows: the scholarship of discovery, the scholarship of application, the scholarship of integration, and the scholarship of teaching and learning.[155] For **faculty** hiring and **tenure** purposes, only the first of these really counts. Publications that count toward tenure are only those that provide novel findings or interpretations to your discipline; anything else "isn't

---

155. Ernest L. Boyer, *Scholarship Reconsidered: Priorities of the Professoriate* (San Francisco, Jossey-Bass, 1990).

really research." In fact, not only do applied research, brilliant literature summaries, and inspired pedagogical writing not help; they may skew a review committee's thinking against your case in a research-focused department. "Who can spare that kind of time instead of making a meaningful contribution to her discipline?" the argument will go. The more research-intensive your college, the more you must focus only on work that advances the knowledge of your field. The other kinds of publication may be worth your while if you're at a **teaching**-focused school, but even there, caution and local advice are important.

As with much in higher education, your publication record will be judged against an invisible standard, and you will always imagine that you've not done enough. And nothing I can say from outside your context will be helpful. I'd like to state with certainty that for the social sciences, having four major journal articles published and a book contract in hand is sufficient for starting your faculty career; or that for the lab sciences, being a **coauthor** on a dozen peer-reviewed articles is a sufficient basis upon which to be considered for a **tenure-track** job. But every college, and every department in every college, has its own standards, which are constantly changing as each successive generation of grad students raises the expectations of the field. Find out the publication record of the most recent successful hires or tenure reviews in your department, and expect that you should exceed that by 20 percent.

Publication contract. There's just something lovely about a book. I've written dozens of articles and enjoyed them all greatly; other academic and popular readers have told me that they've found them useful or engaging. But when I tell people I've written a couple of books, they take my writing seriously. And I take my own writing more seriously. I love magazines and newspapers and good blogs, but writers write (and read) books.

I know that a gentleman never discusses money, and that it's gauche to talk about how much you make. But without somebody being gauche, nobody ever gets any smarter, and my job is to keep you from making the same mistakes I did, which means I get to embarrass myself. So I'll tell you that, while working on this entry, I received in the mail the royalty statement for fiscal 2012–13 for my book *Landscapes of Betrayal, Landscapes of Joy.*[156] During that year, I made $26.52.

When I was working on that first book, I very much wanted to publish

156. Herb Childress, *Landscapes of Betrayal, Landscapes of Joy: Curtisville in the Lives of Its Teenagers* (Albany, NY: SUNY Press, 2000).

with a **trade publisher** rather than an academic press. I believed (and was told by early readers) that the narrative was engaging and widely pertinent, and I wanted to have a broader voice than I'd get by being shelved in academic **libraries**. But no trade publisher would go for it, though a couple said it would make a good novel if I had one central character all the way through it with a major crisis and resolution. I thought that kind of missed the point of its being a nonfiction look at a whole community. So a friend and **mentor** happily acquired it for his series with a university press, and we went through a year and a half of revision and external reviews and proofreading and cover design and contracts, starting in September 1998, for a book released in April 2000.

The press's **editor** was excited about the book and thought that the press would market it substantially outside higher education because she believed that, as others had already said, it had significant popular interest. "It might be our first crossover book," she said.

Or not. I did a book signing and a radio interview in the general region that my book was about, on my own initiative and at my own expense, and saw one copy of the book in one enormous bookstore in San Francisco.[157] But I was never contacted by the publisher to do any promotional work. They just weren't set up to accomplish that, and they didn't push.

I've been told that the contract I signed was particularly abysmal,[158] but one doesn't know these things from the outside, and academic publications rarely attract the interest of literary agents who might be able to push for more advantageous deals. And it was the publisher's standard boilerplate contract, so I assumed, probably correctly, that I made as much money as anybody else there.

The press published a hardcover and softcover edition of my book: the

---

157. I, of course, compressed some other books around it so that I could put mine face-out rather than spine-out. *Vanity, thy name is author.*

158. My wife and I have just turned down a publication contract from another major for-profit academic publisher, one whose terms were even more egregious than the one I'm describing here. They were hoping to sell 800 or, at best, 1,200 copies of the thing at a $100 list price to gullible academic libraries, which would have made them about $50,000 after their discounting; my wife and I would jointly have pocketed about $1,800 at the top end of that scale. But worse, if they'd wanted a second edition, either we would have had to write it ourselves, or they'd hire someone else to write it at our expense, and leave our names on it. If you're on the tenure hunt, this stuff doesn't matter, because the CV line is your payment. That kind of academic publishing really is a great racket: publishers get to sell material at a horrific price after having gotten it virtually free.

hardcover originally at over fifty dollars, primarily for academic libraries, and the softcover at twenty dollars, for individual readers. Author's royalties were based on the net profit of the book—the amount of money the publisher received for each sale of the book—and publishers typically give booksellers discounts of between 20 and 40 percent, depending on how specialized a book is.

My contract specified that I was to receive 5 percent of the press's net (or, assuming a 30-percent average discount to bookstores, about $1.75) for each hardcover sale, and 2.5 percent of the press's net (or about thirty-five cents) for each softcover copy after the first thousand copies were sold. On the basis of my own faith in the work and the press's excitement about the crossover possibilities, I proposed that they keep all the revenue from the hardcovers and give me 5 percent of the paperbacks starting from the first copy. I was told apologetically that the press didn't negotiate royalty computation, because they had a set body of fixed costs that they had to balance.

So, as always, the content provider works on spec, whereas the publisher has to support people with, you know, *jobs* and salaries and stuff. I once heard a radio interview with a noted journalist explaining why, after nearly forty years as a freelance writer that allowed him great independence, he was finally taking a job with a magazine. He said that for his first cover story in the 1960s, he was paid five hundred dollars. And he finally decided to leave freelance life when, in the mid-2000s, he was offered a cover story for a small magazine, and they said they'd pay him . . . five hundred dollars.

From April 2000 through June 2013, my book *Landscapes* has sold 1,883 copies. People who know things tell me that's quite a lot for a social science book from a small university press, though publishers almost never reveal sales information unless they want to brag about achievements at the *Harry Potter* scale.

If your **dissertation** might become a book, the time to understand the contract is immediately after the editor says she likes it and wants it, and *before* you spend time getting it to publishable condition. Once you've even informally signed on, you're spending the time of editors and designers and reviewers, and leaving at that point because you don't like the contract borders on unethical (unless the contract really *is* egregiously bad, leaving you with no possibility of any payment at all). But asking for the terms of a publishing contract before you start the work of editing and revising can be seen as arrogant overreach. So go ahead and be arrogant, but in your kindest and least threatening voice, and see what the press has to offer. When they talk about their publicity plans, ask specific questions about what they've done on behalf of other books and authors, and whether those media efforts might be expected for yours as well. It's your intellectual work, and you deserve to know what's likely to happen with it.

Publisher (trade/academic). My friend and first academic **mentor**, the geographer Paul Groth, used to end his course American Vernacular Landscapes with two images shown side-by-side. "I don't care if you learn nothing else in this course," he would say. "You *will* know the difference between a silo and a grain elevator." He went on to explain that a silo is a farm implement, like a tractor or mower, and that a grain elevator is a tool of capital exploitation more akin to a refinery's pipeline. He later wrote about this difference, one that influenced his own childhood in North Dakota:

> No one explained how the grain elevators that towered over the landscape explained the economic reality of our region. We were a colony of the rest of the U.S.: All the locally grown products were exported a thousand miles away, along with the profits to be gained from them, and everything else was imported, retail.[159]

Publishers are the grain elevators of the world of ideas. They take your words, and the words of thousands of others, and buy them for a few dollars. They then sort, polish, package and transport those words for a dozen or twenty times what they paid you, sending them along to retailers who put them on the shelves for another doubling. The seventeen dollars you just paid for that paperback made its author a buck and a half.

Academic publishing takes this already meager economic exchange and puts a religious spin on it. You, humble farmer of ideas, bring your best goods to the altar and beg that they may be deemed worthy. If they are found acceptable, you are given merely a blessing and a mandate to go forth and produce more. The presumption is that you have an employer, and that your employer pays you to create these goods, so that the clerics of academic publishing needn't reward you in any material way. They take your ideas, nod kindly, and walk away with not only your crops but the basket you brought them in.

You will sell your writing wholesale, and pay your rent retail.

159. Paul Groth, "Tithing for Environmental Education: A Modest Proposal." *Places* 7, no. 1 (1990): 38–41.

When choosing a publisher, you must keep in mind your ultimate goals, both for your **career** and for your particular body of ideas. If you hope to make a little money or to have your words in the broadest possible conversation, you need to put your work in front of **trade publishers**, and you need a literary agent to do it. Trade publishers, the kinds of folks who put books into bookstores, are motivated both by the quality of the work they represent and by the income they might receive from it. So they have good graphic arts departments (that stark silver tie on the *Fifty Shades of Grey* cover has probably on its own made the book five or ten million dollars), they have publicity managers, they have representatives who not only sell books to bookstores but also get the books onto the desks of important reviewers at important magazines. The work still has to be good, or at least good enough to satisfy the consumers of its genre, and you still need to follow up by talking with magazines and radio interviewers and booksellers, but the publisher has the burden of making your book a social and economic success.

If, on the other hand, you hope to go into academic life, publishing with a trade press has inverse effects, marking you as less than serious, a dilettante rather than a scholar. I have one colleague who had to submit a trade-press book to independent **peer review** in five different **disciplines** because her **departmental** colleagues believed that it was merely a "popularization" rather than a piece of serious **interdisciplinary** intellectual work. Any university press would have sufficed, but when she chose W. W. Norton instead of the University of Nebraska, her disciplinary community saw red flags.

There are a few publishers who cross those boundaries, who have public-idea motives and also strong peer review practices and high credibility in the academic community. Routledge, Wiley, Verso, and the New Press are among the best known private crossovers; the university presses of Chicago, California, and MIT do some of that same work from an academic base. Publishing with one of these is the closest you can come to having dual-community success, but they still don't have the marketing power of a Random House or a HarperCollins.[160]

160. If you don't know which category a particular publisher fits into, here's a first hint. Look at the covers of some of their sample books. If they're beautifully designed and feature representational images, they're a trade press. If they're Modernist or abstract art, they're a hybrid house or a good university press. And if they're Microsoft clip art, or sans-serif text on simple blocks of usually pretty horrid colors, they're a for-profit academic publisher. I had a chapter in an edited book with a major academic publisher (the original list price, designed to gouge college libraries, was $250), the cover of which was just a pair of purple rectangles containing white text of the title and the editors'

Publishing your dissertation as a book puts you squarely in the jaws of that dilemma. If you're a pre-tenure **assistant professor**, you just go with the academic press; you already have a salary, and you know upon which side your bread will be buttered. If you're a post-tenure **associate professor**, you can do whatever the hell you want, because you already have a salary *and* a guarantee of continuation. In fact, your future promotion to full **professor** may rely on bringing public recognition to the college, and you'll be more notable if you publish with Farrar, Straus & Giroux than with the University of Akron Press.

But if you're just finished with your dissertation and don't yet have an academic job, you can't fully predict what kind of a career you'll wind up with, and you have to gamble. Once you've placed your chips on red or black and the wheel is spinning, you can't move them; you just have to hope for the appropriate payoff. If you bet academic and go into industry, your work will sink unnoticed; if you bet industry and go into academia, your work won't count for promotion with your employer. This time between the wager and the outcome is where incantations, rabbits' feet, and lucky stones come into play.

This whole discussion is about the publication of single-authored books, of course. Publication of **journal** articles and chapters in **edited volumes** are just free labor, the supplications you must offer to the gods of academia.

---

names, set against a background of the same purple reduced to a more pastel value. I think the design team must have bought a remaindered color that another publisher had found unusable. I unpacked the single contributor's copy I received—my only compensation—and my spirits just sank. If you have any aesthetic aspirations for your writing, if you hope to impart joy as well as thought, the graphic arts departments of academic publishers will put a knife in your heart over and over again.

Rr

R1 (and other Carnegie designations). This is an obsolete designator that was used for so long that it's still part of the vernacular language. An R1 or Research 1 university was a college that awarded a certain number of PhDs and received a certain threshold of federal research funding each year, and thus was considered to be a "major research university." You'll still hear people say "Oh, she got a position at an R1," and others will nod in admiration.

The Carnegie Foundation for the Advancement of Teaching is a think tank that has more than a hundred years of influence in higher education policy. One of its projects has been the Carnegie Classification,™ a framework for understanding what kind of school any particular college might be. There are now dozens of specific categories that a college might fall within, ranging from Assoc/Pub-R-S (a small, rural two-year public college) to Spec/Faith (seminaries, yeshivas, Bible colleges).

Given that you're involved in doctoral education, the school you attend or are considering will have one of three "basic" categories: DRU (doctoral/research university), RU/H (research university / high research activity), and RU/VH (research university / very high research activity, or what used to be called R1s). Those three classifications account for 297 schools, or 6.3 percent of all American colleges (but more than a quarter of all undergraduate students, and virtually all doctoral students).[161] It matters which of the three categories your school is in, because that's likely to determine your job prospects. If you aspire to teach at an RU/VH, you'd better have gotten your doctorate from an RU/VH, as moving upward in hiring is rare. (See the entry on **program rankings/ratings** for more on this.)

The R1 classification is still in vernacular use, as are other designations like PUI, for primarily undergraduate institutions, or state or regional "comprehensive school," to denote one of the many less selective system schools in California, Wisconsin, New York, Michigan and so on that offer

161. You can see the entire array of basic categories and the number of schools in each classification at http://carnegieclassifications.iu.edu, accessed April 29, 2015. In late 2014, the management of the classification system was moved to the Indiana University Center for Postsecondary Research, though they're still going to use the term "Carnegie Classification" for the near future.

mostly undergraduate and some professional or graduate degree programs to communities bounded largely by geographic region. There's a way in which all of these designators act in the same way as your Meyers-Briggs classification or your astrological sign, letting you quickly communicate something about your school's interests and intentions without really saying anything specific. It would be an interesting thought experiment, though, to imagine a state system with sixteen campuses, each of which was based on serving students with a particular Meyers-Briggs profile. Instead of geographical schools like Cal State–Stanislaus, we could have attitudinal schools like Cal State–INFP, the college of the brooding arts.

The biggest difference between all of these classifications, from the standpoint of your **job search** and your early **career**, is that different kinds of schools will judge your professional adequacy by different criteria. Advancement in higher ed relies upon your participation in the holy trinity of teaching, scholarly activity, and college service. But the recipe made from these three ingredients will vary radically from school to school. If you're at an R1, your **teaching load** will be low, and you may be protected from service (**committee** work and so on) until **tenure** ... but you'd better be publishing in top-tier **journals** and winning major research funding on a regular basis. If you're at a community college, you'll be teaching a lot, and you'll probably be on far too many committees, but you will have no responsibility at all for being an active scholar. One of the great frustrations among college **faculty** is when their institution isn't a very good match for their aspirations; neither the teacher at the research school nor the researcher at the teaching school will be happy with their lot. So not only are there not nearly enough higher ed faculty jobs, but you're seriously going to want to throw out half or more of the ones you're qualified for anyway, because they'll make you miserable. So find out the local recipe, and think about whether it's tasty before you buy the *venti* size.

Recommendation, letter of. As a part of applications for graduate school or for academic positions, you will often be asked to submit letters of recommendation from people familiar with you and your work.

You'll typically be asked to provide three letters. Think about how to use them to represent a breadth of your abilities and interests. One letter can relate directly to your scholarly capabilities, another to your professional abilities, and a third to your teaching skills. Or, if the position you're applying for has different criteria, you might have two letters related to your research abilities and a third about your management of a **grant**-funded research project. Just make sure you understand the multiple facets of your desired position, and have someone on your side for more than one of them.

Name recognition can count for something. When I was an undergrad applying to doctoral programs, my discussion section TA in architectural history declined to write a letter of recommendation for me—not because he didn't believe in my capability, but because in his estimation, no review committee would take a TA's recommendation seriously. I don't completely agree with that—I think Greg would have written a wonderfully detailed and relevant letter, since he knew me far better than Spiro Kostof would have in a class of four hundred students—but I understood his argument, given that he was speaking from the vantage point of a doctoral student at a high-powered research university. If you have the opportunity to get a meaningful recommendation from Secretary of State Madeline Albright as you're applying for grad school in public policy (or, really, for almost anything), that's going to make people pay attention. If you've been working with one of the leading scholars in your field, that person's status in the academic community will lift your application to stronger consideration.

But breadth and name recognition are both secondary considerations. Whether asking for or writing letters of recommendation, the foremost characteristic must be genuine and specific enthusiasm. A good letter contains details of particular accomplishments or wonderful traits that the writer wishes the reader to know about. A letter simply stating that the applicant was a good student or a productive colleague will be ignored; a letter about the applicant's remarkable research on working-class marriages, or on the applicant's masterful management of a contentious curricular change, will be far more memorable.

When you ask for a letter of recommendation, make sure that you provide your recommender with any forms that the college uses, and it's a nice touch to provide a stamped and addressed envelope if physical mail is required. The form for recommendation may have a lot of boilerplate questions about how long and in what capacity the reviewer has known the applicant, and sometimes a rating of the applicant in comparison to other students the reviewer has known.[162] But there will usually be the capability of attaching a longer letter of recommendation, and most reviewers will

162. Sometimes these ratings can be quite detailed. The referring writer may be asked whether a student was in the top 10 percent of all students, was in the top 5 percent of all students, or was the best student in that teacher's past five years. You don't want a letter from someone who's wavering between calling you "adequate" or "good."

take advantage of that (and you should as well, when you write your own recommendations).

The form will often have a section for the applicant to fill out, as well as one for the recommender. Make sure you complete it, so that the recommender can just finish it and get it out rather than having to contact you for a signature or for checking off some box. One element the applicant is responsible for will have two check-box alternatives, usually something like "I wish the contents of this recommendation to be confidential" paired against "I retain my right to inspect the contents of this recommendation." You should *always* allow reference letters to be confidential. (All the more reason to know your references well.) You want your recommenders to be honest and candid, not looking over their shoulder knowing that you'll be reading their assessment; your potential grad school or employer wants to see that you have confidence in your capabilities and trust in your colleagues. It's a small box on the form, but choosing the wrong option can mark you as oddly insecure at a time when you want them to think only good things.

If you're asked to write a recommendation for someone else's application, think carefully about whether you should accept that request. As a teacher in the Duke University Writing Program, I was working with students in their first or second semester in college ... not the most relevant source of commentary three years later as they were considering med school or law school. Typically, I wrote letters for them only if they had done remarkable work in my course, or if they displayed some powerful persistence or dedication or curiosity that I knew was likely to still be true of them several years later. On the other end of the scale, if a student had gotten a B-minus in Writing 20 and was still asking me for a letter of recommendation, I knew it didn't speak very well of any further academic relationships he'd been able to build; was I really one of the best three letters he was going to get?

Finally, a plea for understanding if you ever come to be on a hiring committee. Think about how many applicants you're likely to have, and how many you'll eliminate immediately. Please don't ask every single applicant for letters of recommendation as part of their initial submittal package. A good letter writer spends time crafting a recommendation that relates to the specific interplay of the applicant and the position, and you're squandering an enormous amount of time and good will by requiring that of referees for people who will never make the first screening. Wait until you get to the point of the phone interviews or the list of twelve before asking for reference letters; good karma will await you for your generosity.

Regalia. When I was in Catholic high school, the nuns wore religious garb, which we shorthanded as "habits." The word "habit" was actually the collective term for all of the specialized clothing, which included the robe, the coif, the bandeau, and the wimple.

Likewise, what we think of as academic regalia or "the cap and gown" is actually a collection of three items: the robe, the cap, and the hood. At your doctoral commencement ceremony, your **dissertation** adviser will adorn you with your hood; the term "hood" is a misnomer that really indicates sort of a long satin and velvet scarf worn the wrong way round, with the front tight across the neck and the back end dangling down around your butt. In the bluntest possible visual hierarchy, the length of the hood increases by your degree: three feet for the bachelor's; three feet, six inches for the **master's**, and four feet for the **doctorate**. So there.

The color of the robe, the trim, and the hood are all representational according to the school and **discipline** from which you received your highest degree, and are standardized by the American Council on Education, who you'd think might have better things to focus on. The doctoral robe has three velvet bars on each sleeve, and velvet panels on either side of the front zipper; the doctoral recipient also gets to wear the soft puffy velvet Tam o' Shanter rather than the square satin or linen mortarboard. The **president** or the chair of the board of trustees often has a staff or a cane with the school medallion on it. Commencement day looks like a Renaissance faire.

If you are one of the fortunate ones who go on to faculty life, you may be expected to participate in commencement each spring, and to wear the appropriate regalia. Thus, rather than renting it every year, you might consider purchasing your own. You're probably going to spend between five and eight hundred dollars on it, so consider buying a second-hand mannequin for displaying it in your office between ceremonies.

Rejection letter. By tradition and by fear of litigation, the rejection letter for **faculty** positions is one of the most uncommunicative forms of communication ever devised. It will tell you absolutely nothing about how you fared or about why you weren't chosen. They might as well print the single word "no" on a postcard and save themselves some money.

I've had one rejection letter that indicated the number of applicants (140). I've had one rejection letter that spent a paragraph on the press release for the marvelous person they actually hired, which just made me want to reconsider my stance on nonviolence. And I've had at least two schools that never bothered to send me anything at all; I just assumed that after three or four years, they'd probably decided otherwise. Who knows, maybe they're still waiting for me to show up and claim the **office** that's been sitting there vacant all these years.

You can go online and find sample rejection letters that are part of many universities' legally-vetted human resources toolbox. You can also find lots of blogs with pretty amusing examples; my favorite was the **e-mail** message that had the file "reject.doc" attached. There's your happy thought for the day.

There is, though, a second flavor of rejection letter, the one from an **editor** who has declined to publish your manuscript, or from a funding agency that has not funded your proposed project. These letters will be equally damaging to your psyche, but in fact will actually tell you something of use about why your paper or proposal has fared as it has. Counterintuitive advice here: Give the letter to one of your colleagues who can read it more objectively than you can. When *you* read it, it's just one big blinking neon word ... *loser* ... *loser* ... *loser*. But that's not really what it says, and someone else, whose **career** hasn't just been crushed, can read it for its specific advice and bring you back to stable ground.

Research. You'll hear people say that they spent the whole day researching carpet for an interior design project, or researching where to buy woodstove pellets. "Do some research and get back to me" is your boss's way of telling you to find out what other similar organizations are doing about a given problem. But looking things up is not the same as research, though generations of middle-school and high-school students have been taught that it is.

As used in higher education, research is the attempt to advance a **discipline**'s thinking. A doctoral **dissertation**, by definition, is an original contribution to the scholarly work of one's field, and that word "original" is crucial. You can make an original contribution by advancing the applicability of a theory into explaining a new phenomenon, like using subatomic theory to locate and identify some particular little beastie in a collider. Alternatively, you can make an original contribution by theorizing some known but poorly understood circumstance in the world, like how queer kids in rural areas develop social networks and claim physical spaces of belonging.[163]

In 1990, Ernest Boyer, longtime president of the Carnegie Foundation

---

163. Kaila G. Kuban, "That Which Is Not What It Seems: Queer Youth, Rurality, Class, and the Architecture of Assistance," dissertation, University of Massachusetts–Amherst

for the Advancement of Teaching, suggested that we might reconsider our focus on the disciplines when thinking of "original contribution," imagining instead the multiple ways in which research might successfully advance the cause of knowledge.[164] Boyer suggested four categories of scholarly work: the scholarship of discovery, the scholarship of application, the scholarship of integration, and the scholarship of teaching and learning.

As a doctoral student, and probably as an assistant professor, you'd better be doing the scholarship of discovery to the near exclusion of the others. Academia is still a conservative place, and basic disciplinary research is still valued far more centrally than any other mode of thought. But if your heart really lies in one of the other three areas, at least make sure that you're publishing your work in peer-reviewed academic **journals**; without that, it's just not in your positive column at all. Research differs from curiosity at least in part because researchers intend to report their work back to others, and the "others" who count most are in your field.

A subsequent Carnegie publication shortly after Boyer's death attempted to set forth the standards by which scholarly work should be assessed, regardless of which of the four categories it occupied. Scholarly work, they argued, is marked by clear goals, adequate preparation, appropriate **methods**, significant results, effective presentation, and reflective critique.[165] I would like to add that it should start from a socially meaningful question; research is a social endeavor, after all, and every society needs to monitor its spending. If I were king of the world, I'd be spending a lot less on NASA and a lot more on NOAA—not because we don't learn important things from space research, but because what we don't know about the oceans and the climate will soon kill us. Big research follows big money, and the major research universities have long acted as state and federal research-and-development laboratories; we ought to consider our collective research priorities politically, since it's public money that ultimately keeps researchers in business.[166]

(2010), accessed April 29, 2015, http://scholarworks.umass.edu/cgi/viewcontent.cgi?article=1188&context=open_access_dissertations.

164. Ernest L. Boyer, *Scholarship Reconsidered: Priorities of the Professorate* (San Francisco, Jossey-Bass, 1990).

165. Charles E. Glassick, Mary T. Huber, and Gene I. Maeroff, *Scholarship Assessed: Evaluation of the Professoriate* (San Francisco: Jossey-Bass, 1997).

166. We did that once; they're called land-grant universities. That worked out pretty well.

Research agenda. Back in the day of progressive rock, there was a pro-
fusion of what were called "concept albums." The term was intended to
separate them from albums that were simply collections of songs. But even
there, the concepts that held such albums together were pretty different
from each other.

- Genesis's *The Lamb Lies Down on Broadway* was a *narrative* album, a
  story with a plot and sequence. (See also Rush's *2112*, David Bowie's
  Rise and Fall of Ziggy Stardust and the Spiders from Mars, etc.)
- Pink Floyd's *Animals* was a *metaphoric* album, with the players of
  capitalism represented as different animals (particularly pigs as the
  financiers, dogs as the salesmen, and sheep as the rest of us).
- Porcupine Tree's *Fear of a Blank Planet* was a *thematic* album, with
  the songs—mostly through the narration of a middle-school kid—
  exploring twenty-first-century dysfunctions such as ADD, bipolar
  disorder, impermanent/casual relationships, and the emotional
  distancing of technology. (In another genre, and twenty years earlier, Bruce Springsteen's *Nebraska* was similarly thematic, reporting
  on the darkness of a spiritually and emotionally impoverished rural
  America.)
- Rick Wakeman's *Six Wives of Henry VIII* was a *category* album, with
  six different pieces each intended (loosely) to evoke one of Henry's
  six wives. In much the same way, Gustav Holst's *The Planets* and
  Antonio Vivaldi's *The Four Seasons* might be regarded as category
  albums.

In each case, the concept is working to unify and to suggest additional
moves, even though the natures of the concepts are quite different.

Creative **careers** often have concepts. The entire forty-year output of
Kraftwerk is a meditation on the increasing unity of human and machine;
Steely Dan has gotten the same amount of time out of considering the cycle
between decadence and regret; Devo has worked for a similar span to help
us see the regression (or "de-evolution") of humankind toward a nonre-
flective animal state. Likewise, Amos Rapoport has spent almost fifty years
examining how cultures speak through building forms, and Clare Cooper
Marcus about forty years on the ways we communicate and strengthen our
self-identities through manipulating our spaces. The dozens of individual
projects add up to a life project.

When **faculty** search committees are considering a new hire, they're looking for someone who ideally will be with them for decades to come, and they want to see someone who's likely going to be academically productive for a long time. They want to see that your research interests are robust enough to spawn further projects (and, depending on the institution you're applying to, that they're robust enough support a few generations of doctoral students as well). So when they ask you to discuss your research agenda, they're not really asking you to name a sequence of specific projects; they're asking for the concept that underlies your current project, the big impetus that motivates you and will likely continue to motivate you once the **dissertation** is completed. They'll want to hear a little detail on what you're thinking of doing immediately as a second step, but beyond that, you're speaking in thematics.

The prospect of naming one's life project when you're in your early thirties is daunting, and you aren't signing a binding agreement anyway. It's only been recently that I've come to realize that all of my work has at least one common theme, which is that of attempting to bring respect to people and places that are often ignored or actively disparaged. That has led me to write about seemingly dissimilar phenomena—about small cities, teenagers and young adults, research participants, and now grad students looking into academic culture from the outside—but all this work stems from the same seed crystal of desire, employs the same body of intensively ethnographic **methods**, and is aimed at a form of storytelling that speaks in the native language rather than in academic or disciplinary structures. Starting to learn and name your own research agenda is a crucial task, one that you might do in common with your fellow grad students some evening. They'll make connections that you, being too close to the individual projects, might overlook.

If, like me, you take a broad look at the world, you may have to frame your research agenda in covert ways to get the attention of your disciplinary peers. The great Paul Goodman once wrote:

> I have been severely criticized as an ignorant man who spreads himself thin on a wide variety of subjects, on sociology and psychology, urbanism and technology, education, literature, esthetics, and ethics. It is true that I don't know much, but it is false that I write about many subjects. I have only one, the human beings I know in their man-made scene.[167]

---

167. Paul Goodman, *Utopian Essays and Practical Proposals*, (New York: Vintage, 1962), 4.

Goodman's research agenda was to think carefully, and write exuberantly, about the state of lives in the world. You and I, in fitting ourselves to the suit of tenure-track armor, might have to describe ourselves in lesser terms.

Research assistant. It isn't always easy to get a tuition waiver out of an institution to support promising graduate students, so one of the traditional back-door methods has been to name them as a research assistant, the stipend for which almost always equals the expected tuition. And because it's primarily a means of support, it's a position for which the duties are not always adequately predicted by the title.

In the laboratory sciences, a research assistant occasionally *is* a research assistant, working in partnership with a **faculty** member in their lab. Sometimes, on major quantitative social science endeavors, a research assistant does statistical analysis or database management. But just as likely, the position of research assistant is a clerical support job allocated in a department or **research center's** annual budget. Research assistants do filing, make name tags for events, manage mailing lists, set up computer systems, filter **e-mail**, make travel arrangements for incoming guests, order sandwiches, and organize libraries.

When you're offered a "graduate research assistantship" (often shortened to RA or GRA, akin to its partner the TA or GTA or graduate **teaching assistantship**), find out the position's expectations. If a department has more than one GRA slot available, you may be able to angle for the one most amenable to your research goals. But no matter what the responsibilities of the GRA position, you can learn useful things from it.

Lots of GRA positions are seen as simple stipends; there's occasionally a little bit of work to do now and again, some of which might strike you as being beneath you,[168] but mostly you can use the time to keep up with your reading for seminars or work on a problem set. I'd like to encourage you to not do that, for a couple of reasons. The first is that you don't want to get a reputation as a goldbricker, and people do notice whether you're involved or not. But the more important reason goes back to the framework I put forth at the beginning of this book, that **careers** have three components:

168. One of the reasons why executives have assistants is that they have limited time available in their lives, time better spent having big ideas or big conversations than ordering and cataloging books. You wouldn't drive the Ferrari to the hardware store. But you're not a Ferrari yet, so cool down and lower your indignation level when Professor Imperious asks you to arrange lunches for tomorrow's meeting. And remember how to treat people right when you get higher up the hill yourself.

knowledge of content, knowledge of logistics and management, and knowledge of strategy and purpose. You can use your time as a menial GRA to get a fuller understanding of how to manage a complex set of processes, thus building your logistical knowledge.

Let's say that you're helping to organize a **conference** as part of your GRA duties. There are a thousand moving parts in conference organizing, only a few of which have to do with the content. Conferences are successful when the ideas are good and the infrastructure isn't noticed. And for the infrastructure not to be noticed, the rooms have to be scheduled properly, the program has to be accurate, the food and coffee have to arrive on time, the wireless network has to operate easily and have sufficient bandwidth, the registration check-in has to be rapid and friendly, the name tags have to be ready, the schwag bags have to have a couple of cute things in them along with the program and info papers, the accommodations and shuttle buses need to be organized, the VIPs have to be met at the airport, and a vast cell-phone network has to exist behind the scenes so that people can call up resources when small emergencies occur. If you pay attention to these things and learn to do them well, you'll be far better able to lead a team and write a budget when you're a faculty member conceiving of your own conference. The GRA gets no credit when things go well, but gains the tools that will allow her to be recognized for great work once she has GRAs of her own behind the scenes.

As a GRA, keep your ears open for faculty talking loosely about possible projects. If you hear a casual conversation about a potential research area, you might let it be known that you have an interest in that area. One of the things that a good assistantship might result in is **coauthorship** on your boss's paper, but you have to be on the project team to have that opportunity. Be prepared to say yes to work that's somewhat related to your own **research agenda**; it'll broaden your fields of experience and get you a little more exposure (and reputation as a smart, hard worker).

Research center. The most fundamental organizing categories on any campus are its **departments**: groups of **faculty** who share disciplinary fealty, who organize some component of courses or majors or graduate programs, and who advise a body of their pledged students. Departments are funded by the college, and are expected to be eternal elements of the college.

External funding through **grants** adds another roster of organizations to the campus: research groups, centers, institutes, and laboratories. These organizations have power and resources because of their income and influence on reputation, but there is no expectation of permanence, and the funding comes from outside the standard university budgeting.

When I was an undergraduate at Berkeley, three high-horsepower faculty members had garnered enough building-energy research grants to establish a research group that later became the Center for the Built Environment. The CBE now has a permanent staff, remarkable physical and computing resources for energy simulation, and several generations of doctoral students who have spread its thinking throughout higher education and the mechanical engineering and architecture industries.[169] Their money comes not so much from the Berkeley **chancellor**'s office, but from the US Department of Energy, from various utility companies, and from construction-industry partners. The CBE's leaders are still members of the architecture faculty, but their salaries are largely paid through **buyout**, their **teaching loads** are reduced, and their daily work is mostly taken up with CBE research and administration.

Likewise, when I was a doctoral student at UW–Milwaukee, a couple of members of the architecture faculty (and the dean of the School of Architecture and Urban Planning) had worked to receive a major donation from a private foundation to launch the Institute on Aging and the Environment. As with Berkeley's CBE, the IAE's leaders remained members of the architecture faculty, but the IAE was an independently funded entity that conducted research and design consultation with long-term care providers and their architects.

These auxiliary organizations are typically outside the department's governance, except through informal and political suasion by the **dean** and **provost**. They act in many ways as independent nonprofit agencies located within schools. Once established, they become magnets for graduate students—some who come to the college because of the institute's reputation, and some who come to the department for their own reasons but ultimately fall into the gravitational pull of research funding to finish their degrees. At Milwaukee the joke was that you had a lot of leeway with your **dissertation** topic in the architecture department, but to get financial support, its title had to include the words "people with dementia." This led to amusing hypotheticals such as "Contemporary Islamic Streetscapes for People with

169. Center for the Built Environment, "About Us: Industry/University Collaborative Research Solutions," accessed May 4, 2015, http://www.cbe.berkeley.edu/index.htm.

Dementia," "Visual Preferences in Seaside Recreational Community Design among People with Dementia," and "Slum Redevelopment in Calcutta as Experienced by People with Dementia."

Research institutes can be larger or smaller than a single department. Lots of centers span across departments, such as UW–Milwaukee's Center for 21st Century Studies,[170] UMass Boston's Center for Social Policy, Carthage College's Center for Children's Literature, or any of thousands and thousands of similar initiatives. A research group can also be organized and led by a single person, as in the case of a senior researcher's laboratory group. Regardless of size and span, though, the basic commonality among these groups is that they only live as long as the external funding allows, and so are always on the hunt for the next project or partner.

Research misconduct. The Office of Research Integrity, part of the US Department of Health and Human Services, has created a guide to the responsible conduct of research (often shorthanded as RCR), with nine components:[171]

1. research misconduct
2. protection of human subjects
3. welfare of laboratory animals
4. conflicts of interest
5. data management practices
6. **mentor** and trainee responsibilities
7. collaborative research
8. **authorship** and **publication**
9. **peer review**

Frankly, I'd call a violation within any one of those categories a potentially serious form of research misconduct, but from the ORI's point of view, "research misconduct" is a term reserved only for the fatal trio of *fabrication* (making up data or even whole studies), *falsification* ("tweaking" the data, misrepresenting the **methods,** or ignoring inconvenient outliers), and *pla-*

170. Which started back in the twentieth century as the Center for 20th Century Studies. It may become perpetual. Check back in a few hundred years.
171. United States Department of Health and Human Services, Office of Research Integrity, "ORI Introduction to the Responsible Conduct of Research," accessed on April 29, 2015, http://ori.hhs.gov/education/products/RCRintro/.

giarism (claiming credit for the work of others).[172] If you're found guilty of one of those, you can lose your project funding, lose your ability to apply for funding (for a period of time, or forever), lose your job, have your **publications** retracted, and in rare cases go to jail for defrauding the funders financially.

The entire RCR guidelines are worth studying in detail; they raise **methodological** and ethical questions that don't often come up in your academic methods courses. You and your colleagues over lunch will immediately come up with examples of problems from your own field that go far beyond the examples of the RCR training materials, especially if you're outside Health and Human Services' traditional interests in the laboratory sciences.

Research question. Matthew Miles and Michael Huberman opened their book on qualitative research **methods** by saying: "Qualitative research is the practice of successively lowering your expectations." And really, that's true of all research. We might be interested in how people use public space, how air resistance affects cars, or how social class impacts young people's life chances. But although those are important and useful questions, they're also far too large to conduct as single research studies. You'll hear many recommendations about "narrowing down" or "focusing" your research question, without very much direction as to what narrowing or focusing actually means.

What makes a question researchable? When I work with grad students, I try to get them to frame a topic that has a noun, a verb, a context, and a motive. (For those of you in the lab sciences, skip the motive.) And each of those four terms ought to be specific. For instance, let's look at "How do people use public space?" It has three of the four terms: the noun "people," the verb phrase "use space," and the context "public." But all three are far too slick to gain purchase. We might assume that people use spaces differently from one another, on the basis of gender or ethnicity or age or cultural background or social class or any number of characteristics. We might assume that people might behave differently in public space depending on whether that public space is a shopping center or a national park or a NASCAR grandstand. We have no idea what "use" means beyond simple occupancy. And we have no motive at all. A setting even as specific as NASCAR

---

172. You can read some of the more colorful instances of misconduct at US Department of Health and Human Services, Office of Research Integrity, "Case Summaries," accessed April 29, 2015, http://ori.hhs.gov/case_summary.

grandstands is a study in mixed motives: dedicated race fans, the family members they've dragged along, people trolling for dates, and public safety and concessions employees. Each of these people, and likely many more, want something different from their experience.

So if we made "people" into "early-career white-collar men," "use" into "have personal and professional conversations," "public space" into "Cleveland urban parks," and added the motive of taking a midday break from work, you'd have a study of professional social life in a big city that would advance our understanding of the physical context of engagement and **networking**. It would be a good nine- to twelve-month project worthy of a **dissertation**.

I have a friend who's studying the experience of Union loyalists in the South during and immediately after the Civil War. She's in the process of narrowing down all of these terms as her interests become illuminated through study in relevant archives and landscapes. "Union loyalists" might become soldiers, civilians, former soldiers, local/regional civic leaders; "the South" is probably going to be one region of southern Alabama and northern Florida, her childhood home. The context, "during and immediately after the Civil War," is probably going to have to be more closely described; during the political struggles marking the period between the dissolution of the Confederate government and the Compromise of 1877, maybe. What's missing altogether so far are the verb and motive. Engaging in political action? Participating in everyday civic or economic life? Protecting the safety of their families and property?

My own thinking is that if you start too soon with all four terms precisely named, you've cut off lots of potential avenues for growth; you need to define each of those areas in response to your growing sophistication and to areas that become especially exciting. But ultimately, the shift from "interest" to "dissertation topic" will be made only once the noun, verb, motive, and context have been fully formed.

As you're considering a doctoral program, look at the titles of the most recent dozen or so dissertations completed there. That'll give you a great idea of what your prospective **department** considers a research question, as well as giving you a pretty concrete sense of whether your own interests will be comfortably accommodated or grindingly misfit.

Résumé gap. If pressed, I could probably tell you where I worked during every month of my adult life. But if I'm applying for work in higher ed, I'm not going to tell you that I worked as a bowling alley mechanic from

October 1978 through May 1980, at which point I took over the snack bar operation for another nine months or so before running the pro shop. I'm probably not going to bring it to your attention that I dropped out of college at all, and I'm going to list my bachelor of arts at Berkeley as though I went straight there out of high school as everybody else did—not that I went to Michigan Tech for two years, worked for seven, went to community college at Laney College for three semesters, and only then transferred and finished my BA at **age** thirty-one. I'm not embarrassed by any of that, and in fact think that it's helped me to be a smarter, more empathetic, and more versatile scholar than I otherwise would have been. But that's something I'm going to argue in person, not let you try to intuit from reading my résumé.

If you look at the entry for **curriculum vitae**, you'll see that I emphasize "all of the qualifications you have obtained and work you have done that pertain to your professional and intellectual life." So I'm not going to go back to age twenty and talk about working in a bowling alley; that's not pertinent. But for many of us, there's also some lumpiness within our **careers**, and when applying for a **faculty** position, smooooooooth is what you want. No lumps, no detours, no delays. Think hollandaise, not country gravy.

So, although I'm not going to include the bowling alley or the sporting goods store or the running shoe store that supported me prior to completing my BA, I also have to figure out how to portray an odd couple of years within my later life. I finished my doctoral coursework at Milwaukee and defended my **dissertation** proposal in 1994, and moved to northern California to do my fieldwork.[173] I did field research and wrote my dissertation in a very efficient two years; I was supported by the university for the first field year, but not the second. I knew myself well enough to know that if I took a demanding job during the day, it would be difficult for me to gin myself up to write for four or six hours every evening. So I got a job selling furniture, which allowed me to go run in the morning, show up at the store at quarter to ten, lock up at 6:05 p.m. and leave it behind for dinner, and then write from 7:30 until midnight or 1 a.m.

I took that furniture job in fall 1995 when my fellowship ended, and I defended my dissertation in November 1996. So far, so good. On the CV, that's just listed as being in a doctoral program from 1991 through 1996,

---

173. Why? Because I'd always wanted to live in Arcata, and this was my chance to do it. In retrospect, I obviously should have stayed in Milwaukee and had my ear to the academic ground; but instead I moved to a beautiful, isolated, and decidedly unacademic environment.

smooth as hollandaise. But the lumps soon appeared. I trudged up the hill to the Humboldt State library every Thursday afternoon to read the ads in the latest *Chronicle of Higher Education*, usually getting it handed to me directly from the library mailroom, never before opened ... and trudged back down, empty-handed, two hours later.[174] I did that for two years. Finally, though I never really wanted to, I took a position with a design-research firm in January 1998, thinking that at least it was closer to what I wanted to do than selling futon frames.

So what do I do with calendar year 1997 on my CV? I wasn't involved in academia at all, nor was I involved in a meaningful professional connection. I was assembling office chairs and selling rugs.

Fortunately, a CV is organized categorically rather than merely chronologically, so the education is in one area and the work history in another. The hole in the "related work history" from 1991 to 1998 more or less corresponds to the 1991–96 plug of the doctoral program, and like a framing carpenter, you hope your customers don't notice the relatively small misfits that have no bearing on structural integrity. But CVs are read by intelligent people, and I'm sure that some folks have done the matching exercise and discovered the gaps between components.

There's a noted architectural theory book called *A Pattern Language*, which purports to have identified 253 universal patterns of good design, things that appear over time and across cultures.[175] One of them is called "half-inch trim," the idea being that large structural things almost never align perfectly, and that's why trim boards and moldings exist. How can you conceal résumé gaps with the career equivalent of half-inch trim?

You can conceal small gaps by citing your experiences by years only rather than years and months. You can add nonemployment work you did during the gap period if it's relevant: volunteer editing or community organizing work for a nonprofit. (Make sure you don't misrepresent it as a job, though; you can call the work section of your CV "Experience" instead of "Employment," which is accurate in both fact and spirit.) Ideally, you can find a named post-doc or ongoing **research assistantship** to cover the gap, even if it doesn't cover your rent.

Your CV has to be dead accurate; if you fabricate any part of it, you're

174. There were three postings that year for faculty positions in turf grass management, as I remember. 1996–97 was a good year for golf course agriculture, but a bad year for me.

175. Chris Alexander, Sara Ishikawa, and Murray Silverstein, *A Pattern Language: Towns, Buildings, Construction* (Oxford: Oxford University Press, 1977).

in danger of being caught out years later, and you'd feel bad about doing it anyway. But you can be accurate and still present yourself in the most advantageous way possible. If there are gaps in your relevant history, figure out how to portray them quietly so that they can become interesting stories you tell at your interview rather than blockages that keep you from being interviewed at all.

Ss

Sabbatical. Let's say that your **dissertation** has been published into a book, and has gotten you a **tenure-track** job. Let's further say that you've done a lot of research during your **assistant-professor** summers, and that too has finally coalesced into a second contracted book. You're safely through the gates of **tenure**, but you've kind of trampled down the ground of your original research ideas. You've been at that topic for a decade or more, you're more than a little **burned out** on it, and there isn't much more for you to say. What now?

The university, as a centuries-old model of scholarly life drawn from religious traditions, has anticipated your intellectual ennui. That's why it's instituted the sabbatical. Every seven years (biblically) or so (collegiately), you're entitled to apply for a semester's or a year's leave to open a new line of research or utterly immerse yourself in an ongoing project. The school pays your salary and benefits—often 100 percent if it's a semester, maybe two-thirds if it's a full year—while you go off to engage in some fresh scholarly pursuit. In a way, it's not unlike doing your doctoral program again; a year of fieldwork freed from other responsibilities, leading toward a dissertation-quality new work.

Because of that expectation of scholarly productivity, a sabbatical is never automatically granted. The application process, like a **job search**, starts about a year before the work you hope to undertake, and you have to apply for it just as seriously as you would any other research funding. You have to make the case for why the disciplinary community and your own college will benefit from the work; you have to get sign-offs from your department **chair** and **dean** and **provost**; and you often have to sign an agreement that you'll come back to the college for at least a year or two of continued work after the sabbatical has ended, so that you don't use your "visiting scholar" gig at another school to get yourself a permanent **offer**.

After the sabbatical, you have to report on the work you did and the **publications, grant proposals,** or other scholarly products that are likely to come from it. If you spend the year in circus school or painting on the beach in Mallorca and come back with nothing, it's unlikely that you'll be punished or be made to refund the money, but it's equally unlikely that your dean or provost will ever entrust you with anything again. I've heard a provost from a mid-sized university say directly, "We've wasted so many sabbaticals . . . ." That just means that any other **faculty** from his school will have to work twice as hard to demonstrate that their plans are both achievable and beneficial. A year's sabbatical, at an **associate professor**'s rate of pay and benefits, is at least a hundred-thousand-dollar investment in your intellectual growth. Don't mess it up.

Scholarship / scholarly activity. It's rare to have a PhD in architecture. Almost everyone else I worked with has an M. Arch; research **doctorates** in architecture are pretty uncommon, mostly located in subfields like architectural history or energy-use management or structural/material sciences (or, like mine, in environment-behavior studies). And frankly, a lot of the people teaching those specialties come from other **disciplines** anyway: they're architectural historians trained in art history, building energy analysts trained in mechanical or electrical engineering, or structures experts from civil or structural engineering or materials science.

But because architecture schools exist mostly as departments of larger universities, rather than as stand-alone trade schools, the research expectations common to higher education can act as a significant **career** barrier to those in the professional or artistic fields. Professional architects create buildings, not **peer-reviewed** academic papers. Likewise the professor of choreography or clarinet, the novelist, and the sculptor; the form of excellence their field demands is something other than a **journal** article.

Universities are slowly coming around to understanding what scholarly productivity means in nonresearch fields, and the phrase "research, scholarly, and creative activity" is starting to gain ground. The equivalent of **peer review** for a painter is a gallery or museum that agrees to show her work, the professional critic who writes a review of her exhibition, the art journal that publishes her career retrospective. If other professional artists and art critics respect her work, that's peer review. Likewise, if Sony Classical gives an artist a recording contract and he's invited to do eighty performances a year with a dozen different orchestras, those are pretty decent indicators of his capability as a pianist. And, like journals, these venues will have relative rankings. A painter whose work is shown at the Oakland Museum of California gets different career credit than a painter whose work is shown at the Starbucks down the block from the museum.

In professional or arts fields, the **CV** section having to do with **publications** will often include a significant number of publications that some other writer has written about you, not publications you've written yourself. Instead of the researcher's sections labeled "Books," "Journal Articles," and "Chapters," the musician's CV might have "Recordings," "Performances," and "Reviews"; the sculptor's CV might include "Commissions," "Gallery Representation," "Reviews"; the architect's CV might have "Commissions," "Competition Victories," "Reviews." All of those things are akin to the more traditional scholars' peer review; they're indicators that your work is a meaningful part of the dialogue in your field.

Once you have started on the track toward a research doctorate, your own published writing will be the currency upon which you live. It's not often that we think about this carefully, but if you're a research scholar, no matter what your field, you are fundamentally a writer. No writing, no **publications**, no **grant proposals**, no job. But if you have or are attempting to have another form of **terminal degree**, your version of scholarly productivity will be different as well. Examine what the leading lights of your field have accomplished, and how they represent those accomplishments on their CVs (and frankly, you'll only find CVs from professionals whose primary employment is in higher education; if they're day-to-day practitioners, their relevant representational genre is the résumé).

Seminar. Early in the semester of a graduate historical research methods seminar, our professor opened a class with the following question: "If you had to choose one city to study that you would use as a metaphor for the entirety of American history, which city would you choose?" A thought-provoking question. One of my fellow students said, "New York City. It's the city of immigration, the preeminent metropolis, the city of finance and money ...."

The professor smiled the smile of a man who had just pretended to throw a ball and was now amused at his dog's confusion. "Thaaaaaat's interesting," he said, stroking his metaphoric beard. "But really, if you could only choose one city ..."

I ventured forth. "I might choose Los Angeles. It's really the city of the twentieth century, with westward migration, huge suburbanization, focus on media and image, wasteful use of water and other resources. . . ."

"Thaaaaaat's interesting . . . but really, if you could only choose one city . . . ."

Well, we were onto his game now, and we just barked like crazy. "Albuquerque!" "Toledo!" "Boise!" Finally, someone said, "Washington, DC." "Iiiiiiiiiii think that's a very interesting choice," he said, and then proceeded to tell us for the next ten minutes why Washington would do nicely as a proxy for the entire nation.

This was not a seminar. What is a seminar? Anyone? Anyone?

That's right; a seminar is a class structure that encourages collective deliberation of difficult and unsettled ideas, rather than conveying the instructor's specific and fixed content. I couldn't have said it better myself.

If you have the chance to teach a seminar, please remember what they're for. [176] Bring material to the table that you personally are interested in and find unsettling or surprising. Ask questions that reveal your own uncertainty, or frame different ways of thinking about the problem at hand. And try to facilitate conversation among your students, rather than have them constantly responding to you.

Any seminar can be thought of as the most fundamental methods course for almost all interpretive **disciplines**, because the methods most often used in that mode of scholarship are close and careful reading, connection of one thinker's ideas with the ideas of others, and the tentative, provisional positioning of oneself in that conversation. Fields that study *tame* problems, to use Rittel and Webber's formulation, have little need for seminars, because wrong answers are demonstrably wrong.[177] But for fields with *wicked* problems, dissimilar ideas can each have merit and utility, and seminars are how the work of refinement and deliberation gets done.

---

176. This will raise terminology issues on most campuses. Often, courses are listed in official materials as *lecture*, *seminar*, and *laboratory*. But these have little to do with the conduct of class, and more to do with the enrollment size and the student products of class. In a lecture, the products are most often tests. In a seminar, products are term papers. And in a laboratory, products are experimental reports. Just because a course is called a seminar, that doesn't mean that seminar methods will be your best strategy—especially when, as is too often the case, seminars have twenty-five or thirty students arrayed in oppositional seating, with all of them facing one of you.

177. Horst Rittel and Melvin Webber, "Dilemmas in a General Theory of Planning," *Policy Sciences* 4 (1973): 155–69.

Short list (noun) / Shortlist (verb). In the United States, there are 351 Division 1 men's college basketball teams, but only about a fifth of them get invited to participate in the NCAA Championships. The ones that get into March Madness either have won their division tournaments or have been chosen as among the best in the country by a collection of athletic directors. So just being allowed to enter the tournament means that you've been judged to be better than 80 percent of all other big-time teams.

And you still might be Long Island University, and get beaten by twenty-two points in the first round by Michigan State.

A **faculty** search has much in common with March Madness, including the general time of year in which it takes place. You start your season in the fall, getting your materials in front of as many selection committees as makes sense. You're one of hundreds, and you need to show yourself as best you can.

Eighty percent fall away, and you make the big dance in the new year. But that's not the short list.

Another winnowing takes place, and you survive to the Sweet Sixteen. But that's not the short list either. It's often called the long list, and it comprises the people who will get screening interviews by telephone, by video meeting, or at disciplinary **conferences**.

After more competition, the Sweet Sixteen become the Final Four. That's the short list. If you hear someone say they were *shortlisted* for a position, they really ought to mean that they were one of the three to five people invited for a campus interview.

The NCAA Final Four, men's or women's, are truly elite teams; any one of them could beat any of the others on a particular day, and college athletic departments crow about how many Final Fours they've made, not merely how many championships they've won. I've been shortlisted seven times, five times for jobs I haven't gotten, and once the pain of the final **rejection** wears off,[178] I can look back and have empirical evidence that a search committee saw me as intellectually and interpersonally viable for a job that I wanted. But you can't put a shortlist on your CV, even though it obviously shows that you were among the best one or two percent of all candidates for a given position, the equivalent of scoring 700-plus on an area of the SATs. It would just remind another review committee that you were a loser somewhere else, an image you do *not* want in their heads at that particular moment.

178. It never does.

Soft money / hard money. Colleges make money in a lot of ways. The one you're most familiar with is tuition and fees, which you've been paying for many years. But they also make money from real estate holdings, from licensing fees for sports and logo schwag, from renting the dorms over the summer to youth soccer camps and "college exploration weeks," from **intellectual property** rights to inventions and patents, and from **grants** for the conduct of specific projects.

The term "soft money" or "soft-money employee" refers to a program or position funded only because of the existence of a grant; the contrast is "hard money," written into the college's ongoing operational budget. Any project that has grant funding can be staffed in one of two ways. Through **buyouts**, the college can be reimbursed for some or all of a faculty member's normal salary and benefits; in exchange, that employee's normal workload in teaching or service is reduced, and that workload shifts to the grant project. The idea is that the college will need to pay someone else to temporarily cover those courses or that service, and thus must pay extra; that "extra" comes from the grant. The other way of funding a project is to hire someone directly through payment from the grant funding itself, which of course means that the position will end once the funding ends.

Often, the project leader(s) (see **PI**) will have a buyout arrangement in a project, since they're likely to be **tenured** or otherwise long-term college employees; it's more likely that the lower-level researchers, **research assistants**, and **administrative staff** are soft-money employees, working diligently until the project ends or the money runs out. 'Twas ever thus.

Soft-money positions can be converted to hard-money positions if the college becomes convinced that the project should become a lasting part of its work. That's one of the ways in which administrative growth and "mission creep" occurs: the college gets funding to develop an eating-disorders program or a young-faculty **mentoring** program, and if the program is successful, the college can hardly give it up once people rely upon it. Cautious administrators will occasionally decline to sponsor a grant proposal, even if the project it describes is intelligent and useful on its own terms; it's important to be wary about extending the college's long-term commitments in ways that might become permanent.

Sponsored research. The late-night-movie version of the researcher is the hermit who cobbles together lab materials from found objects, who sits in front of the old manual typewriter or stands scribbling at the dusty blackboard, ignored and ignorable until at last the importance of his work can no longer be denied.

Those folks are still around, but most research costs money. At the very least, there's the cost of keeping your apartment lit and warm while you write. But artists need studio space and materials, historians need visits to distant archives, archaeologists need **research assistants** and their trips to the field sites, and astrophysicists need zillion-dollar computer-managed telescopes and armies of technicians to maintain and operate them.

As in any creative endeavor, there are at least three ways of organizing the economics of your research work. You can work on spec, making something and hoping it'll get bought; that's what all unknowns do, whether writers or scientists. You can work on contract, having convinced someone to pay you up front on the promise that your work will be of high benefit and high quality. Or you can work for a patron, someone who simply cares enough about your craft (and about his own name recognition) that he'll pony up and support you.

If you do your work the first way, sitting in the garret and working in the cold until the novel is published, you'll get some recognition from your **department** come **tenure** time, but you'll be invisible to the institution as a whole. Once you enter the second or third modes, though, you'll be engaged in sponsored research and thus be beloved by your **dean**. Sponsored research is good for colleges because the contract or award is something they can publicize, because it relieves the college's burden for some of your salary, and because significant funding carries with it the **overhead** support that makes your work a net plus to the institution's finances.

Major research universities (and smaller schools that aspire to research activity) will often have an office of sponsored research. These are the folks on campus who know who the grant makers are; know the best possible funds or programs for you to apply to, and how to manage your application; and know how to get the right permissions from your **administration** and the right information from your accounting office. If you want your **career** to move, learn how sponsored research is facilitated on your campus, and stop by for a preliminary chat before you head off on any particular intellectual excursion.

A word of caution, though. The federal government and its big-science agencies have for decades been the endless buffet that fed the academic world, and sponsored research offices are well prepared to assist with **grant** applications to the National Science Foundation, the National Institutes of Health, and the US Departments of Energy, Agriculture, or Commerce.

They may be less aware of the hundreds of thousands of family foundations or state and local agencies that can fund small, career-launching projects. So allow yourself to be guided by your sponsored research professionals, but be prepared to do your own legwork as well. And beware also of industry-sponsored research; even if the corporate manufacturer of pesticides or GMOs or cigarettes keeps their hands off your work—and they don't always—you'll always operate under the cloud of reasonable suspicion that your findings are artificially friendly to your sponsor.

Start-up costs. To follow on our conversation of **sponsored research**, let's imagine the categories of things you might need to spend money on. You might need equipment and supplies and materials, computing hardware and software, **research assistants**, **travel** and archive access, professional memberships and **journal** subscriptions, licensing or patent fees, **publication** fees (if your journals charge page fees or charge for the inclusion of certain kinds of graphics), or laboratory or other work space outfitted in a particular way. As part of your initial job **offer**, you may receive a certain set amount of start-up costs, usually pretty low (a few thousand bucks at most), as a standard package from the university. But if you have specific needs for scholarly success, you can't manage without them.

A school is not going to give away significant start-up funds to make some bland "contribution to knowledge." The institution takes a very cold-eyed look at return on investment; and the more you ask for, the more you need to be able to return to the college through external funding. Because of this, different colleges and their expectations for academic productivity will make different kinds of start-up support available. At Southern Illinois University at Edwardsville, for instance, the standard start-up is $3,500,[179] whereas for a high-powered science research program, a start-up package of half a million bucks for a new **assistant professor** wouldn't be unreasonable.[180] If a research university wants to recruit a senior researcher from another school, the start-up could be well into the millions if the faculty member has a proven record of major funding and the school thinks it can recoup its expenses more

179. Southern Illinois University Edwardsville, Office of Research and Projects, "Research & Development: New Faculty Start-up," accessed December 31, 2014, http://www.siue.edu/orp/internalgrants/startup.shtml.

180. See for instance Ronald Ehrenberg, Michael Rizzo, and Scott Condie, "Start-Up Costs in American Research Universities," Cornell University Digital Commons Working Papers 33 (March 2003), accessed December 31, 2014, http://digitalcommons.ilr.cornell.edu/cgi/viewcontent.cgi?article=1039&context=workingpapers.

quickly. The numbers don't come from nowhere; the incoming faculty member is essentially writing a business plan with anticipated expenses and anticipated income, and with the university as the business partner.

If you're a poet, your income and expenses will be low, and start-up will be a marginal part of your job negotiations even at a major research institution. If you're in molecular biology or particle physics, though, break out the spreadsheet and get serious about the argument you'll present for your start-up package; it may make a far larger long-term contribution to your happiness than your starting salary.

Tt

Teaching. We all have a handful of teachers whom we can look back upon with great joy, and whose work somehow inspired us to change our path or to recommit to a path we'd already chosen. I can name ten or twelve teachers, of the dozens I've had in twenty-two years of classroom education, who had that kind of life-changing effect.[181] Those are the people who have most influenced my own repertoire as a teacher, the ones whose examples became my training manual.

Who else among us has that kind of impact on so many lives? Who else is privileged to work directly with people who entrust us with their curiosity?

Because of that responsibility, I have almost as many books on my shelf about teaching as I do about my own content area. I'm good at teaching, but I'm not as good as I want to be, and I never will be. I love to read biographies of teachers, essays by teachers, polemics by teachers. I learn from each what makes them impassioned, and the tricks they've discovered to make the patchwork of learning run another day. I don't bother so much with handbooks and training guides, which are too sanitized to be trustworthy.

You're going to be a teacher. And you're going to start out being a less-than-good teacher. It's important to know that, to acknowledge it, and to

---

181. I would encourage you to make that list for yourself. It'll make you happy, help you remember why you embarked upon all this in the first place, and give you something to post on your computer monitor for strength in dark hours.

embrace it as a first step on your mission to *become* a good teacher. Here are a few things to remember about that voyage.

First, your students are pretty resilient, and you won't break them if you come to the work with good intentions. I can name that top 10 percent or so of the teachers who've changed my trajectory; I can also name the 10 percent or so who were truly awful due to **burnout**, malice, or their privilege of procedure above learning. The other 80 percent did me no harm, and most of them were probably useful to other students with different agendas.

Second, you have to believe that teaching can be learned. If you assume that class isn't going well because your students are wastrels who just want to drink, text, and get laid, then it's all out of your hands and there's no point in continuing. If, on the other hand, you assume that class isn't going well because you're irretrievably incapable of the work, then it's equally out of your hands and there's no point in continuing. You have to believe that class isn't going well because you're not doing some things as well as you could and your students aren't doing some things as well as they could, and that all of those skills can be acquired.

Third, you can't learn teaching (or anything else) systematically. Learning is a nonlinear experience. You stagnate, and then have a sudden period of improvement. You have days when even a good course goes poorly, days when the spark just won't take. You find yourself particularly frustrated by a particular component of the teaching life, and you seek help with that; that work improves, and your concern turns to another area of inadequacy. You learn what you need to learn, when you need to learn it. (This will be true for your students, too, regardless of what your carefully planned syllabus says.)

Fourth, your teaching is not independent from the rest of your life. I was not a good teacher during the year I was getting divorced. I wasn't terrible, but I don't think I made anybody's life list that year; I was limping along as best I could during a time of reduced capability. You'll have times when your teaching isn't good because nothing is good, other times when your teaching is just one aspect of a life that seems whole and strong. Likewise, your students' learning is not independent from the rest of their lives, and their performance in your class is only a three-hour sliver out of a dense and emotional week.

Fifth, your teaching will be far too private. Invite people in to watch how class unfolds, and to tell you what they saw and heard. When I observe someone else's teaching, I try hard not to offer advice. Instead, I attempt to be a reporter and to point out things that they may have missed in the flurry of the class. "Almost all of the participation in seminar came from four people out of the twelve; there was a moment when one student redefined a term you'd been using, and that seemed to unlock the next ten minutes; I saw very few people taking notes, even though they seemed mostly to be paying careful attention to your lecture." You need coaching, just as any elite professional needs coaching, and the core skill of coaching is precise observation.

Sixth, enthusiasm is infectious. When I was doing my dissertation, I asked a lot of teens and adults what they loved to do and how they got started with it. In nearly every case, they started because someone they knew and liked was enthusiastic about that hobby, and because it just looked like their friends were having fun doing it. If you walk into the classroom aflame with your topical material, more of your students will follow you into the fire; if you're tepid about the work, you'll catch nobody.

Seventh, you won't catch them all, no matter how good you are. The same student who loves her lab classes may be halfhearted at best about literature; the talented history student may never fully engage with statistics. And that's fine. I've never understood our valorization of the 4.0 student; all that means is that her **curriculum** has never yet been demanding enough for her to discover where her limits are. Once her **grade** drops from an A to a B, we've discovered something she needs to work on; or perhaps we've discovered something she never needs to do again.

Finally, not all of your students will be equal, and the inequality may have nothing to do with their intelligence. I believe that all kids are born curious, wanting to know. They have a certain amount of kindling waiting to be ignited; some have more than others, to be sure, but all young people carry the capability of bursting into flame.

Some of those kids are raised in flammable environments. They're surrounded by books and magazines, sent to schools with impassioned and challenging teachers, nurtured by families who value ideas and argument. Those kids' kindling is lit from birth, and all you have to do when they show up in your class is throw another log on the fire.

Some kids are raised in pretty airless homes: stable and loving families, to be sure, but with lots of television, no serious thinking or discussion of civic life at the table, dull schools without purpose, no sense of possibility. The kindling is all there but it's inert, it's never been struck. When one of those kids comes into your class, you have to search for the spark that might ignite their particular arsenal of interests.

And some kids have had their kindling pissed on their whole lives.

They're told that school is for sissies, or that girls can't do science, or that they'll never succeed in school because they're black, a factory kid, a redneck, an immigrant, you name it. Or they were raised with violence that left them untrusting, or were sent to schools that were little more than feedlots. When those kids arrive in your classroom, they may be too wet to burn; there may be nothing you can do that will help them overcome their fear, their disdain, or their resistance. Your job is to help them dry out, at least a little. They may not succeed in your class, but there will be others to come in their lives, and you can be one of the first people who doesn't demean them or tell them those same old stories. You can be someone who offers them safety and trust, so that a later teacher might find the right spark.

When I was a kid, I loved the pastor of our church. Lutheran minister was the first job I ever aspired to. Forty years later, I didn't become a pastor; in fact, I've left that faith altogether. But for a few years, I got the job I wanted. I got to study important texts and think about their meaning; I got to write and do public speaking; I got to reach out to people in need, and help them across difficulties in their lives; I got to have the office that people stopped into when they had a problem or a question.

I got to be a teacher.

Teaching assistant / TA. The key word here is "assistant." As an assistant, you might just make photocopies. You might take attendance, or keep the gradebook. You might load PDF documents onto the **learning management system**. You might do some of the grading, especially the grading of exams for which there are answer keys and little judgment to exercise. Those are all the housekeeping of teaching, the chores that must be done.[182] But you might be allowed some additional discretion. For instance, in a huge lecture class, teaching assistants lead smaller subdivided sections to discuss and clarify major points of the lectures and text. You might read and grade the research papers of the students in your discussion section. And you might be permitted to prepare and deliver two or three lectures during the course of the semester.

As a graduate student aiming yourself toward a faculty **career**, you want teaching experience. If you get a year-long TA-ship, work with your faculty supervisor to set up a sequence of increasing responsibility, so that in the

---

182. Like any housekeeping, teaching chores can be done with inattention or with grace. If these kinds of tasks are "all" you're given, do them with care and you'll learn some things anyway.

fall semester you're focusing on logistical work, and in the spring you have the opportunity to take on more facets of course preparation and conduct. Make it clear to your supervisor that this **mentorship** is as important to you as the scholarly mentorship, and that you're in this to learn something about the craft of teaching as well as to pay for another year of school.

Learn the history of the course. When did it originate? What course came before it? Who else has taught it, and how does it change when it's in someone else's hands? Which elements of the course are this instructor's emphasis areas, and which are constant?

Learn the placement of the course within the larger **curriculum**. What other courses are students expected to have taken before this class, and what will they take after it? What are the core skills that these students' next round of instructors will expect them to have?

Learn what's unsatisfying about the course as it stands. What would your supervising instructor do with this course if the decision were entirely within her purview? Which part of the course seems somehow "broken" or less satisfying than it should be? Offer to take on some research to revise that element of the course. If that offer isn't accepted, just nod and go on about your work, but consider for yourself how you might reframe that course component if you had the chance.

If you treat your assistantship as another course you're taking, you will build professional capability in ways that most graduate students and early-career faculty will have never considered. You'll be prepared to engage in your **department**'s pedagogical deliberations, prepared to take on new courses more quickly. Think of your TA-ship as an apprentice period, and be active in framing what you want to learn and what your instructor might have to offer.

Teaching load. It's interesting that of **tenure**'s big three—scholarship, teaching, and service—teaching is the only one that is spoken of in terms of "load." You may think that's because teaching is seen as particularly burdensome, but a more generous understanding is that it's the only one of the three that can be adequately quantified. Nobody can say just how much research you'll need to fulfill your responsibilities, or how much service on committees and task forces, but we know exactly how many courses you have to teach.

You'll hear things in casual conversation like "I don't know what the hell he's complaining about; he's only got a three-two load," or "I'm not sure about taking this position; they're expecting a four-four." Although they may sound like fractions or musical time signatures, what these designators actually mean are the number of courses a **faculty** member is expected to teach over the course of an academic year. Usually, the two numbers are equal: three courses in the fall and three in the spring is a 3/3, for instance.[183] Some colleges structure their teaching such that faculty have a lighter load in one semester, so that they can do some work on their research; and you'll hear about a 4/3 or 3/4, depending on which semester is lighter.

Some (typically the teaching-focused) colleges frame teaching load in terms of the number of credits one is responsible for, either by semester or by year. So a college might expect a twenty-four-credit teaching load, which would be the equivalent of a 4/4: eight three-credit courses over an academic year. An individual faculty member will determine with her department **chair** how to spread that out over fall and spring, and in some cases summer.

Although the teaching load is made explicit at almost every college, there's an often unspoken paired variable, which is the number of *different* courses you might be teaching. Teaching four sections of first-year writing is an easier task than teaching one section of first-year writing, one section of nineteenth-century English romantic poetry, one section of the contemporary American novel, and one section of women's memoir. Each of those requires its own unique preparation, and faculty members often talk about how many "preps" they have in a given semester. In some colleges, the number of preps is included in the formal teaching load, but that's hardly standard practice. And not all courses are worth three credits: some schools give one-third of one credit for leading an independent study, for instance, or three credits for teaching the lecture and one credit for leading the lab section. It can get pretty complex pretty fast.

So how much *should* a faculty member be teaching? Well, those expectations vary enormously across the spectrum of higher ed. There are high-powered research appointments that carry a 1/1 load, with the expectation that one of those is a broad required course and the other is a graduate seminar in one's own research specialty. The counterpoint is that those "overpaid, underworked" professors bear gigantic expectations for their research productivity and **grant** funding prowess. Research-focused universities in general tend toward 2/1 and 2/2 loads, whereas at the stronger

183. No matter what the numbers are, you'll pronounce them as sequential words, such as "four-four" or "three-two." In text, most often you'll see the slash or sometimes a hyphen between them.

Table 3. Implications of teaching loads for your academic lifestyle

Teaching load	College type	Research expectations	Will you be in your office for office hours?	Will you have graduate students to advise and lead?
1/1	Research-centered departments in research-centered universities	Internationally acknowledged as an authority in your field	Once in a rare while; don't count on it	Only a handful of the very best, who will be supporting you in your own research endeavors
2/2	Research-centered universities	Consistently published in your field	Probably, though things do come up...	Yes, that will be a primary expectation
3/3	Private liberal arts colleges of highest reputation	Published enough in your field so that you're a recognizable name	Yes	Yes, unless your college is *really* undergraduate-focused, in which case you'll be leading senior theses and creative projects
4/4	State comprehensive colleges, less prestigious liberal arts colleges	Published enough in your field so that we might find you in a quick database search	Yes, unless you're at yet another governance committee meeting	Probably not; you'll be teaching in mainly undergrad programs
5/5	Community colleges with a decent union	None	Yes; you'll be there constantly, grading away	There won't be any.
6/6	Community colleges in nonunion systems	None	No; you'll be in another class-room, or trying to eat a sandwich somewhere.	There won't be any.

liberal arts colleges that expect scholarly productivity, a 3/2 or 3/3 is the norm.[184] Teaching-focused colleges like the smaller state schools and non-elite liberal arts colleges tend to center around 4/4. At community colleges, where faculty members typically carry no expectation of scholarly productivity, 5/5 is not uncommon, and I've heard of 6/6.

184. See the entry for **buyout** to learn more about the ways that research funding can reduce the contractual teaching load even further.

The **faculty handbook** at any school should be explicit about the expectations for teaching load; what happens if you have an overload (teach more than enough courses in a given semester); how giant enrollments or courses with more credit hours or graduate courses are counted differently; and what happens if a scheduled course doesn't run due to low enrollment. More important than the raw numbers, though, is what these teaching loads imply for your life. Knowing that exceptions abound, we can characterize it as shown in table 3.

These two little numbers carry enormous implications for what kind of a life you're going to lead, and what "being a faculty member" will really mean on the ground at any specific school. When you're considering taking a new position, it's important to understand what kind of faculty life you're dreaming of,[185] and whether the workload of your proposed position is anything like it. If you aspire to do groundbreaking research, be wary of a 4/4. If you love the idea of classroom interaction, be careful of the 2/2. And don't think that "getting your foot in the door" at a 4/4 gives you a leg up on getting an appointment at a 2/1 later. To borrow from the apocrypha of elite architects, beware of taking early jobs designing kitchens; you'll become known for great kitchens, and never get a more important project. If your first faculty job is at the University of Wisconsin–Stevens Point, forget about the University of Wisconsin–Madison. The world of higher education, supposedly focused on critical thinking, is actually very quick to judge and slow to reconsider.

Telephone/video interview. In our discussion of **shortlisting**, I talked about how the candidate pool is filtered and strained until there are roughly a dozen or fifteen whom the committee believes are viable and interesting. That list becomes the **short list** of four or so through some kind of a screening process, either in person at a national **conference interview** or, more often, through a virtual interview via phone, Skype, Google Hangout, WebX, or any number of other electronic connections.[186]

185. The colleges we most often see in the movies, with the avuncular professors, ivy-covered walls, and elbow-patched sport coats, are probably 3/3s.

186. Even just naming these software programs will soon date this entry; videoconference protocols change all the time, and the school you're interviewing with will almost certainly be using one that you're not familiar with. All of them work haphazardly, at best, without a lot of practice and immense technical support. Cross your fingers and hope they just use the phone.

The telephone requires only a few brief preparations. Use a landline if possible, a cell phone only under duress. Don't use the speakerphone feature; the sound quality is usually worse. Make sure that no interruptions are possible: have your computer sounds off, your cell phone silenced, and your family, cats, and fellow students exiled. Have a notepad next to the phone and space to write, and keep your watch next to the notepad so you can track the time. Note the names of the committee members as best you can, and their genders if possible, so that you might have a sense of who's asking which question.

A video conference requires all of those precautions plus several others. Foremost among them, make sure that your understanding of the conferencing technology is completely bulletproof. Find out what protocol they use, and practice making and receiving video calls with it until it's as easy as opening the fridge. Dress as nicely as you would for an in-person interview, since your shirt, tie, and jacket will all be visible on screen.

An often overlooked part of video conferencing is the placement of the camera. You'll be watching them on your monitor, and they'll be watching you via your webcam, which is probably that little dot at the top of your monitor. Experiment with the angle and placement of that camera to ensure that your face is right at the center of the screen view; I've been part of an interview where someone was using their laptop and started with the screen opened all the way back, which meant that their webcam was giving us an unobstructed view of ceiling tiles.[187]

You will have the illusion that the monitor is a sort of window through which you and the committee are communicating, but it's crucial to clear that mistake up right now. You see them through the monitor, they see you through the camera, and those two things are not in line with one another. Eye contact is just as important in a video interview as it is in person, and you make eye contact by looking directly into the camera. If you're looking at the monitor, your eyes will seemingly be averted from your viewers, and you'll look shifty. Look at the monitor when they talk to you, that's fine; but look directly into the camera when you talk to them. (If you have a stand-alone webcam, you can place it so that it's right in front of the monitor;

---

187. And make sure that the room you're in is adequately lit. Otherwise, the only illumination will be that sickly blue light of the computer monitor making your face look ghostly and putting a huge reflection into your glasses. Really, this is *theater!* Make yourself look good.

they won't be able to see it, and you'll be looking at the camera and the committee at the same time.)

Five or six committee members will be on one end of the phone, and they'll introduce themselves around the table they're gathered at; write down their names and **departments**. They've called you, so there's no need to introduce yourself. You'll usually start by being asked to describe why you're interested in this particular position. Use no more than 10 percent of the total time to do this—not more than three minutes of a half-hour call, not more than five minutes of an hour-long call. (See the entry on **elevator/ airplane talk**). You can script this if you like, though you shouldn't read it. Pay attention to your watch.

The chitchat, the introductions, and your soliloquy will have taken eight to ten minutes. You'll then be asked a series of uniform questions that the committee is asking of all of their candidates; most often, each of the committee members will be allotted one question, and they'll take turns. Listen carefully to each question, and respond to it in not more than sixty seconds—maybe ninety seconds if it's a particularly important response that reveals a lot about your capabilities and intentions, but you don't want to go on at length. And even though you'll probably diverge somewhat to be able to talk about your strengths,[188] make sure you've answered each question.

After the scripted questions, there'll be a couple of questions related specifically to something you've said, or to some unique element of your background. Those can be engaging, but be sure that your answer is as concise there as it was for the others.

Finally, if the committee is practiced at their role, they'll stop with about a third to a quarter of the time remaining, and ask you if you have any questions for them. You'd better; anything less and you'll come off as unprepared and casual. This is a moment to remember the truism that you're interviewing them just as much as they're interviewing you. You're a colleague, not a grad student. So ask them interpretive rather than factual questions about their department:

188. In political speech, this is called "the pivot." Reporter: "Senator Jones, there are rumors circulating that you're having an affair with your chief-of-staff's daughter . . . Do you have a comment?" Senator Jones: "I'm glad you've asked me that, Paul. Good relationships are so important to our nation, and that's why I find it so disturbing that my opponent has consistently opposed marriage for gay and lesbian couples." Practice your pivot (better than that one) so that questions become opportunities to talk about other great things you've done and are capable of doing for this new college.

- How would you describe the core values or goals of your program?
- Where do you imagine the program will be in five years?
- What's surprised each of you the most about working at your institution?

You'll get them thinking, you'll discover alliances and fault lines among the committee members, and they'll leave the conversation feeling as though they've just had an interesting dialogue.

The committee chair or spokesperson should tell you what the next steps in the process are. That's usually something like, "We're in the midst of doing telephone interviews now, and that process will conclude in the next two weeks. We'll meet as a committee to discuss those interviews, and will invite finalist candidates to a campus visit, probably sometime in March." If the committee doesn't provide this overview, it is perfectly acceptable to ask directly, "Can you tell me the next steps in the process and what you imagine the timeline might be?"

Finally, once goodbyes are said all around, make absolutely, utterly sure that you're disconnected before you sigh, swear, or otherwise emote. Congratulations on getting through it. The committee now has something to talk about, and if you've done well, they'll be speaking positively and making the appropriate mark next to your name on the list. Write a thank-you to each member of the committee.

Tenure/P&T. Tenure is one of the most hotly debated aspects of the structure of higher education. In briefest form, its proponents speak of tenure as the guardian of **academic freedom**, ensuring that a **faculty** member cannot be released from her or his position because of unpopular academic or political stances. In briefest form, its opponents speak of tenure as a featherbed, as guaranteed lifetime employment at a pretty good salary with more than pretty good benefits. Thousands of opinion pieces, both within the higher ed community and in the media at large, have ingested millions of words in support of one position or the other, without a lot of nutrition to show for it. Demagogues use the concept of tenure to attack public education in particular and public service in general. Other demagogues use their own achievement of tenure to simply be pests and gadflies, offensive for the sake of offending.

Let's take a clear look at what tenure does. When a young faculty member is awarded tenure, several specific things happen. First, she has received a promotion and her title changes, from **assistant professor** to **associate**

professor. It's like becoming a partner in a law firm; Dr. Vita R. Vetted is now an *associate* of the college, with the expectation of a full-**career** relationship. And there's an accompanying pay raise, one that goes beyond her annual cost of living increase and sets Dr. Vetted onto a new plateau perhaps ten thousand dollars or so higher than before.

The tenure decision welcomes Dr. Vetted into a long-term relationship with the college. And colleges tend to be pretty long-term enterprises. At the very least, students show up expecting to embark on a four-year journey, so we want them to have a relatively stable **curriculum** and **mentorship**. We want a group of established leaders whose reputation attracts graduate students and professional renown. In some fields we outfit laboratories for particular kinds of research, and so expect to be able to amortize that expense over a long service life; we want the ongoing income from **overhead** payments that come from their **grant**-funded research. Higher education is not quick-turnover work, and the institution benefits from the expectation of stability as much as the tenured faculty member does.

That stability, of course, has drawbacks as well as advantages. A culture's interests change over the course of a thirty-year career, and if Dr. Vetted doesn't keep pace, her work may become irrelevant. More problematically, whole departments may be based on topics that go stale, and the burden of their upkeep may prevent the college from opening newer departments of more current interest. Ford doesn't make the Pinto anymore, not even an updated and improved version; they were able to let it go as an organizational decision in favor of the internationally sourced Escort. In part because of tenure structures, colleges don't have the commensurate ability to drop departments that have become less productive or less interesting, and the enterprise grows by accretion.

Although scholars are indeed employed by their colleges, there is a way to think about tenure as something other than an element of an employment **contract**. A college faculty has significant similarities with a polygamous family, whose primary goals are to live in fealty to the faith and to raise a *lot* of children. So the academic family recruits new potential mates from among a broad pool of candidates, and then the initiate goes through six years of elaborate but pertinent courtship rites. We want to see if she's kind to her colleagues, if he's good with the kids, if she upholds the rites and rituals of the **discipline**, if he gets his work done.

At the end of that six years, the initiate asks for a formal declaration of marriage—first from his immediate partners in his department, then from the elders who sit on the P&T (promotion and tenure) **committee**, and finally to the **provost**-bishop who has the final word on admitting new members to all the families within her institution.

Marriage and family membership are not intended to be a revocable status. It may be that the marketplace shifts and fewer students choose computer programming as their major, preferring the raw materials of electrical engineering instead. When that happens, tenure systems generally ensure that, although we're not adding to the computer science family at the moment, we're not going to jettison any of our current members. And we all know that courtship is hard work, and that after a few years of marriage, it's tempting to sit on the couch in your shorts and socks and watch *NFL Sunday Doubleheader*. But most families, and most family members, are a little better than that, and continue trying in good faith to be strong and supportive partners.

And divorces do happen. Scholars find more attractive positions, or have breakdowns of ethical performance, or just get sick of hanging around with the same people over and over and over, any of which can lead to a formal parting of ways. You can leave a position before or after having received tenure; but the position can only leave you before tenure, after which you have to do something particularly egregious to be fired.

Tenure track. There are a hundred kinds of teaching jobs in higher ed, but they can be divided into two fundamentally different tracks. For those on track one, teaching is a form of back-room support, with low autonomy and high pace. Its participants are still responsible for the success of the team and the welfare of all involved, but they'll not make much money, no one will contribute to their retirement or healthcare, and no one will ask their opinion. They won't be invited to participate in panel discussions at the big events, and won't be interviewed by the media when expert opinion is sought. And the day they're too ill or too disgusted to take another assignment is the day they will no longer work in the industry.

Those driving on track two are the public face of the enterprise, the enduring representatives of the organization. Their pay is not merely assured, but is easily double or more than that of anyone in the first group—and it's bolstered further by insurance, an office, retirement contributions, research infrastructure, and travel and professional development expenses. Members of group two are asked to take an active role in the management of the larger organization, to plan its strategy and implement its agenda. If a member of group two gets sick or needs family leave, the organization will plan around them and cover their absence, for months or even years if need be. And if they meet the institution's expectations over their first six years or so, they will be offered **tenure**—a permanent, irrevocable spot in the roster.

There are at least a few things to say about this state of affairs, only some of which are even remotely polite and only a handful of which are related to the purpose of this book, which is the understanding of academic culture for people who'd like to be part of it. So I will use the metaphor of the tracks literally, and limit my remarks to the following:

1. Job ads for track one will employ varied terminology, typically an adjective implying impermanence (**adjunct**, temporary, contract, contingent, visiting, guest) followed by a noun (instructor, faculty, lecturer, scholar). A job ad for track two will use specific language: it will be called tenure-track, or tenure-stream, or ladder-rank, and its first rung will be called **assistant professor**.[189] An assistant professor is presumed to be "on track" to become tenured; everybody else is off the track, engaged in service work.
2. There are a lot more people behind the scenes in group one than on the track in group two.
3. If you begin your post-PhD **career** off the tenure track, it will be exceedingly difficult to find your way onto that track later. You will be traveling on the service roads that rarely connect to the super-speedway.
4. Persons in group one will be more or less invisible to persons in group two, just as the winning NASCAR team owner doesn't publicly thank his pit crew's left-rear-tire man after a big win.
5. We have known about this two-tracked system, and about its emotional and economic impact, for decades. We not only accept it, we not only perpetuate it, we have accelerated it. It is neither accidental nor unexpected.

When you look at a job ad in higher education, these five elements form the underlying structural conditions that apply not to a particular job, but to all

189. The tenure track is a superspeedway, with only three curves: turn one, assistant professor; turn two, associate professor; and turn three, full professor. All the other tracks are behind the scenes, often underground, where the tractor-trailers and the food-service trucks come in.

jobs. They are the unspoken text behind every visible line. Do not imagine that being the very best left-rear-tire man in NASCAR history will ever get you behind the wheel.

Terminal degree. Throughout this book, I've talked blithely about the connections between pursuing a PhD, obtaining a PhD, and getting an academic job. But there are some fields in which PhDs are rare as rubies, and most of the **faculty** members have other sorts of degrees.

A terminal degree is not an academic diagnosis of pending fatality. It simply means the degree that is the highest customarily awarded in a particular field. If you're an art historian, the terminal degree is the PhD, because your field is based on research. If you're a performing artist (whether theatrical, visual, or textual), the terminal degree is the master of fine arts (MFA). If you're an architectural historian or building materials scientist, the terminal degree is the PhD, because your field is based on research. If you're a practicing architect, the terminal degree is the master of architecture (M. Arch).

The terminal degree aimed at professional practice will in most cases be a master's degree. If you're teaching in a practice- or performance-based **discipline**, the terminal master's degree will suffice for consideration for a faculty position. It'll always be looked upon with a little disdain by colleagues in other **departments**, though, and **tenure** is somewhat more difficult because the **P&T** committee will be made up of people from across the school who are used to looking at the **publications** section of the **CV** first, rather than at professional outcomes. There's a push to the PhD in some professional, artistic, or clinical disciplines simply as academic self-preservation; that's led to some unfortunate individual decisions to pursue **doctorates** through shady institutions that offer online convenience, and to some unfortunate institutional decisions to offer doctorates not grounded in rigorous advancement of a field's thinking.

If you have a nondoctoral terminal degree, you can ask the hiring committee what their attitude is toward terminal degrees in their field, but you should also investigate what the promotion history has been. It may be that although the department thinks you'd be a good fit, the college as a whole doesn't often offer tenure to faculty members without PhDs. Don't set yourself up for a surprise a few years after hire; learn up front whether your proposed employer values your degree enough to defend it during promotion decisions.

Thesis. In England and other nations with a longer history of higher education, it's common to speak of someone writing their doctoral thesis. That's not the customary usage in the United States, though. In the American context, there's a hierarchical and categorical division between the thesis and the **dissertation.** A thesis, which is the capstone document of a **master's** program (and often of particularly good undergraduate programs as well), demonstrates that a student has broad mastery of the concepts and techniques of her field; it's proof not only that she knows how to get the work done, but knows how to stay current with the research in the field and to continue investigating intellectual advances. A dissertation, on the other hand, *makes* those intellectual advances, does work that currently does not exist, moves a body of knowledge forward.

Think of it this way. A thesis compiles, analyses, categorizes, and integrates the known work of a field; the argument is based on what's known to date. A dissertation *starts* with a thesis, and then carries it into investigations that have never before been done.

TIAA-CREF. Say each of the first four letters independently and then pronounce "cref" as a single word rhyming with "chef," and you've named the retirement plan for higher education.

The Teachers Insurance and Annuity Association was launched by Andrew Carnegie in 1918, and was followed after World War II by the College Retirement Equities Fund. Carnegie wanted a pension system that would do two things: make the profession of higher education teaching economically competitive and thus capable of drawing the best and brightest; and enable older **professors** to retire with safety instead of hanging on for those last few unproductive years.[190]

As with most employers and their retirement programs, your college will contribute some percentage of your salary and you can contribute some percentage of your salary, and all that money goes into the pool, building a little at a time over the decades. You don't always need to be part of the **tenure-track** faculty to participate; I was part of Duke's TIAA-CREF plan

---

190. The end of mandatory retirement at age sixty-five has indeed pushed the actual faculty retirement age upward; it seems to be centering around seventy-one now. This is yet another source of generational tension between the young adjunct population and the seemingly immovable elders. See, for instance, Colleen Flaherty, "Working Way Past 65," *Inside Higher Ed*, June 17, 2013, accessed April 29, 2015, http://www.insidehighered .com/news/2013/06/17/data-suggest-baby-boomer-faculty-are-putting-retirement.

when I was a **postdoc**. Many other classes of a college's employees are part of the pool; you might even be eligible as a graduate **teaching assistant** or **research assistant**.

One of the other nice elements of TIAA-CREF is that its ubiquity across higher education makes it likely that if you change schools, your new employer will just carry on with the same general plan, and you can treat your retirement funds as a unitary account rather than having 401k's and 403b's spread around in a half-dozen brokerages. Unless you treat investing as a hobby, it's nice to have a single trustworthy source to deal with, and TIAA-CREF has been about as trustworthy as investment houses can be.

Time suck. We all have those things we do when we aren't doing anything else: Facebook, Sudoku, YouTube, **e-mail**, gardening, television. Those are all important elements of our mental health. If you were on duty every waking hour, you'd soon find yourself in pretty deep intellectual ruts, sacrificing surprise for efficiency, opportunity for productivity. You'd be a Frederick Taylor bureaucrat, counting up "time on task" and educational minutes.

That said, you want to be aware of the things you do when you're afraid of a project, or bored by it. You don't need to keep a diary, but you should take note of those days or weeks when little seems to be accomplished and you've played too many hands of solitaire. What's behind that? It's not usually that solitaire is all that compelling; rather, it's a way of not doing something else.

The worst kinds of time suck are the ones that actually seem productive but keep you from doing something significant. Signing up for another **committee**, volunteering to do some data analysis or review best practices—those things make you feel helpful, give you quick tasks that you can check off the list, but they can also prevent you from doing the work you've really set out to do. Think about what you'd be proud to have accomplished in the coming year, and put the top three or four on a list on the wall over your computer. When the **chair** asks for volunteers for yet another task group, look at your list and ask yourself whether it will help advance those big goals. If not, try to resist the impulse to step forward. You'll feel like you're shirking your responsibilities, but if nobody else wants to do it either, then it might not be worth doing, or it might be that everybody recognizes that it has the danger of consuming time without strong benefit. You don't always have to be the one who steps up to fix a problem.

I'm personally susceptible to this. Like a lot of kids, I played a lot of sports informally, and I always jumped at the chance to be the goalie or the catcher. It wasn't because I was terrific at those things (though I was a pretty good catcher). In retrospect, I see that I wanted to be the one who stood observant, ready to try to save things when all the other defenses had failed. There's a lot of unfortunate family dynamics at play there, but goalie syndrome has influenced too many of my on-the-job decisions, usually at the expense of my larger intentions. You can't fix all things for all people.

I'm not one usually given to quoting Reverend Rick Warren, he of *The Purpose-Driven Life*, but I once heard him say something in a National Public Radio interview that's really stuck with me. "We overestimate what we can do in a year, and underestimate what we can do in forty years." Keep those big items in view, and let the smaller ones fall away as much as possible.

Travel budget. Going to a **conference** is a pricey proposition. Conference registrations are almost always more than $300 these days, and often above $500. If it's a national conference, assume airfare at $400 minimum, not counting the ground transport on both ends. If the conference runs for four days, you'll have at least three nights of lodging, and conferences are usually in major metropolitan areas where the hotels aren't cheap; let's add another $600 for that. And you have to eat while you're away; breakfast might be free at the hotel, but lunch and dinner won't be. So going to one national conference in your **discipline** each year is easily a $1,500 event, probably closer to $2,000.

Most research-participating colleges will attempt to send each faculty member to one chosen academic conference per year; other, more teaching-oriented colleges might put a dollar cap on travel for each faculty member, so that any expense beyond that is on that faculty member's own tab. If you want to do something that goes beyond this normal contribution—attend a second conference, or get coverage for a particularly expensive city or regis-tration—you absolutely have to get prior approval. You don't get to just decide that something will be a good experience, and then submit your re-imbursement form and a pile of receipts when you get back. Be prepared to offer some sort of significant justification to your department **chair** and/or **dean** before registering, and be prepared to be turned down. If you want the best chance of having your proposal be funded, you need to make the case that the college will benefit from your travel. If you're presenting a paper, that brings prestige to your school;[191] if you're part of an organiza-

191. Dirty little (not so) secret, though: Conference organizers at all but the most elite conferences are actually pretty loose about whom they'll accept for presentations or

tional steering **committee**, that may help your school build partnerships or influence disciplinary policies. If travel is part of a **grant**-funded research project, that travel should be written into the proposal budget as a direct cost, so that the funding agency takes responsibility for it.

Regardless of your campus's largesse, you may personally find it important to attend professional meetings that go outside your official travel budget. It's worth paying out-of-pocket to attend a conference *if* you have a strong history of **networking** with that community, *if* that conference is the most likely location of employment interviews or recruiting, or *if* it offers professional development you can't get in any other way. Pay for it as a **professional expense**, just like your personal books, subscriptions, home computer and internet access, and work clothes, and don't hesitate to claim it if you itemize your income taxes.

Two-body / two-career / trailing-spouse problem. Let's consider a married couple; call them Margaret and Eileen. Margaret is a corporate loan manager at Citibank who makes $120,000 per year. Eileen is a graphic designer for Random House who makes $70,000 per year. Between the two of them, they make enough money to have bought a loft condo in the Red Hook neighborhood of Brooklyn. Nice life.

Margaret gets offered a promotion to manage the West Coast Citibank corporate lending program, at the San Francisco office. Good gig, with a bump from $120K to $180K. Eileen knows that San Francisco has lots of publishing work, as well as web design and product design industries, and her strong **portfolio** will almost certainly land her at least interesting work within a couple of weeks.

Now let's stick with Margaret and Eileen, but change their jobs. Margaret is a relatively new **assistant professor** of cultural geography who makes $65,000 per year at John Jay College. Eileen is finishing her PhD in molecular pharmacology at NYU's medical center, with a research stipend of $45,000. Between the two of them, they make enough money to rent a tiny one-bedroom apartment in Alphabet City, down near Chinatown. Things are tight but okay.

But Eileen hits the academic jackpot in her first year on the market, and is offered an assistant professorship at the Molecular and Cellular Biochemis-

---

posters. They know that presenters are more likely to actually register and attend, and conference registration fees constitute a meaningful percentage of organizations' operating budgets.

try Department at Indiana University Bloomington. Great gig, with a bump from $45K to $80K, especially in moving from Manhattan to Indiana; they might finally be able to buy a home. But what the hell is Margaret supposed to do? It's not as if she can carry her cultural geography portfolio, stellar though it might be, into all of the colleges in the Bloomington area (which isn't quite as many as the colleges of New York) and walk out of one of them with a job **offer**. The IU Geography program only has a few **faculty** lines, all of which are thoroughly occupied; if one were to come open, there'd easily be a hundred or more applicants for it.

Academia is a particularly tough world for a two-**career** couple. Almost all the decent jobs are subject to **national searches**, and you don't get to be regionally picky. If you're in different fields, the college where one person gets a job may not even *have* the other **department**; if you're in the same field, there's no way that two positions will both be open at once. Promotions in private industry usually result in moving from smaller to larger places; major cities all have lots of employers, and the job market is in constant turnover. Colleges offering great opportunities aren't always in major cities, and even metropolitan schools have much more rigid job markets (after all, we're trying to get jobs that offer lifetime affiliation).

There are already all the normal locational stresses that would occur when any normal family gets transferred for work. "Indiana? You want to move to Indiana?!"[192] But add to this the possibility that one **partner** may not be able to practice her profession at all, and the situation is grim at best.

The more well-heeled colleges can afford to manufacture work for "the trailing spouse" if a candidate is particularly desirable, up to and including creating a new faculty line.[193] That's nice, but everybody on campus knows that the trailing spouse got a gift that others would (sometimes almost literally) kill for, and he'll never be taken seriously by his colleagues. And the vast majority of schools can't afford that kind of largesse anyway. I was a semifinalist for a **provost**'s position at a small liberal arts college in Wisconsin—provost, a vice-presidential-level position!—and was told clearly

---

192. Don't write me nasty letters; it's just an example. I was a finalist for a dean's position in Manhattan, and I absolutely couldn't imagine myself living in New York. Fortunately, I was the runner-up, and didn't have to make that decision. My wife, who's *from* Manhattan, would faint dead away at the prospect of living near my hometown in Michigan. Your mileage may vary. Also, a married couple named Margaret and Eileen may feel somewhat less comfortable living in some parts of the country . . . .

193. God help them, though, if Eileen subsequently gets tenure and Margaret doesn't.

that there was no spousal-hire provision. If a new provost can't get academic work for his or her partner, good luck in the hoi polloi.

Pretty much everything in your life is supposed to wait for **tenure**. Don't say anything controversial, don't have kids, don't fall in love, don't get married. Just do your work, get your job, go through promotion, and then feel free to live as you please.

Two-community problem / The two cultures. There's a substantial divide in most fields between theorists and practitioners. It may have its roots in the divide that Sartre identified when he divided the **intellectual** class into two camps, organic intellectuals (supported by and serving capital) and critical intellectuals (serving justice and the oppressed, and supported too often by no one). Or it may be more simply divided between those who have time to study a problem in detail and those whose engagement with a problem is determined by the billable hour.

Whatever the root cause, practitioners complain that academics dwell in the ivory tower and don't understand the "real world," and academics complain that practitioners operate by habit and intuition rather than being informed by research. These mutual complaints are present in law, policy, psychology, architecture, education, medicine, business and economics, criminology, theology, and pretty much any academic **discipline** that has a profession adjacent to it. Engineering is applied physics (or $E = P/\$$), but practicing engineers don't keep up with developments in theoretical physics all that well. Law is applied philosophy, but lawyers don't read much contemporary analysis. Real estate development is applied architecture or urban planning, but developers don't read design research; pastoring is applied theology, but parish pastors don't engage in high-level theological debates. And in all of these cases, too, the scholars aren't reading a lot about what's happening in the grind of professional life. In any field, the two communities have independent reading lists and information sources. They hold different values, work on different time frames, are rewarded in different currencies, and achieve fame for different products.

I've done so-called research within the professions, which often begins with the answer and merely fills in the local color. Any fact about the world that can't be learned in eight hours just takes too long to know, runs counter to "best practices," and holds the risk of pissing off the client. And I've lived for a long time within academia, which (as I wrote in the *Acknowledgement of Limitations*) can theorize masculinity while failing to appreciate either the valor or the necessity of men clearing tree damage off your deck in icy weather.

Similarly, fifty years ago, C. P. Snow delivered a lecture called "The Two Cultures," in which he attempted to understand why science and the humanities had diverged so strongly in their goals.[194] That dichotomy has been expressed as positivism versus hermeneutics, quantitative versus qualitative, rigor versus impressionism, reductive versus contextual thinking, truth and accuracy versus fuzzy relativism. In many ways, the division between science and the humanities mirrors the blockages between academics and professionals.

But why must we consider one of these to be the best way to understand the world and the other to be the lesser? What if we were to consider them different tools for different jobs, the equivalent of a power grinder and a microscope? If you asked people whether the power grinder or the microscope was the better tool, they'd either respond by asking "better for what?" or by telling you which one fit the kind of work they liked doing. Some people are power grinder people, and some people are microscope people.

The best way of thinking about this that I've ever encountered comes from the design researchers Horst Rittel and Melvin Webber, who said essentially that there are different kinds of problems in the world, and that we make grave mistakes if we try to solve one kind of problem with the other kind of tools.[195] Some problems have rules, like trigonometry; others have few or no rules, like dating. Some problems, like engineering, would be defined in the same way by everyone looking at them; others, like race relations, would be described very differently by different observers. Some problems, like chemistry, have right answers; others, like foreign policy, have no answers at all. Some problems, like a computer program, can be finished; others, like cities, can never be finished. Rittel and Webber dichotomized their formulation as well, calling one body of problems *tame problems* and the other *wicked problems*, but their main contribution was in helping us to be aware once again that the hammer is not the only tool in the box.

The problem is not that there are different ways of approaching different kinds of problems; it's that most people are so bound up with studying one way of addressing one kind of problem that they lose the capability of being reflective about the others, and then start to believe that the model they and

194. Charles P. Snow, *The Two Cultures* (London: Cambridge University Press, 1959).
195. Horst Rittel and Melvin Webber, "Dilemmas in a General Theory of Planning," *Policy Sciences* 4 (1973): 155–69.

their colleagues employ is "natural" or "obvious" or "clear" (which immediately relegates everybody else to artificial, arcane, and muddy).

So a historian reads the **CV** of a chemist up for **tenure**, and says, "Why is she always the third or fourth **author** on every one of these articles? Can't this person think on her own?" And the chemist reads the CV of the historian and says, "Only three papers in six years? Really? What the hell has she been doing?"

And the professional employer sees the academic **career** and says, "Uh boy, another one of those head-in-the-clouds types who can't survive in the real world." And the academic hiring committee sees the professional career and says, "Uh boy, another one of those ill-informed commercial types who isn't interested in ideas."

The problem, of course, is that we have to live together, run schools together, set policy together, and teach students together. We have to learn that our own assessments and our own definitions are not the only ones that might be pertinent, that others have goals they find worthy even if we might not.

This understanding is the hidden wisdom behind liberal education, in which we are asked to take up not merely different topics, but different ways of thought. We are asked not to think about physics, but to think like physicists; not to think about literary criticism, but to think like critics; not to periodically take a PE class, but to imagine and enhance the wisdom of our bodies.

We all had those experiences as undergrads, if we went to good schools that emphasized thought rather than content. But two things are happening that get in our way. The first is that college is increasingly defined in terms of content, in terms of preparation for a particular job (or worse, simply in terms of preparation to be a droplet in the labor pool and avoid unemployment). The second is that the further we go with our education, through **master's** and **doctorate** and **postdoc** and **faculty** life, the more we surround ourselves only with people who are equally captivated by our small problem set and the habits our field has formed. We forsake all others, dedicating ourselves only to our chosen intellectual partner. And I believe that we fall out of the practice of considering, of deliberating, of purposefully putting on the ideas and attitudes of the other to reflect on what a problem must look like to her.

One of the gravest problems you will encounter as a graduate student, when looking for your first faculty post, or when applying for **tenure** is rigidity of thought—yours *and* theirs. You'll be measured against inapt criteria, you'll set a single outcome as the correct one, you'll be labeled with an incomplete definition—and no one will recognize that they're doing it, or that there are alternatives to their thinking. Events that we label as secrecy, obstinacy, or misunderstanding are so often traced back to closely held and rarely examined assumptions about good ways of living and thinking.

When you're in a high-stakes moment like a **job search** or a **tenure** review or a dissertation **defense**, it's hard to remember that your responses are cultural, and so are those of the panelists you face. If you can depersonalize what's going on around you, and think anthropologically about the language and the definitions and the underlying goals that are manifesting themselves in particular ways, you'll have far more vocabulary and repertoire with which to respond. Practice this ethnography when the stakes are lower—when, for instance, your bartender brings the wrong drink, or you get cut off in traffic. It will make you more capable when the risks and the rewards are great.

Uu

Undergraduate research. So here's a moment for a plug. For the past twelve years, I've been a member of the Council on Undergraduate Research, an organization which attempts to foster everything that was missing from my first iteration at college. The goal of undergraduate research (or UR, to shorthand) is to allow students to experience the power and delight of real investigation, of doing something where the answer isn't already known. That, after all, is the joy of scholarly life: wandering off the playground and into the wilderness, discovering something unplanned and unscripted.

Thirty years ago, UR was rare. But now it's widely acknowledged to be a "high impact practice," capable of increasing retention and graduation, leading toward higher grad school enrollment and better employment opportunities. More and more colleges have active UR programs, and **deans** and **provosts** are pressing their **departments** for greater and more systemic participation.

As a doctoral student, you'll likely have the chance to teach. If you can get experience in leading undergraduate research projects, that becomes an important element of your **CV** and your **cover letter**; it sets you apart from the great mass of TAs who only ever see their students as students; and it indicates that you have some sense of intention about your teaching mission. Check on your own campus to see if there's an office of undergraduate research; if there is, find out how you can get involved. It's gratifying to see the lights come on in a student's eyes, and that's terrific preparation for your own life as an academic **mentor**.

Union / collective bargaining unit. I come from a union family. My dad was a member of the machinist's union at his factory, and I knew some important things about how the power of the many could counteract the power of the wealthy. But I thought that unions were for men who wore blue shop uniforms; it wasn't until many years later that I understood that unionization could be a force in all forms of employment.

We can go back and forth all day about the relative benefits and evils of unions and "right to work" states and so on. For the purposes ahead of us here, I simply want to say that you need to know whether the college you're considering working for is unionized or not. If it is, the union and the college will have negotiated standard working agreements, which cover not merely salaries but also **tenure** and promotion rules, **course load** expectations and course allocation, **faculty** governance and its relation with university governance, vacation and research release and **sabbatical** policies, and benefits packages. If you join a unionized faculty, you will be required to have union dues withheld from your salary; the amount will probably feel significant unless you compare it against the hypothetical but likely lower salary, poorer benefits, and reduced job security that come with nonunionized life, all of which you are protected from whether or not you personally believe in labor organization.

If your prospective college is unionized, find out who's included in the collective. It's likely that **adjuncts** will not be included, **postdocs** will not be included, and graduate **research assistants** and graduate **teaching assistants** will not be included. As is true in industrial workplaces, one strategy that management employs when they can't be rid of unions altogether is to sharply limit the numbers of people who can be members; another is to play the fears of the established older workers against the needs of the younger generation, as in the United Auto Workers' decision to allow two-tier wages so that employees hired after the wage agreement could be paid half the hourly wage of pre-agreement workers in exchange for experienced workers being retained at higher pay and benefits. The same dynamic occurs in higher education, where the protected tenure-track occupants have little motive to speak on behalf of their colleagues on the wrong side of the moat.

If your prospective college is *not* unionized, there will still be some sort of **faculty handbook** that outlines most or all of the above working conditions, but the college's **administration** will have a greater and more unilateral hand in writing and amending it. I worked for a college that simply one day decided to stop contributing to its employees' retirement packages, and that regularly changed its employee-review processes. Instead of "New Deal," the contemporary labor slogan seems to be "Deal with it."

You may intuit from my comments that I am in fact a fan of unions. And I sort of am, although academic unions can get themselves wound up into a constant state of oppositional paranoia, protect truly poor employees as a reflex, and try to negotiate constant standards on small issues that render the college more rigid and less interesting. But I'm more worried about massive institutions operating within a system of labor oversupply. When wages and working conditions are completely unregulated, we're on a race to the bottom. We're already seeing that in the high proportion and low pay of adjuncts, in the horrible conditions of teachers at the for-profit colleges, and in universities salivating over the prospect of selling online seat time to the masses with only a single instructor for tens of thousands of students.

If you're thinking about joining a doctoral program at a major public research university, you may find that there's actually a grad-students' union. The question of whether grad students are eligible to unionize is far from settled yet, with teaching and research assistants claiming that they're employees, and colleges claiming that grad assistants are merely recipients of student financial aid. State laws regulate state colleges, and the National Labor Relations Board has gone back and forth with regards to the status of student workers at private schools.

Any union at a local college will typically be affiliated with a larger consortium of unions: the American Association of University Professors, the American Federation of Teachers, the National Education Association. But there's no reason why your union has to stay with an industry-based organizer. If you need to play hardball, you can affiliate with the Teamsters.

Ww

White Paper. Not just the stuff you stick in the photocopier. In business and academia, a white paper is a research-based briefing with recommendations, prepared to help decision makers be better informed (and ideally to take your side of the argument). It's called a white paper because, although it can be lengthy and rigorous enough to be a monograph, it either isn't bound at all or just has a plain-paper cover.

A white paper can be thought of as a miniature master's **thesis**. It has a topic, a **literature review**, discussion or implications, and a bibliography. But its purpose is not the neutral advance of knowledge. Rather, white papers are strategic. They lay out the landscape that is germane to a problem, analyze benefits and drawbacks of possible actions, and offer recommendations.

White papers are an underutilized form of scholarly production. Just as a terrific literature review has huge benefits for other scholars in the field, a good white paper can clarify an organization's options and advocate intelligently on behalf of a particular course of action. If you have the opportunity to work with an industry- or profession-linked research group, get involved in the creation of its white papers. They force you to look carefully and broadly at a problem, imagine an array of solutions, and argue your case. The ability to do policy work, organizational leadership, or think-tank collaboration is just another tool in your intellectual arsenal, and it can expand your **postdoctoral** opportunities.

Afterthoughts

I'm writing this from my home, a home I never thought I'd find, set among the timberlands of the Green Mountains. Our trees are profligate: every fall brings hundreds of thousands of acorns and maple seed pods, a vast array of pinecones, innumerable apples each bearing twenty or thirty seeds. Only a few of those seeds, those precise and costly repositories of DNA, will become the next generation of trees. Most of the acorns will be eaten by squirrels or deer, most of the maple pods stored away by chipmunks and cracked open by chickadees. Those seeds that aren't eaten immediately are mostly dissolved into the soil, and never sprout. The handful that sprout are nibbled away at soil level by rabbits and groundhogs.

All of this could be seen as a tragedy if we imagine that the destiny of the acorn is to become an oak, the destiny of the apple seed to become an apple tree. But the fact is that most acorns become deer, and most deer become venison. Most maple seeds become chipmunks, and most chipmunks become snacks for hawks or foxes. And whatever isn't consumed by identifiable animals is consumed by unidentifiable bacteria, becoming an increasingly enriched soil that nurtures generations to come.

In order not to go insane, we have to believe that our work matters. But "having our work matter" may look different than we imagine. Our acorns may never become red oaks; but they may result in well-fed deer and a tourist economy that brings hundreds of thousands of visitors to Vermont. Whether those visitors see the red oak leaves or pursue the deer, the acorn is fulfilled in either case.

We may never know how our work is used. That may not be our right. We may only know that we've been true to ourselves—that, as Kipling put it, we've filled "the unforgiving minute with sixty seconds' worth of distance run." That is not enough, I know. And yet, that is all we have.

Here are some useless comments you might hear.

"Well, you have only yourself to blame. You should have known."

Yes, we all should have known. And yet we didn't.

Everything we know, we learned somehow. Some people learn to be faculty members by growing up with one or two of them at the dinner table; others learn by doing it and making lots of mistakes along the way. When you're entering a new culture, you don't even know what's important to know; you don't follow the customs, you miss the signs, you come into the curve too fast.

Then there is the seemingly more reassuring "Everything happens for a reason." This isn't firmly attributed, but is most often thought to have been said by Marilyn Monroe:

I believe that everything happens for a reason. People change so that you can learn to let go. Things go wrong so that you appreciate them when they're right. You believe lies so you eventually learn to trust no one but yourself, and sometimes things fall apart so that better things can fall together.

That's what you tell yourself when you're trying desperately not to be miserable.

And the fact is that when we don't get the grad-school seat or the faculty position, we go on with our lives and do our best, and often come out fine in some unpredictable way. We tell our stories backward, and we recognize that any change in our past would have led us to a different present location.

Here's an exercise I often share with my incoming freshmen students. I give them a list of every paid job I've ever held.

- setting out and stacking folding chairs at my high school for Saturday bingo
- dishwasher at Mr. Steak
- house painter
- college bowling instructor
- canvasser for R. L. Polk city directory research
- bowling alley mechanic's assistant
- bowling alley snack bar attendant
- bowling alley pro shop operator
- retail sporting goods manager (for two different companies)
- architectural energy simulation analyst

- newspaper critic in architecture and urban planning
- architectural energy technical and specifications writer
- architecture teaching assistant
- architecture research assistant
- furniture salesman
- architectural pre-design consultant
- K–12 school reform researcher
- college writing postdoc
- college administrator (one school, three different roles in seven years)

This is not the TripTik route that AAA would have reasonably planned for me to wind up at a destination called "college dean," not a path that the high school guidance counselor would have laid out for us. We have a body of talents and interests; we have work that we do diligently because it matters so much to us; we have social commitments to families or to places that are key parts of our identities. The world presents us with a certain array of opportunities, and we put all of those variables together in whatever way seems best at each moment. And we don't know—we can never know—the alternate realities that might have come about had we chosen differently. All we can do is to take the greatest possible advantage of every circumstance we find ourselves in. I learned elements of human relations in retail sales that later made me a good administrator; I learned things by trying to be a professional bowler—things like careful observation, patience, and the pleasure of precise execution—that I continue to rely upon as a writer.

This doesn't mean that I don't have regrets or missed opportunities. Had I had better advice before college, or before grad school, or on the faculty search, I'd have made different choices. There's no guarantee that I'd have had better outcomes, or that I'd be the kind of person who defined "better outcomes" in the same way that I do now. Nonetheless, I would like to have been Kathy Merkey's boyfriend during high school. I would like to have been six inches taller. I would like to have had a sister. And I would like to have gotten a traditional tenure-track faculty position at a small liberal-arts college.

All of those things would have put me in an entirely different place in my life. Better? It's hard to say, but it's also hard to imagine; I'm mostly happy with what I have and can do, and I'm closer to being comfortable with who I am than I've ever been since I was thirty years old and immersed in the newfound joys of architectural history.

In the novel *Siddhartha*, Hermann Hesse portrays a late-life meeting between Siddhartha, the man who will ultimately be recognized as the Buddha, and Siddhartha's childhood friend Govinda, a monk who has charted an unstinting life of service and devotion as compared with the varied and unscripted path that Siddhartha has taken. Govinda asks Siddhartha, whom he does not now recognize, to share the sources of his seeming maturity and wisdom. Siddhartha correctly identifies Govinda as a "seeker" of enlightenment, and replies:

> When someone is seeking, it happens quite easily that he only sees the thing that he is seeking; that he is unable to find anything, unable to absorb anything, because he is only thinking of the thing he is seeking, because he has a goal, because he is obsessed with his goal. Seeking means: to have a goal; but finding means: to be free, to be receptive, to have no goal.[196]

I pretend no greater wisdom in life than the Buddha. But as I think of you now occupying some of the places I've been, I think it's good to have a goal; you just can't become so attached to it that you lose sight of other possibilities, or of the joy you can take from the work you're doing now. We place all of our emphasis on the attainment of some outcome, and ignore the value of the experiences that constitute it.

Right now, you're seeking, and I hope that the knowledge you've gained from my experience will help you in that quest. But more than anything, I hope that your intelligence and your opportunities allow you to *find* ... to find engagement, joy, and satisfaction, and to recognize them as they become present to you.

---

196. Herman Hesse, *Siddhartha*, trans. Hilda Rosner (New York: Bantam, 1971), 140.

Bibliography

"A Saudi Prince's Controversial Gift." Harvard Magazine, March-April 2006, http://harvardmagazine.com/2006/03/a-saudi-princes-controve.html.

Aad, G., et. al. (2008.) "The ATLAS Experiment at the CERN Large Hadron Collider." *Journal of Instrumentation* 3 (August 2008). http://iopscience.iop.org/1748-0221/3/08/S08003/.

Alexander, Chris, Sara Ishikawa, and Murray Silverstein. *A Pattern Language: Towns, Buildings, Construction*. Oxford: Oxford University Press, 1977.

American Association of University Professors. "Figure 1: Trends in Instructional Staff Employment Status, 1975–2009." Accessed April 27, 2015, http://www.aaup.org/NR/rdonlyres/7C3039DD-EF79-4E75-A20D-6F75BA01BE84/0/Trends.pdf.

American Council on Education. "Leading Demographic Portrait of College Presidents Reveals Ongoing Challenges in Diversity, Aging." Accessed April 29, 2015, http://www.acenet.edu/news-room/Pages/ACPS-Release-2012.aspx.

American Federation of Teachers, Higher Education. "American Academic: The State of the Higher Education Workforce 1997–2007." Accessed May 4, 2015, http://www.aftface.org/storage/face/documents/ameracad_report_97-07for_web.pdf.

Barnishaw, John, and Samuel Dunietz. "Busting the Myths: The Annual Report on the Economic Status of the Profession, 2014–15." *Academe* 101 no. 2 (2015): 4–19. http://www.aaup.org/reports-publications/2014-15salarysurvey.

Beall, Jeffrey. "Beall's List: Potential, Possible or Probable Predatory Scholarly Open-Access Publishers." Accessed May 4, 2015, http://scholarlyoa.com/publishers/.

Boyer, Ernest L. *Scholarship Reconsidered: Priorities of the Professoriate*. San Francisco: Jossey-Bass, 1990.

Butler Hospital. "Instructions for Submitting Documents to the IRB Office." Accessed May 4, 2015, http://www.butler.org/irb/instructions.cfm.

California State University Office of the Chancellor, Human Resources. "Report on 2011 Faculty Recruitment and Retention Survey." Accessed April 27, 2015, http://www.calstate.edu/hr/FacRecSurvRep11.pdf.

Center for the Built Environment. "About Us: Industry/University Collaborative Research Solutions." Accessed May 4, 2015, http://www.cbe.berkeley.edu/index.htm.

Childress, Herb. "Seventeen Reasons Why Football is Better than High School." *Phi Delta Kappan* 79, no. 8 (1998): 616–19.

Childress, Herb. *Landscapes of Betrayal, Landscapes of Joy: Curtisville in the Lives of Its Teenagers*. Albany, NY: SUNY Press, 2000.

Chronicle of Higher Education. "Assistant Professor, Massachusetts Institute of Technology, Program in Science, Technology and Society." Accessed May 4, 2015, http://chronicle.com/jobs/0000790595-01.

Conway, Jill Ker. *True North: A Memoir*. New York: Vintage, 1994.

Costello, Elvis, with Scott Simon. "Elvis Costello Gets a Little Bluegrass." National Public Radio Weekend Edition Saturday, December 12, 2012. Accessed May 5, 2015, http://www.npr.org/templates/story/story.php?storyId=105326845.

Costello, Elvis. "Satellite." *Spike*. Warner Brothers, 1989. Audio CD.

Dews, C. L. Barney, and Carolyn Leste Law, eds. *This Fine Place So Far From Home: Voices of Academics from the Working Class*. Philadelphia: Temple University Press, 1995.

"The Disposable Academic: Why Doing a PhD Is Often a Waste of Time." *Economist*, December 16, 2010, http://www.economist.com/node/17723223.

Duke University & Duke University Medical Center Animal Care & Use Program. "Policy, Species Covered Definition." Accessed May 4, 2015, http://vetmed.duhs .duke.edu/PDF/Policies/IACUC%20Process/policy_on_definition_of_a_covered _species.pdf.

Dunn, Syndi. "U. of Colorado at Boulder Names Steven Hayward Its First 'Visiting Scholar in Conservative Thought." *Chronicle of Higher Education*, March 13, 2013, http://chronicle.com/article/U-of-Colorado-at-Boulder/137895/.

Ehrenberg, Ronald G., Michael J. Rizzo, and Scott S. Condie. "Start-Up Costs in American Research Universities." Cornell University Digital Commons Working Papers. Accessed May 4, 2015, http://digitalcommons.ilr.cornell.edu/cgi /viewcontent.cgi?article=1039&context=workingpapers.

Eisner, Elliot. "Educational Connoisseurship and Criticism: Their Form and Functions in Educational Evaluation." *Journal of Aesthetic Education* 10, nos. 3–4 (1976): 135–50.

Fatsis, Stefan. *Word Freak: Heartbreak, Triumph, Genius, and Obsession in the World of Competitive Scrabble Players*. New York: Penguin, 2001.

Flaherty, Colleen. "Working Way Past 65." *Inside Higher Ed*, June 17, 2013, http://www .insidehighered.com/news/2013/06/17/data-suggest-baby-boomer-faculty-are -putting-retirement.

Gladwell, Malcolm. *Outliers: The Story of Success*. New York: Little, Brown and Company, 2008.

Glassick, Charles E., Mary T. Huber, and Gene I. Maeroff. *Scholarship Assessed: Evaluation of the Professoriate*. San Francisco: Jossey-Bass, 1997.

Glassie, Henry. *Passing the Time in Ballymenone: Culture and History of an Ulster Community*. Philadelphia: University of Pennsylvania Press, 1982.

Goodman, Paul. *Utopian Essays and Practical Proposals*. New York: Vintage, 1962.

Graff, Gerald, and Cathy Birkenstein. *They Say, I Say: The Moves That Matter in Persuasive Writing*, 3rd edition. New York: W. W. Norton, 2014.

Grasso, Maureen, Melissa Barry, and Thomas Valentine. *A Data-Driven Approach to Improving Doctoral Completion*. Washington: Council of Graduate Schools, 2009, http://www.cgsnet.org/cgs-occasional-paper-series/university-georgia/chapter-1.

Groth, Paul. "Tithing for Environmental Education: A Modest Proposal." *Places* 7, no. 1 (1990): 38–41.

Guay, F., J. J. Matte, C. L. Girard, M. F. Palin, A. Giguère, and J. P. Laforest. "Effect of Folic Acid and Glycine Supplementation on Embryo Development and Folate Metabolism during Early Pregnancy in Pigs." *Journal of Animal Science* 80, no. 8 (2002): 2134–43.

Hall, Donald. *The Academic Self: An Owner's Manual*. Columbus: Ohio State University Press, 2002.

"Harvard University Endowment Delivers 15.4% Return for Fiscal Year 2014." Harvard Gazette, September 23, 2014, http://news.harvard.edu/gazette/story/2014/09/harvard-university-endowment-delivers-15-4-return-for-fiscal-year-2014/.

Hesse, Hermann. *Siddhartha*. Trans. Hilda Rosner. New York: Bantam, 1971.

Higher Ed Jobs, "Higher Education Employment Report, Fourth Quarter and Annual, 2014." Accessed April 27, 2015, http://www.higheredjobs.com/documents/HEJ_Employment_Report_2014_Q4.pdf.

Hossler, Don, Doug Shapiro, Afet Dundar, Mary Ziskin, Jin Chen, Desiree Zerquerya, and Vasti Torres. "Transfer and Mobility: A National View of Pre-Degree Student Movement in Postsecondary Institutions," February 2012, http://nscresearchcenter.org/wp-content/uploads/NSC_Signature_Report_2.pdf.

Hubka, Thomas C. *Big House, Little House, Back House, Barn: The Connected Farm Buildings of New England*. Hanover, NH: University Press of New England, 1984.

Huma, Ramogi, and Ellen J. Staurowsky. "The Price of Poverty in Big Time College Sport." Norco, CA: National College Players Association. Accessed May 4, 2015, http://www.ncpanow.org/research/body/The-Price-of-Poverty-in-Big-Time-College-Sport.pdf.

Indiana University Bloomington, Center for Postsecondary Research. "The Carnegie Classification of Institutions of Higher Education.™" Accessed May 4, 2015, http://carnegieclassifications.iu.edu.

Jackson, Joe. "Is She Really Going Out With Him?" *Look Sharp!* A&M/Polygram Records, 1978. Audio CD.

Jackson, John L. Jr. *Racial Paranoia: The Unintended Consequences of Political Correctness*. New York: Basic Civitas, 2008.

Jaschik, Scott. "Bias against Older Candidates." *Inside Higher Ed*, December 17, 2008, https://www.insidehighered.com/news/2008/12/17/age.

———. "Unhappy Associate Professors." *Inside Higher Ed*, June 4, 2012, https://www.insidehighered.com/news/2012/06/04/associate-professors-less-satisfied-those-other-ranks-survey-finds.

Jinha, Arif E. "Article 50 Million: An Estimate of the Number of Scholarly Articles in

Existence." *Learned Publishing* 23, no. 3 (2010): 258–63, http://hdl.handle.net/10393
/19577.

Klein, Hugh. Adolescence, Youth, and Young Adulthood: Rethinking Current Conceptualizations of Life Stage. *Youth and Society* 21, no. 4 (1990): 446–71.

Kuban, Kaila G. "That Which Is Not What It Seems: Queer Youth, Rurality, Class, and
the Architecture of Assistance." Doctoral dissertation, University of Massachusetts–
Amherst Department of Anthropology, 2010.

Lin, Jessica. "Unraveling Tenure at MIT." *The Tech* 130, no. 28 (June 11, 2010). http://
tech.mit.edu/V130/N28/tenure.html.

Lubrano, Alfred. *Limbo: Blue-Collar Roots, White-Collar Dreams.* Hoboken, NJ: John
Wiley and Sons, 2004.

Marquette University Department of Philosophy. "Ph.D. Comprehensive Exam Information and Reading List." Accessed May 4, 2015, http://www.marquette.edu/phil
/documents/phdcomps.pdf.

Massachusetts Institute of Technology. "MIT Facts 2014: Financial Data." Accessed
May 4, 2015, http://web.mit.edu/facts/financial.html.

Menand, Louis. "Live and Learn: Why We Have College." *New Yorker*, June 6, 2011,
http://www.newyorker.com/arts/critics/atlarge/2011/06/06/110606crat_atlarge
_menand.

Michigan Technological University. "Patent, Research, and Proprietary Rights Agreement." Accessed May 4, 2015, http://www.mtu.edu/hr/current/docs/patents.pdf.

Morrissey, Susan R. "Starting Salaries." Accessed May 4, 2015, http://cen.acs.org
/articles/90/i23/Starting-Salaries.html.

Nasar, Jack. *Design by Competition: Making Design Competition Work.* Cambridge: Cambridge University Press, 1999.

National Center for Education Statistics. "Fast Facts." Accessed 12/28/2014, http://nces
.ed.gov/fastfacts/display.asp?id=31.

National Science Foundation. "Science and Engineering Doctorates: 2011." Accessed
May 4, 2015, http://www.nsf.gov/statistics/sed/2011/data_table.cfm.

Penn State University, Vice Provost for Academic Affairs and Office of Planning and
Institutional Assessment. "Faculty Tenure-Flow Rates: 2009–10 Annual Report,"
January 2010, http://www.psu.edu/president/pia/planning_research/reports
/spring10-tenureflow.pdf.

Rittel, Horst, and Melvin Webber. "Dilemmas in a General Theory of Planning." *Policy
Sciences* 4 (1973): 155–69.

Rogers, Jenny. "3 to 1: That's the Best Ratio of Tenure-Track Faculty to Administrators,
a Study Concludes." *Chronicle of Higher Education*, November 12, 2012.

Ross, Andrew S. "In Silicon Valley, Age Can Be a Curse." SFGate (San Francisco Chronicle web portal), August 18, 2013, http://www.sfgate.com/business/bottomline
/article/In-Silicon-Valley-age-can-be-a-curse-4742365.php.

Sartre, Jean-Paul. "A Plea for Intellectuals." In *Between Existentialism and Marxism*,
trans. John Matthews, 228–85. New York: Pantheon, 1974.

Sartre, Jean-Paul. *The Emotions: Outline of a Theory*, trans. Bernard Frechtman. Secaucus, NJ: Citadel, 1975.

Smith, Ryan E. "The Bass Grant: Why Yale Gave $20 Million Back." *Yale Herald*, March 24, 1995, http://www.yaleherald.com/archive/xix/3.24.95/news/bass.html.

Snow, Charles P. *The Two Cultures*. London: Cambridge University Press, 1959.

Southern Illinois University Edwardsville, Office of Research and Projects. "Research & Development: New Faculty Start-Up." Accessed May 4, 2015, http://www.siue.edu/orp/internalgrants/startup.shtml.

Stanford University Department of Economics. "Comprehensive Exam Archive." Accessed May 4, 2015, http://economics.stanford.edu/graduate/current-phd-student-resources/comprehensive-exam-archive.

Strong, Michael. *The Habit of Thought: From Socratic Seminars to Socratic Practice*. Chapel Hill, NC: New View Publications, 1997.

United States Census Bureau. "Educational Attainment in the United States: 2014–Detailed Tables." Accessed May 4, 2015, http://www.census.gov/hhes/socdemo/education/data/cps/2014/tables.html.

United States Department of Education, National Center for Education Statistics, Institute of Education Sciences. "Employees in Postsecondary Institutions, Fall 2010, and Salaries of Full-Time Instructional Staff, 2010–11."Accessed April 29, 2015, http://nces.ed.gov/pubs2012/2012276.pdf.

United States Department of Health and Human Services, Office of Research Integrity. "Responsible Conduct of Research, General Resources." Accessed May 4, http://ori.hhs.gov/general-resources-0.

United States Department of Health and Human Services, Office of Research Integrity. "ORI Introduction to the Responsible Conduct of Research." Accessed May 4, 2015, http://ori.hhs.gov/education/products/RCRintro/.

United States Department of Health and Human Services, Office of Research Integrity. "Case Summaries." Accessed May 4, 2015, http://ori.hhs.gov/case_summary.

United States Department of Labor, Bureau of Labor Statistics. "Earnings and Unemployment Rates by Educational Attainment." Accessed May 4, 2015, http://www.bls.gov/emp/ep_chart_001.htm.

University of Alaska Fairbanks Center for Research Services. "Institutional Review Board Protocol Review." Accessed May 4, 2015, http://www.uaf.edu/irb/faqs/protocol-review/.

University of California Berkeley Library Collections. "Hot Topic: Publisher Mergers." Accessed May 4, 2015, http://www.lib.berkeley.edu/scholarlycommunication/publisher_mergers.html.

University of California Berkeley Library Collections. "Monograph and Serial Expenditures in ARL Libraries, 1986–2005." Accessed May 4, 2015, http://www.lib.berkeley.edu/Collections/pdfs/monser05.pdf.

University of California Office of the President. "UC Tenured Faculty, New Appointments 2006–07 to 2010–11 & Academic Availabilities (1990 to 2004 National Doctoral Degree Recipients) Universitywide." Accessed May 4, 2015, http://www.ucop.edu/academic-personnel/_files/newhire_tenuredgender.pdf.

University of California Office of the President. "UC Tenured Faculty, New Appointments 2006–07 to 2010–11 & Academic Availabilities (1990 to 2004 National Doc-

toral Degree Recipients) Universitywide." Accessed May 4, 2015, http://www.ucop
.edu/academic-personnel/_files/newhire_tenuredethnicity.pdf.

University of California, Moffitt Library, Media Resource Center. "Spiro Kostof
Lectures: Architecture 170B, Spring 1991." Accessed May 4, 2015, http://www.lib
.berkeley.edu/MRC/kostof.html.

University of Connecticut Office of the Vice President for Research. "IRB Policies and
Procedures." Accessed May 4, 2015, http://research.uconn.edu/wp-content/uploads
/sites/351/2014/09/IRB-Policies-and-Procedures.pdf.

University of Pennsylvania, Division of Vice Provost for University Life. "8–13 Year Out
PhD Alumni Survey." Accessed March 21, 2015, http://www.vpul.upenn.edu
/careerservices/8-13yearphdsurvey.php#Question3.1.

Virginia Tech University. "Campus Buildings: Physical Plant." Accessed May 4, 2015,
https://www.unirel.vt.edu/history/physical_plant/campus_buildings.html.

Wasserstrom, Jeffrey. "Expanding on the I-Word." *Chronicle of Higher Education* 52, no.
20, (January 20, 2006): B5.

Wolflinger, Nicholas H., Mary Ann Mason, and Marc Goulden. "Problems in the
Pipeline: Gender, Marriage, and Fertility in the Ivory Tower." *Journal of Higher Education*, 79, no. 4 (2008): 388–405.

Index

Boldfaced terms are those included as main glossary entries; boldfaced page numbers are the locations of those entries.